LAWLESS

Rampant abuse, hate speech, censorship, bias, and disinformation – our internet has problems. It is governed by technology companies – search engines, social media platforms, and infrastructure providers – whose hidden rules influence what we are allowed to see and say. In *Lawless*, Nicolas P. Suzor presents gripping examples of exactly how tech companies govern our digital environment and how they bend to pressure from governments and other powerful actors to censor and control the flow of information online. We are at a constitutional moment – an opportunity to rethink the basic rules of how the internet is governed. Suzor offers a vision of a vibrant, diverse, and flourishing internet that can protect our fundamental rights from the lawless rule of tech. The culmination of more than ten years of original research, this groundbreaking work should be read by anyone who cares about the internet and the future of our shared social spaces.

NICOLAS P. SUZOR is principal research fellow in the Queensland University of Technology School of Law and Digital Media Research Centre, where he leads a program of work on the governance of digital platforms and internet intermediaries. He has published over forty articles and book chapters. He is deputy chair and a founding board member of Digital Rights Watch in Australia.

D1453817

Lawless

THE SECRET RULES THAT GOVERN OUR DIGITAL LIVES

NICOLAS P. SUZOR

Queensland University of Technology

CAMBRIDGE
UNIVERSITY PRESS

CAMBRIDGE
UNIVERSITY PRESS

University Printing House, Cambridge CB2 8BS, United Kingdom

One Liberty Plaza, 20th Floor, New York, NY 10006, USA

477 Williamstown Road, Port Melbourne, VIC 3207, Australia

314–321, 3rd Floor, Plot 3, Splendor Forum, Jasola District Centre, New Delhi – 110025, India

79 Anson Road, #06–04/06, Singapore 079906

Cambridge University Press is part of the University of Cambridge.

It furthers the University's mission by disseminating knowledge in the pursuit of
education, learning, and research at the highest international levels of excellence.

www.cambridge.org
Information on this title: www.cambridge.org/9781108481229
DOI: 10.1017/9781108666428

© Nicolas P. Suzor 2019

First published 2019

Printed in the United Kingdom by TJ International Ltd. Padstow Cornwall

A catalogue record for this publication is available from the British Library.

Library of Congress Cataloging-in-Publication Data
NAMES: Suzor, Nicolas P., 1981– author.
TITLE: Lawless : the secret rules that govern our digital lives / Nicolas P. Suzor.
DESCRIPTION: Cambridge, United Kingdom ; New York, NY : Cambridge University Press, 2019. |
Includes bibliographical references and index.
IDENTIFIERS: LCCN 2018058444 | ISBN 9781108481229 (hardback) | ISBN 9781108740470 (paperback)
SUBJECTS: LCSH: Internet–Law and legislation. | Internet governance–Law and legislation. |
Social media–Law and legislation. | Copyright. | Privacy, Right of.
CLASSIFICATION: LCC K564.C6 S875 2019 | DDC 343.09/944–DC23
LC record available at https://lccn.loc.gov/2018058444

ISBN 978-1-108-48122-9 Hardback
ISBN 978-1-108-74047-0 Paperback

Contents

Acknowledgments

First, this book is dedicated to the memory of my father, Gabriel Suzor, who read every word I ever published, and whose advice to write more simply I should have followed long ago.

This book has been a long time coming. It started over ten years ago, when I started my PhD research on the governance of virtual worlds. A lot has changed since then, but I am always grateful for the excellent research training I received and the amazing opportunities I was given. Brian Fitzgerald was my supervisor and mentor, and it is his work on "digital constitutionalism" that animates the ideas in this book. I grew up, academically, in the Australian Research Council (ARC) Centre for Creative Industries and Innovation (CCI), among legal experts and media and communications scholars, and I could never have asked for a better home. Over the last decade, I have benefited from the advice and support of many great colleagues – far too many to name – from the CCI and the Queensland University of Technology (QUT) law school. Early on in my career, Stuart Cunningham and Ros Mason generously provided crucial time for me to extend my research past my PhD on extended research leave, and Judith McNamara and Matthew Rimmer have supported my work over the last four years. I want to particularly thank Judith for her outstanding leadership of the School of Law and all her support over the past few years. Parts of this book have been published, in modified form, in outlets including the Melbourne University Law Review, Social Media + Society, Policy & Internet, International Communication Gazette, and the International Journal of Communication.

Most of this book draws from the last three years of my research, which has been supported by an ARC Discovery Early Career Researcher Award fellowship (project number DE160101542). Over this time, I have been housed in the amazingly vibrant and generative intellectual environment of the Digital Media Research Centre. To say I am both extraordinarily grateful and extraordinarily lucky for these opportunities is a massive understatement. I am grateful beyond words to the close knit communities of scholars, here at QUT, nationally, and internationally, that have given so much of their collective time to help me in my research and in my academic development. I am enormously thankful for the leadership work that Jean Burgess has put into making the DMRC such a welcoming, caring, fun, and stimulating community.

Much of this book has been inspired by the great people I am fortunate enough to work with: all my colleagues at the Digital Media Research Centre and the Faculty of Law that have helped to work through and refine the research and argument in this book. The students and postdocs in our lab have played a huge role in pushing forward our research on platform governance in interesting and highly innovative ways, and I am very grateful to have learned so much from their work – including, particularly, Stef Dugauy, Ariadna Matamoros Fernandez, Andrew Quodling, Alice Witt, Rosalie Gillett, Natalie McIntosh, and Joanne Gray. I am particularly grateful to my collaborators on a lot of the research underpinning this work, including Jean Burgess, Sarah Myers West, Jillian York, Molly Dragiewicz, Bridget Harris, Pat Aufderheide, Michael Guihot, Anne Matthew, and Patrik Wikström.

I am grateful for excellent research assistance in bringing this book together. Particularly, Rosalie Gillett, but also Tess Van Geelen and Bobbie Seignior. Many people were generous enough to read parts of this manuscript in various forms, including Suzy Wood, Ricky and Nina Grafton, Sean and Peter Ridgewell, Hope Johnson, Terry Flew, Tom Cochrane, and Alice Witt. I had the benefit of expert editorial assistance from Brendan Dabkowski, Jackie Lipton, Melissa Gold, and the Cambridge University Press team: Matt Gallaway, Emma Collison, Andrew Ward, Abigail Neale, and Shaheer Husanne.

Thanks to Ross, for endless support and diversion, and thanks to Ricky, Nats, Lucas, and Jared, for listening to me talk about this work. Thanks to Pia and Patrik for great times, great food, and great support. Thanks to my mother, Martine. And, most of all, for her unending patience and insight, thank you always to Kylie.

PART I

A Lawless Internet

1

The Hidden Rules of the Internet

In August 2017, several hundred white nationalists marched on the small university town of Charlottesville, Virginia. The rally turned tragic when one of the protesters rammed his car into a crowd of counterprotesters, killing 32-year-old Heather Heyer. The *Washington Post* characterized the protesters as "a meticulously organized, well-coordinated and heavily armed company of white nationalists."[1]

Heyer's death was mourned across the United States, but to people on the Nazi website The Daily Stormer it was reason to celebrate. Stormer editor Andrew Anglin wrote that Heyer was a "Fat, Childless 32-Year-Old Slut" and that "most people are glad she is dead."[2] On the site's forums and in its private chat channels, participants spewed hateful memes and made plans to send armed Nazi agitators to Heyer's funeral.

Rampant abuse and hatred on digital networks is not new. The pressure to combat hate is strongest on such ubiquitous social media platforms as Facebook, Twitter, and Reddit. Governments and civil society organizations worldwide have complained for years that, even though their terms of service generally prohibit abuse and hate speech, these platforms do not do enough to enforce their rules. Social media platforms are responding to increasing pressure by more clearly articulating their standards of acceptable behavior and banning users and groups that spread hatred and abuse. These rules are not yet uniformly enforced, but they are becoming enforced more regularly.

As the large and well-known networks begin to crack down on abuse and hate, hate groups are moving to less mainstream sites. The Daily Stormer is a perfect example. It is one of the larger neo-Nazi sites, described by the nonprofit Southern Poverty Law Center in 2016 as the "top hate site in America" and "the most popular English-language radical right website in the world."[3] Southern Poverty Law Center senior research analyst Keegan Hankes explains that the site "took its name from *Der Stürmer*, an astoundingly vile and pornographic Nazi newspaper started by Julius Streicher and specializing in attacking Jews. Streicher was later hanged for war crimes at Nuremberg."[4] Like many extremist sites, The Daily Stormer operated on the safety of its own domain and hosted its own site, which meant it was free to follow its own rules.

Even on the open web, away from the policies of social media platforms, there are always points of control on the internet. Each website must have a hosting service for its hardware or virtual servers, lease a network connection, and register a domain name. Everyone who wants to use the internet has to enter into an agreement with an internet service provider (ISP). The contracts for these services usually contain a clause that allows the provider to cancel the agreement at any time. This means that companies that provide infrastructure services on the internet can make decisions about who is allowed to speak and participate online. Still, it's rare for an internet infrastructure service provider to get involved in public debates about the content that people distribute over their networks. Many of these infrastructure companies see themselves as neutral, and the presumption that they shouldn't get involved in debates about content is as old as the internet itself. This means that, even though an ISP might cancel an account on occasion, hate groups have not traditionally had difficulty finding a host that will accept their content.

Charlottesville was a game changer. During the media storm about the rise of domestic extremist groups, infrastructure companies made unprecedentedly concerted moves to disconnect The Daily Stormer. GoDaddy, a well-known domain registrar, informed The Daily Stormer that it would no longer host the site's domain name. The Daily Stormer moved to Google's domain management service and was kicked off within hours. In addition, Google placed a "hold" on the site, which prevented it from moving to a different registrar and effectively confiscated the main domain. This was a serious problem for the Stormer; without a well-known domain name, websites are extremely difficult to find. The site operators then attempted to register a series of other domains, including through registrars in China, Russia, and Albania, each of which was canceled only hours later.

The most significant move came when Cloudflare, a content distribution network, canceled its contracts with The Daily Stormer. Cloudflare is not a host, but a security and content distribution company that accounts for nearly 10 percent of the world's internet traffic.[5] It makes copies of its clients' websites and distributes them worldwide so that they are faster to access and protected against hackers and other security breaches. Most of us never think about companies like Cloudflare because they exist in the background of the internet and, although they are what allow sites we access every day to function smoothly, we would have little to no reason to interact directly with the company. Companies like Cloudflare not only make the web faster, they provide crucial protections from attackers who routinely try to force websites offline. A distributed denial of service (DDoS) attack works by flooding a web server with so many fake requests that it becomes unable to respond – effectively shutting the website down. DDoS attacks are so commonplace now that any high-traffic or controversial site must use a content distribution network or risk being blasted off the internet by malicious attackers. Very little technical skill is needed to coordinate a DDoS attack. Without the protection of a service like Cloudflare, a site like The Daily Stormer could be easily taken offline by anyone who disagreed with its hateful content. In fact, it was a would-be attacker that first contacted Cloudflare and asked it to drop The Daily Stormer as a client: "Get out of the way so we can DDoS this site off the Internet."[6]

Cloudflare historically shied away from making decisions about which sites should stay online. It has a policy to follow the law and only remove accounts or provide identifying information subject to a valid court order in the jurisdictions in which it operates. Since 2013, it had prominently stated that "Cloudflare has never terminated a customer or taken down content due to political pressure," and it assures users that it will "exhaust all legal remedies" to try to protect its users before it terminates a customer account.[7] The decision to drop The Daily Stormer was an important one. The site could have continued shopping around for hosts and domain registrars, but without the protection offered by one of a small number of content distribution networks like Cloudflare or its competitors it was unlikely to survive on the open web.

After running out of options, The Daily Stormer moved to a part of the "dark web."[8] The dark web is almost like the internet's alternate universe; it's not findable by search engines and can only be accessed through special anonymizing browsers, like Tor, that are designed to be private and resilient. Tools like Tor have become relatively easy to install, but they still require technical skills, knowledge, and some determination to use. Even without the dark web, it is almost impossible to completely remove any site from the internet; there will always be people willing to create copies and archives of content that others try to block. But censorship doesn't have to be perfect to be effective. By making The Daily Stormer difficult enough to find and getting it off the mainstream of the open web, anti-racism advocates hope that they can substantially slow its influence and starve it of attention.

The decisions by major internet infrastructure companies to remove The Daily Stormer from the open web have been extremely controversial. The strongest critics are not the people who want to support the site's vile propagation of hate; rather, it's those who worry about the implications of putting public pressure on infrastructure companies and how that affects regulation of speech in the future. The Electronic Frontier Foundation (EFF), a civil society group dedicated to protecting freedom of speech online, took a hard line in response: "Protecting free speech is not something we do because we agree with all of the speech that gets protected. We do it because we believe that no one – not the government and not private commercial enterprises – should decide who gets to speak and who doesn't."[9] The EFF and others worry about the precedent set by these decisions, particularly as major internet companies are facing a lot of pressure to do more to police the internet on an ever-widening set of issues. It points out that decisions made at the infrastructure level – like the domain name system, crucial backbone links, or the massive pipes operated by content distribution networks – will always be somewhat crude. The companies that operate this infrastructure cannot target single posts or individual pieces of content; they only have a blunt ability to refuse to host an entire site or domain. This power, many free speech advocates believe, should almost never be exercised because it will inevitably censor more than the specific posts or content targeted.

What makes this so difficult is that infrastructure services are sometimes the only viable option to target some websites. The standards for hate speech are very different outside the United States, and The Daily Stormer website would probably be illegal in countries like Germany or France, which have strong laws designed to ensure that people cannot publicly advocate genocide. Without tackling internet infrastructure on some level, these laws are basically unenforceable – sites like The Daily Stormer can easily move to a jurisdiction that will give them the protection that they seek. Infrastructure may not be the best way to tackle harmful content, but sometimes it is the only option.

The crux of the issue is not really about speech but due process. Due process is the difference between enforcing a legitimate law in a careful and accountable way and making an arbitrary or capricious decision that can have serious consequences. When Cloudflare announced it had dropped The Daily Stormer, Cloudflare's CEO Matthew Prince blogged about his deep ambivalence about the decision. He stood behind the decision but worried about the precedent it set for the future: "Law enforcement, legislators, and courts have the political legitimacy and predictability to make decisions on what content should be restricted. Companies should not."[10] In a memo to the company, he elaborated:

> This was my decision. Our terms of service reserve the right for us to terminate users of our network at our sole discretion. My rationale for making this decision was simple: the people behind the Daily Stormer are assholes and I'd had enough.
>
> Let me be clear: this was an arbitrary decision. It was different than what I'd talked with our senior team about yesterday. I woke up this morning in a bad mood and decided to kick them off the Internet. I called our legal team and told them what we were going to do. I called our Trust & Safety team and had them stop the service. It was a decision I could make because I'm the CEO of a major Internet infrastructure company.
>
> Having made that decision we now need to talk about why it is so dangerous. I'll be posting something on our blog later today. Literally, I woke up in a bad mood and decided someone shouldn't be allowed on the Internet. No one should have that power.[11]

This is what I mean when I say the internet is governed in a "lawless" way. The rule of law is the difference between arbitrary decisions and decisions that are fair and accountable. Cloudflare, like many other companies that influence what we see and say online, operates within the law. But when such companies make decisions about who uses their networks and how, they have almost unlimited discretion. They are accountable only to the market; there are no checks and balances on how they wield their power. Whether we agree with the outcome or not, Cloudflare's decision to disconnect an entire website was based on the personal whim of its CEO. Prince is right: no one should have that power.

PROCESS MATTERS

This is not an isolated example. For as long as the commercial internet has been available, concerns about bullying, harassment, hate speech, and abuse have prompted calls for internet companies to better police the web. Civil society organizations are constantly lobbying for social media platforms to better protect vulnerable people, and users themselves are threatening to leave social media platforms that have become toxic with rampant abuse. Executives at these companies know that they need to take these issues seriously. Hosting company DigitalOcean terminated web hosting for both The Daily Stormer and pro-hate speech crowdfunding site Hatreon; it said in a statement that "[t]his is a terrible situation, but DigitalOcean believes that tech has a role in preventing hate crimes and violence from spreading, and takes that responsibility seriously.[12]" Undoubtedly, tech companies are going to continue to face more demands to take action against users who are spreading hatred.

Technology companies are facing mounting pressure from many different directions to do much more work to police what their users do online. New laws are being introduced around the world – and particularly in Europe – that impose tough new requirements on the way the industry deals with personal data, hate speech, copyright infringement, and other issues. The recent revelations of foreign interference in the 2016 US presidential elections has led to increasing calls for social media platforms and search engines to filter out disinformation and to crack down on fake accounts. The copyright industries have been lobbying for years for the power to require domain name registrars to confiscate the domains of sites that facilitate piracy, to prohibit payment processors from forwarding donations or payments for advertising, and to require ISPs to block their traffic.[13]

The issue of due process has not yet been solved. In the past, due process would involve the courts, which are set up to ensure fairness. It's not realistic to think that courts will have a primary role in the future of the internet, though. They're too expensive and too slow to make a real dent in online abuse and hate, or copyright infringement, or many other problems that involve user-generated content on a massive scale. Technology companies have become the preferred way to enforce the law online because they are able to cheaply influence large numbers of users, but this efficiency always comes at the cost of due process.

When technology companies make decisions that affect their users, there are few avenues of redress for people who feel that they have been treated unfairly. US federal law provides technology companies immunity for their decisions to moderate their networks, and absolves them of liability for what their users say online. Their power to control their users is protected by the First Amendment, but the First Amendment does not protect users from the decisions of technology companies. The First Amendment only prevents the US government from interfering with speech; US tech companies are private entities and are free to decide whether or not they provide services to a particular person or group. US tech companies are not obliged, under the First Amendment, to respect free speech rights of users.

The absence of government regulation is not freedom. This book is called *Lawless* because so many of the decisions about what we can do and say online are made behind closed doors by private companies. This is the opposite of the standards we expect of legitimate, legal decision-making in a democratic society. Where governments do not set laws to regulate the internet, platforms and other powerful telecommunications providers are constantly making decisions about what types of speech they will carry. The major social media platforms all have rules about the content they deem acceptable, and many of these have expressed limits on hatred and abuse. Without law, though, these rules are not enforced in any way that can be called legitimate. There's no easy way to ensure either that the rules are consistently enforced or that they are enforced in a way that is fair and free from bias.

Technology companies exercise an unprecedented degree of power over how we share information, who we communicate with, and what news we see. Search engines have a massive degree of influence over the information we find and how we connect with other individuals and businesses. Social media platforms like Facebook, Twitter, YouTube, and Instagram constantly make decisions that directly influence what we can see and share. Infrastructure companies can prioritize certain types of internet traffic and block access to services and websites. Hosting companies store the websites, files, and documents we share and make them available to the world. These companies "govern" our online social lives. They don't govern in the way that governments do, through binding laws and armed police, which means we shouldn't hold them to the same standards as governments. But their rules do influence how we communicate with each other, what we can say, and what information is available for us to see. We don't currently have any useful ways to think about how they govern or how we should limit their power.

This is a book about the future of our democracies and shared social spaces. Governments in countries across the world are trying to regulate internet companies. Governments will inevitably continue to try to make them responsible for removing hate speech or preventing foreign governments from interfering in elections or reducing abuse and bullying. Unfortunately, these kinds of laws often create new problems because they focus on various questions about content and not the *processes* of governing how users behave.

The core point of this book is that process matters. These challenges of governance are *constitutional* problems – in the sense of rules that set out how our shared social spaces are *constituted* and how decisions that affect our lives are made.

For several years, pressure has been mounting steadily for powerful technology companies to wield their power over us more responsibly. We are now at a constitutional moment, a time of profound potential change, where we all have an opportunity to demand more from those who rule over our digital lives. Sir Tim Berners Lee, inventor of the World Wide Web, has called for a Magna Carta for the digital age. The metaphor is an excellent one: In 1215, the Magna Carta marked an historic turning point when the barons of England demanded legal protection from the king's tyranny. It was a declaration that the king was not above the law – that his power had to be exercised in a way that respected the fundamental rights of his subjects. Now, many people think that we too deserve better from our digital rulers.

This book takes seriously the challenge of making the decisions of technology companies more legitimate: more fair, more predictable, and more accountable. Ultimately, I argue that we need a new constitutionalism – a new way of thinking about the power that technology companies wield and the discretion they exercise over our lives. To constitutionalize power means to impose limits on how rules are made and enforced. Constitutionalism is the difference between lawlessness and a system of rules that are fairly, equally, and predictably applied. We should expect the technology companies that rule over us to take on the hard work, now, to develop their own constitutional protections that can help ensure that *our* rights are protected.

With this book I hope to provide a guide to what more legitimate digital governance might look like. The pressure to regulate is strong, and laws are being implemented around the world that will impose new obligations on technology companies. Not all of these laws are well designed, and some even try to enlist tech companies in illegitimate spying and censorship on behalf of governments. Meanwhile, many of the people in the major tech companies are now working hard to improve how they make decisions, and some companies are realizing that it is best if this sort of change comes from within. This book outlines how tech companies can improve their own systems, how governments can enact better laws, and how we can all work to hold power to account. Real change will require the active participation of a broad range of civil society groups, activists, journalists, academics, and regulators. It will be hard work and require many difficult public debates with no easy answers, but there is a great deal at stake. For those who believe in a vibrant, flourishing, competitive, and innovative internet that is governed fairly and accountably, we have an opportunity and an obligation to work together to develop a new constitutionalism.

2

Who Makes the Rules?

In 2009, Facebook CEO Mark Zuckerberg announced that the massive social network would become more democratic. Responding to criticism over controversial changes to its privacy policy, Zuckerberg pledged that from then on Facebook users would have direct input on the development of the site's terms of service. These terms were "the governing document" for Facebook users across the world, Zuckerberg said; "Given its importance, we need to make sure the terms reflect the principles and values of the people using the service."[1] Facebook committed to ensuring that users would be consulted on any changes to its rules and that the company would in future defer to the popular will of its users through a new voting process.

This experiment with direct democracy did not last long. Facebook set the threshold for voting at an unrealistically high level – it would only be bound if 30 percent of its active users voted. On a platform the size of Facebook – with billions of active users – this target is almost impossible to reach. When the time came to vote on another set of changes in 2012, Facebook's rules meant that 300 million people had to engage in order to change Facebook's mind. Over 600,000 users voted, and 88 percent of those opposed the changes, but this was less than 1 percent of the platform's total user base. After the vote, Facebook rolled back its commitment to direct user input. Zuckerberg's comments were quietly disavowed – Facebook even went to the trouble of altering the 2009 blog post's byline to attribute it to a former employee.[2]

How platforms are governed *matters*. Platforms mediate the way people communicate, and the decisions they make have a real effect on public culture and the social and political lives of their users. Facebook's experiment with democratic ideals neatly illustrates the disconnect between the social values at stake and the hard legal realities. In law, terms of service are contractual documents that setup a simple consumer transaction: in exchange for access to the platform, users agree to be bound by the terms and conditions set out. The legal relationship of providers to users is one of firm to consumer, not sovereign to citizen.[3] In legal terms, it makes little sense to talk of "rights" in these consumer transactions.

Generally speaking, terms of service documents allocate a great deal of power to the operators. Particularly for large, corporate platforms these terms of service are written in a way that is designed to safeguard their commercial interests.[4] They reserve absolute discretion to the operators of the platform to make and enforce the rules as they see fit. Terms of service documents aren't designed to be governing documents; they're designed to protect the company's legal interests.

In the United States, the language of constitutional rights has almost no application in the "private" sphere; constitutional law applies primarily to the "public" actions of state actors and organizations in which the state is directly involved. This means that constitutional rights – freedom of speech and association, requirements of due process, rights to participate in the democratic process – where they exist all apply only against the state and not private against actors. It is a basic truth of US constitutional law that the First Amendment, like many other constitutional rights, applies against the government and not private companies like Facebook or Google. The words are clear: "Congress shall make no law," the First Amendment begins, "abridging the freedom of speech, or of the press." The framers of the US constitution were fundamentally concerned about government tyranny, not about the decisions of private individuals or media firms. So, technically, there is no real concept of legally protected freedom of speech on Facebook. The government can't order Facebook to remove a picture you post (unless it's obscene or illegal for some other reason), but Facebook can implement whatever rules it likes. The reasoning is simple: the government is powerful – it has a monopoly on the use of force and we have no choice but to obey, so its powers must be restricted by law and carefully limited by the courts. But since nobody is *required* to use Facebook, the constitution has little to say about how Facebook operates.

The legal reality is that social media platforms belong to the companies that create them, and they have almost absolute power over how they are run. The terms of service agreements of each major platform have a clause that sets out the basic rule: your access to the platform can be terminated at any time for any or no reason.[5] From this basic rule everything else stems. Your use of the platform signals acceptance of whatever rules the platform may set, and its decision is always final. Having accepted and adopted these terms, users are legally bound by them.

This hard-line legal approach may be technically correct, but for many people it feels somehow wrong to say that values like freedom of speech do not apply in social media. Particularly for the major social media platforms, which sometimes feel like public spaces and sometimes feel like *our* spaces,[6] it seems strange to say that the spaces *belong* to the firm that operates the platform. In part, this is exactly the way that social media has been marketed to us: they're our profiles, our walls, where we can connect with our friends, express ourselves, and share our lives. Even the executives who run these platforms talk about them in these terms – Dick Costolo,

Twitter's former CEO, once called Twitter a "global town square,"[7] and Zuckerberg has spoken about Facebook's core role as developing "the new social infrastructure to create the world we want for generations to come."[8]

Social media platforms provide the space for us to connect and communicate with each other, and they set the rules for participation. There is no such thing as a "neutral" platform; all platforms make decisions, in their rules and in their technical design, that shape the kinds of content that people can post and the kinds of content made visible. Because the major social media platforms have become so central to our lives, the decisions they make have a very powerful impact.

Consider how important social media has become to democracy. Zeynep Tufekci is an academic who studies how people use social media to organize political action. She shows how social media has empowered social movements by allowing people to rapidly form large groups of protestors with a shared goal. Social media platforms provide a way for ordinary people to spread news and draw attention to causes they care about to an extent, and at a speed, that has never before been possible. The ability to participate in social media, then, has become critical to effective political action. Tufekci writes about an activist whose Facebook account was repeatedly disabled because of a conflict between Facebook's policy that users have to use their real names and its policy that prohibits offensive words in a name. The activist was trapped: she couldn't use her real (non-English) name, because in English it was a vulgar word, and she couldn't use a nickname, because she wasn't able to prove to Facebook that it was her real name. Politically active people on Facebook are often at risk of being reported by people who disagree with their views, and the activist had to deal with many exhausting cycles of getting suspended, sending her passport to Facebook, and trying to explain her situation to someone who could help her. Tufekci explains the very real impact that such an experience can have on the ability of people to participate in modern society: "She was finally able to reinstate her account after much effort, largely because she was connected to people who could alert Facebook to the issue. For others, such an ordeal might mean that they are, in effect, banned from the biggest public square in the world, which is also the biggest private social network. The stakes could hardly be higher."[9]

At the same time, social media platforms often feel like our own, private spaces. When we talk to our friends through our Facebook walls, share moments of our lives through Instagram or Snapchat, or talk through instant messaging apps, it often feels like we are in control. Massive platforms are not communities – they're much too big and too diverse for that.[10] But they do host many real communities of people who come together around many different shared interests. When people come together and develop real personal connections and their own norms about how they interact with each other, they create a shared identity and real personal connections.[11] These interactions are all mediated through the platform, but they are real and direct connections between people that take place within a space that is neither fully private nor public. When we are talking and sharing among our friends and our communities, the governing role of the platform often fades into the background in the face of these real personal connections. Unless we are really paying attention or something goes wrong, we often don't experience online social spaces as places that are owned by the platform – they feel like ours.

The law is quite clear in this area. The networks that we use every day to communicate with each other are owned by their operators. Legally, we only have the rights that are in the contracts we agree to when we sign up with a new service. Almost nobody ever reads these, and for good reason. Not only are they often written in dense legalese, but there is no opportunity to negotiate the terms anyway. They are almost all very careful to promise nothing and reserve almost absolute discretion to the owner of the network.

Although the law is clear, it is at odds with how these networks feel, and it is a bad fit for how important they have become. Zuckerberg was right when he said that terms of service have become governing documents. His proclamation recognizes a truth that the law does not: contractual terms of service play an important role in the governance of everyday life. They are constitutional documents in that they are integral to the way our shared social spaces are constituted and governed. Like constitutions, terms of service documents now set the rules for how we participate in online social spaces. But unlike constitutions, they almost never impose any rules or limits about how those in charge should behave. They provide users with no rights, except for the ultimatum: if, for any reason, you disagree with the rules or how they are enforced, you can always leave.

Increasingly, it seems that the gap between what the law says and how we experience online spaces is causing a great deal of tension. Every few days there are news reports about social media platforms making mistakes in their policies or unfairly enforcing their rules. Some of these turn into major investigations, where the CEOs of tech companies are hauled in front of the Congress of the United States to explain and apologize. The law is definitely on their side – these companies can basically do what they want – but clearly people now often feel uneasy when social media platforms make decisions that seem biased or somehow wrong.

WHOSE VALUES APPLY?

Celeste Liddle is an activist, a black feminist member of the Arrernte Indigenous Australian people. On International Women's Day in 2016, she gave a speech at the Melbourne Writers' Festival about how Facebook had suspended her account for posting pictures of "topless desert women painted up for ceremony engaging in traditional dance."[12] Liddle's speech points to the double standards of contemporary Western culture that celebrates nude depictions of women that fit a certain cultural ideal, but does not tolerate images of older Aboriginal women taking part in women's culture. The charge here is familiar. Western media firms have a long history of presenting highly sexualized images of the feminine ideal – popular media is saturated with skinny-waisted, big-busted women who are partially clothed or whose nipples and genitals are only just obscured. Depictions of women of color, women of average or larger body weight, or women with disabilities are much less visible in mainstream media. If women "are going to be semi-naked," Liddle pointed out, "it needs to be for the enjoyment of men."[13]

Liddle's speech was picked up by a news organization, *New Matilda*, which shared it on Facebook with an illustration of Aboriginal women performing at a public ceremony. The image showed two women from the remote Central Australian community of Ampilatwatja performing at a public ceremony, protesting against harsh laws that limited the autonomy of remote Australian towns. The two women wore skirts and had traditional body paint on their bare torsos. The post was quickly removed by Facebook for violating its community standards that prohibit nudity. Liddle and others who shared the post found that their accounts were suspended – and Liddle was told by Facebook that she was a repeat offender for her history of posting nude images.

Also for International Women's Day, *Esquire Magazine* ran a feature on Kim Kardashian, accompanied by a picture of the celebrity also "painted up" in the desert. Kardashian's full-body nude portrait is sexualized, but carefully avoids showing her nipples or genitals. *New Matilda* was quick to point out that Facebook did not censor *Esquire's* post, while Liddle was again suspended, for a week this time, for sharing other media articles covering her original suspension.

The irony was not lost on readers. More than 20,000 people signed a petition started by Liddle, asking Facebook to review its community standards, which Liddle and many others perceived as "blatantly racist, sexist and offensive."[14] Facebook eventually reinstated Liddle's account, but offered a distinct nonapology for the way it moderates content:

> We are aware that people sometimes share content containing nudity for reasons like awareness campaigns, artistic projects or cultural investigations. The reason we restrict the display of nudity is because some audiences within our global community may be sensitive to this type of content – particularly because of cultural background or age. In order to treat people fairly and respond to reports quickly, it is essential that we have policies in place that our global teams can apply uniformly and easily when reviewing content. As a result, our policies can sometimes be more blunt than we would like, and restrict content shared for legitimate purposes. We encourage people to share Celeste Liddle's speech on Facebook by simply removing the image before posting it.[15]

This is one example of many controversies about how social media platforms create and implement rules about what content people are allowed to view and share. When these controversies arise, the curious and apparently inconsistent decisions that platforms make are exposed. These are moments of opportunity for people to ask and debate what we want from social media and how we want our online social spaces to look and feel and be governed. Social media platforms have become so important to so many different aspects of our daily lives that the decisions they make have a substantial effect on how we perceive the world and how we communicate with others. Most of these decisions happen quietly, almost invisibly, and most people will rarely, if ever, be suspended or banned from social media platforms for the content they post. But controversies like this, where decisions look clearly biased or simply inexplicable, can capture the attention of a group of people sufficiently large to send a shock through the system. More recently, these shocks seem to be coming more frequently, and more and more people are calling for change in the way that social media platforms moderate content.[16] For their part, social media platforms are getting better at dealing with and defusing these controversies as they arise.[17] Sometimes policies are tweaked; other times apologies are made and promises to review and improve are given. Real change, however, is slow to come and may require us to rethink some basic assumptions about how the internet is governed.

THE MODERATION PROCESS

Platforms work hard to limit the extent to which they are seen to be interfering with user content. By presenting themselves as neutral intermediaries, mere carriers of content and facilitators of conversations, platforms try to avoid being held responsible for what their users do.[18] At the same time, curation and moderation is a vital part of the experience of commercial social media platforms. Tarleton Gillespie, a social media researcher at Microsoft Research, explains that curation and moderation of content is essentially the core commodity that platforms offer: "Though part of the web, social media platforms promise [to] rise above it, by offering a better experience of all this information and sociality: curated, organized, archived, and moderated."[19] Their revenue comes from selling ads and increases the longer they can keep people engaged. This means that they have a strong incentive to exercise control over the content each of us sees – if they can keep presenting us with relevant content that we enjoy, we will stay longer and engage more. When they don't enforce rules about what people can post or provide tools for users to curate for themselves, large platforms quickly get overrun with spam and toxicity.[20] Moderation and curation is an important function that platforms must provide in order to deliver a valuable experience for their users – doing this well is critical to their ability to survive.

Most moderation happens after a post is published. The meteoric rise of social media is founded on a certain sense that it is organic and genuine and, well, *social* – generated by our friends. This means, generally speaking, that content is usually not approved in advance. For any major site, the costs of monitoring content as it is uploaded are far too high. Even if it were possible to screen content in advance, many sites rely on the immediacy of conversation. Real-time moderation by humans would introduce serious enough delays between posting that it would stunt conversations and reduce engagement. The general principle is usually that platforms will publish almost everything that is posted, but will later review content that other users complain about or that is flagged as potentially prohibited by an automated system.

When a post is flagged by users who think it is inappropriate, it goes into a queue for review by employees or agents of the social media platform – or, sometimes, other users who act as community moderators. For large commercial sites, this job is typically outsourced to people in developing countries who are tasked thousands of times a day with making decisions about whether to ban a piece of content. The work can be mentally challenging. Sometimes moderators have as little as ten seconds to make a decision. Most of the work is mundane – repetitive and poorly paid. It can be empowering work.[21] But it can also be soul-destroying at times. These are the people tasked with reviewing some of the worst content the internet has to offer. From abusive and harassing posts, to gruesomely violent videos, to images of sexual abuse against children, these minimum-wage employees constitute one part of the armies of moderators on the frontlines of a battle to clean up the most repulsive material on the internet.[22]

Some decisions can't be made by these frontline moderators, and they get escalated to management. There are teams of people within most large social media companies, often based in Silicon Valley, who set the rules, sort out difficult complaints, deal with public controversies, and ensure the system runs as smoothly as possible. Like many firms in Silicon Valley, these groups are more likely to consist of white, educated, well-off males, and they come under a lot of criticism for setting or upholding policies that inadvertently entrench existing biases against minorities or inadequately promote diversity. This is obviously something that major platforms are very sensitive about, and some are better than others at building diverse teams with diverse perspectives, but change is slower than many would like.

One of the most difficult parts for users to understand about these content moderation systems is how decisions are actually made. Paradoxically, social media platforms often want the absolute power to curate, moderate, and control their networks while not wanting to look like they're moderating. Social media platforms try to maintain their neutrality – they want to be seen as merely providing the technology for people to communicate and share their thoughts and content. To maintain this veneer of neutrality, they hide the massive and mundane processes of moderating content and responding to complaints. This means that when platforms moderate and curate content, they often do it invisibly to sustain this fiction. Most moderation is done in secret, and the rules of platforms are enforced in a way that is usually well hidden from public view. For most major platforms, their content moderation processes are "black boxes."[23] They're designed to be opaque and hidden.

This is partly because the platforms don't want to disclose their processes to the scammers, spammers, and trolls who constantly try to skirt the rules. But mostly this is because it's difficult to please everyone when platforms make decisions. Decisions about content are almost always contentious in some way. For any given piece of content that goes through moderation, at least the person who posted it and the person who complained about it are likely to have opposite opinions about whether it should be permitted. These disagreements extend along familiar political divides, and platforms often understandably want to avoid as much scrutiny as possible about how decisions are made, because, inevitably, some group will be upset whether the platform chooses to remove content or leave it up.

The result, unfortunately, is that it becomes hard for users to get good information about how content is moderated. Almost everything we know about content moderation comes from leaked training documents, isolated controversies that draw widespread media attention, and some clever reverse engineering by civil society groups and researchers. Real evidence is made available infrequently. The news blog *Gawker* was able to get its hands on a set of cheat sheets developed to help Facebook's outsourced moderators apply its rules back in 2012, revealing peculiarly specific interpretations of the general rules. Crushed heads were OK, but moderators should censor images that contained prominent camel toes, for example.[24] A few years later, *The Guardian* released a series of articles on secret documents it dubbed "The Facebook Files," showing that Facebook had become more organized in its training, but that moderators still had to learn very specific interpretations of the site's complex rules.[25] *ProPublica*, in 2017, was able to obtain and analyze what it described as "a trove of internal documents" that shed "new light on the secret guidelines that Facebook's censors use to distinguish between hate speech and legitimate political expression."[26] All of these documents are littered with what Gillespie calls the "tombstones" of past disputes: special rules that have developed, over the years, to deal with particular controversies: Nazi hate speech, bullying, revenge porn, self-harm and pro-anorexia content, and live streaming of gruesome crimes.[27]

BIAS AND ACCOUNTABILITY

Because they moderate in secret, social media platforms are vulnerable to allegations that they are in some way biased. The sheer scale of material posted every day means that platforms need to employ moderation systems that are cheap and efficient. The modern social web doesn't work if interaction is slow and content is vetted in advance. But at this scale and speed, mistakes are common. The secrecy of content moderation ultimately works against platforms. It leads to a great deal of suspicion when it looks like a platform is biased in some way.[28] Users frequently complain that the rules are unevenly enforced, overly restrictive, or not restrictive enough. Trying to find a logic in what platforms ban is tough; without good, clear information participants turn to folk theories and explanations that range from the platform's incompetence to its outright capture and corruption by vested interests.[29] And without knowing whether a particular decision is just a rare misclassification or a symptom of a deeper trend, users have good cause to be suspicious.

Sometimes, the bias in moderation is a visible and deliberate policy choice by the platform. Take, for example, the long-running controversy over how Facebook and its subsidiary Instagram deal with images of women's nipples and other depictions of the female form. Both platforms ban women's nipples in their terms of service, a policy that activists who cluster around a campaign called "free the nipple" reject as inherently discriminatory. They complain, particularly, that Facebook's policies entrench a particular ideology: the particularly American view that finds nudity offensive but permits violence and gore (a view that is precisely the opposite of similar community standards in Europe). Facebook and Instagram users who were turned into activists when their content was removed or account was suspended for sharing images of their bodies complain that the platforms are full of content that is excessively violent or abusive.

Instagram and Facebook's policies about nudity have shifted in recent years in response to complaints. The organized and sustained complaints of breastfeeding advocates have secured an exception in Facebook and Instagram policies prohibiting women's nipples for "women actively engaged in breastfeeding."[30] This concession came after many protests over the years were picked up by the press, and eventually the platforms were forced to change by the tide of public opinion. Even still, breastfeeding mothers regularly complain that their images have been removed, presumably either accidentally or because the baby was not suckling "actively" enough. Other exceptions have been carved out from the general prohibition on nudity in response to the particular concerns raised by users and the media. Facebook and Instagram allow women's nipples in images that show postmastectomy scarring or other medical issues; photos of people protesting; and photos of paintings, sculptures, and other art.

This more nuanced position is still deeply controversial. Activists continue to complain that Facebook has not correctly drawn the line between acceptable and prohibited nudity. To many, the prohibition still seems unjustifiably restrictive and sexist, since men's nipples are not treated as taboo. These are everyday issues of concern for many people, and, particularly for transgender and nonbinary people, these types of distinctions create restrictions on how people can express themselves online that seem arbitrary and hurtful.

These conflicts raise real questions about what sort of content should be permissible on social media platforms, and who gets to decide the rules. Take, for example, a recent controversy over hate speech documented by Julia Angwin, an investigatory journalist who specializes in uncovering hidden biases in the technology that shapes our lives, from Facebook's news feed, to Amazon's pricing models, to the secret (and deeply racially prejudiced) machine learning algorithms deployed by courts to determine whether offenders should go to prison and for how long.[31] After a terrorist attack in London, a US member of Congress called for the slaughter of radical Muslims on his Facebook page:

The free world ... all of Christendom ... is at war with Islamic horror. Not one penny of American treasure should be granted to any nation who harbors these heathen animals. Not a single radicalized Islamic suspect should be granted any measure of quarter. [...] Every conceivable measure should be engaged to hunt them down. Hunt them, identify them, and kill them. Kill them all. For the sake of all that is good and righteous. Kill them all.[32]

This post, Angwin writes, does not violate Facebook's rules against hate speech because it targets only a subset of Muslims, not all Muslims. If the post had called for the slaughter of all Muslims it would be prohibited as hate speech; if it called for the murder of a particular person, it would be prohibited as a direct threat. But under Facebook's rules, it's permissible to dehumanize and call for the mass murder of a *large group of individuals*.

Angwin was able to obtain internal documents that Facebook uses to train its moderators. A striking example is a slide that explains how Facebook's complicated rules about hate speech work to protect only some subsets of groups. The training image released by Angwin is a quiz that asks whether Facebook protects (1) female drivers; (2) black children; or (3) white men. The correct answer is that Facebook protects white men, but not black children or female drivers from hate speech. The logic is complicated: Facebook treats race as a protected characteristic, but not age. Under Facebook's rules, for a post to be removed, if it targets a subset of a group, both the broader group and the particular subset have to be protected groups. Posts disparaging white men are classified as hate speech because both white people and men are treated by Facebook as protected groups, but slurs against black children are explicitly allowed because they only target a subset of a group that Facebook protects. Angwin points out that this rule leads to results that look very questionable, like when poet and activist Didi Delgado had her account suspended for a week for writing "All white people are racist. Start from this reference point, or you've already failed."[33]

To create workable and reliable rules, platforms have to draw distinctions that reasonable people might disagree on. Sometimes, though, the distinctions are very hard to justify, and it is only through the laborious work of investigative journalists that the rules are made public in a way that can lead to a useful debate. Angwin's work was vitally important in documenting how Facebook's attempt to develop neutral rules that can be consistently applied served, in practice, to provide protection for groups that need it less, while disadvantaging the speech of already-marginalized groups. After the public outrage that followed Angwin's story, Facebook had to tweak its policies to make *age* a protected characteristic.[34]

Social media platforms end up developing complex rules to help their moderators identify when content is not acceptable. Usually, they're trying to find rules that align with what their users expect – they want to provide users with a good experience, and they want to avoid, as far as possible, disappointing users for either censoring too much or too little. But for any network with more than a few people, there will always be disagreement about what, precisely, the rules should allow and prohibit.

For many platforms, the rules start off as informal standards, developed and enforced by a small team. The rules solidify and become more specific as the size of the networks increase and it becomes necessary to hire dedicated teams of moderators. The initial approaches of these teams were very much informed by the values of the people who were in charge of developing policy.[35] Kate Klonick, a law professor at St. John's University, explains that for Facebook, Google, and Twitter there was a common trend where "American lawyers trained and accultur-ated in First Amendment law oversaw the development of company content moderation policy."[36] This led those content moderation teams to try to develop standards that sought to emphasize American freedom of speech values, which were frequently in conflict with demands from people both inside and outside the United States who wanted to see them take more responsibility for removing harmful content. While the platforms were still growing, there was a great deal of flex in these rules, as new problems continuously emerged.

In a widely read story for *The Verge*, Catherine Buni and Soraya Chemaly shone a spotlight on the early days of content moderation at YouTube. A group of ten people, mostly young graduates, were tasked with the job of keeping YouTube clean – but they had to make up the rules for the new site as they went. The team had to make quick decisions about rules and exceptions to rules – like whether a cell-phone video of an Iranian pro-democracy protester who was shot and killed during a demonstration should be allowed because of its political significance, despite its graphic content.[37] The story is the same across most social media platforms in their infancy: small groups of people, predominantly young white college graduates in California, work to guess what rules would work best to satisfy the company's legal obligations, the demands of its users, the tastes of its advertisers, and the moral stance of the staff themselves. The influential law professor Jeffrey Rosen, in an article for *The New Republic*, explained how these "positions give these young people more power over who gets heard around the globe than any politician or bureaucrat – more power, in fact, than any president or judge."[38]

The flexible standards that platforms develop, Klonick explains, eventually had to be codified into complex rules that could be taught to the much larger group of outsourced moderators who took on the job of handling complaints as the platforms grew. The result is a sometimes confusing mess of rules and exceptions that reflect particular ideologies and value judgments. These complex rules are then applied mechanically by workers who have to deal with hundreds or thousands of items a day, leaving little room for debate about context or interpretation.

Setting rules that clearly and predictably explain what, exactly, is prohibited is not an easy task. The challenge of moderating at a massive scale means that rules need to be written very specifically if we are to expect moderators to make consistent decisions. There is a crucial trade-off here between certainty and nuance: for a system of moderation to work efficiently and predictably at this scale, it may not be able to deal with complex contextual information that could inform better, more tailored moderation decisions. The work of setting rules and exceptions is almost never-ending – there will always be new cases that do not clearly fit within established categories. It is unavoidable that companies like Facebook will have to navigate difficult issues as they adapt their rules, and it is impossible to please everyone whenever a particular line is drawn. The biggest problem, however, is that the process of crafting rules and detailed exceptions happens behind closed doors, with little accountability.

Facebook has more than doubled the size of its content moderation workforce in recent years to keep up with demands that it improve the speed and accuracy of its moderation processes. There are more than 10,000 moderators now who make up what Angwin says "may well be the most far-reaching global censorship operation in history."[39] It is also, she continues, "the least accountable: Facebook does not publish the rules it uses to determine what content to allow and what to delete." There are some promising signs that this is changing, as platforms become more aware of the problems that arise when their users do not understand the rules. After criticism by Angwin and many others, Facebook has provided a more detailed explanation of its content moderation processes that includes a redacted version of the internal guidelines it provides to moderators. Other companies have made promises that additional information will be forthcoming. Platforms are getting better at providing understandable explanations of their rules. But there is still a major problem of accountability as rules continue to become more complex. There is a growing disconnect between the simple version of the rules that are published for users to see and the complicated series of tests and exceptions that are actually applied by moderators in practice.

The lack of accountability in moderation systems often leaves users confused about why their content was deleted or their accounts suspended. Sarah Myers West is a researcher with the OnlineCensorship.org project, which documents reports from users about content removals on social media platforms. Trawling through these reports, her research shows just how opaque the content moderation systems of modern platforms are. Users are frequently provided little to no information about why their content has been removed, and it is exceedingly difficult to reach someone at the platform to explain the decision or complain about it. Because of the lack of information available, West explains, users are left guessing about why their post was removed or their account suspended. The most common guess is that one of their contacts complained about a post by flagging it "in the midst of a contentious discussion [...] about politics, religion, or interpersonal relationships"[40] – literally, that they were arguing with someone who took offense and complained to the platform. Others felt discriminated against – Muslims and transgender people, for example, complained that their content was targeted by strangers who wanted to harass or bully them. In other cases, users blamed the platform – like supporters of US President Donald Trump who felt that their posts were removed from Twitter or their accounts suspended "either because Twitter management is protecting [Hillary] Clinton, or her campaign has called for censorship." Facebook found itself in the middle of similar accusations during the last US election after its employees wondered aloud whether the platform should be doing more to support Clinton.[41] In a separate incident, Facebook fired the journalists responsible for curating its highly influential "trending topics" section, which directs users to the high-profile news stories of the day, after workers claimed that the mostly liberal journalists routinely failed to include popular pro-conservative stories.[42]

Platforms also have to deal with organized campaigns by malicious actors who are determined to skirt and undermine their rules. An extensive report by Alice Marwick and Rebecca Lewis from the Data & Society Research Institute documents how far-right political groups have learned to exploit the algorithms that influence visibility on social media platforms to increase the circulation of propaganda and "fake news."[43] This is a major challenge that platforms are still working out how to address. Whatever they end up doing, they're likely to upset certain groups. If platforms rely on old signifiers of reliability – like whether the story came from an established news agency or outlet – they could limit the reach of digital upstarts, citizen journalists, and other important outlets for marginalized voices.[44] If they try to make decisions about the truths of individual articles, they will no doubt quickly become mired in complaints about the interpretation of particular facts and events. But remaining neutral is not an option; if they do nothing, our feeds and mainstream media outlets will continue to be influenced by a flood of disinformation designed to sway the course of our democratic elections.[45]

For many, the rules of social media platforms represent arbitrary value judgments about particular standards of decency that limit their ability to express themselves and perpetuate harmful prejudices. When poet and performer Rupi Kaur posted a photograph of a fully clothed woman lying in bed with a period stain on her trousers, Instagram promptly deleted it, explaining the photo did not follow their community guidelines. Instagram's guidelines say nothing about menstruation, but the platform provided no further information.

Instagram's decision to remove the image sparked outrage. People recognized in this takedown the undercurrent of a misogynist society that shames women for menstruating. Kaur's post to Facebook about the takedown was quickly picked up by media outlets and reposted by thousands of social media users:

> Thank you Instagram for providing me with the exact response my work was created to critique. You deleted my photo twice stating that it goes against community guidelines. I will not apologize for not feeding the ego and pride of misogynist society that will have my body in an underwear but not be okay with a small leak. When your pages are filled with countless photos/accounts where women (so many who are underage) are objectified, pornified, and treated less than human.[46]

Kaur's complaint resonates because it is a powerful personal reminder that the rules that social media platforms develop are not democratically selected nor subject to review by an independent judiciary that is empowered to strike down rules that are unfair or overly restrictive. The content moderation process is human and fallible, like real laws are, but it is not surrounded by an infrastructure designed to lessen the influence of individual decision-makers and the chance of bias.

Data from the OnlineCensorship.org projects shows that people are routinely discouraged from appealing decisions to remove their content or suspend their accounts. Many reported that they found it too confusing to work out what process they needed to follow – something the platforms have not expended a lot of effort to clarify. Others assume that they will have little chance of making their case to the platform and decide not to bother contesting mistakes. Of the people who have taken the time to submit reports to OnlineCensorship.org, only half said that they had appealed the decision to remove their content. Of those, many users reported that they received no response, or, if they did, they received a standard form response that merely restated the initial decision. As West points out, this is deeply frustrating to users, who are left with little information about what, if anything, they did wrong and no way to fix the problem or ensure it does not happen again. For users who rely heavily on their social media presences for business, for activism, or for personal use this can be deeply distressing.

Frustratingly, different rules often seem to apply to the small proportion of users whose stories get picked up by the media and large numbers of other users. Kaur's images were restored after public outcry – a common story that seems like one of the only reliably effective ways to get mistakes addressed. Instagram quickly apologized for removing the image, noting that it was a mistake in the operation of its moderation processes. For many, however, it is a symptom of a larger problem with the way that the rules of social media platforms are enforced. Mistakes in moderation happen all the time, and people rarely have the ability to have removed content reinstated.

Even more frustratingly, special rules seem to apply to celebrities and highly influential people. The policies of both Twitter and Facebook technically prohibit much of the hatred and abuse that Trump posts, but the companies have carved out exceptions to avoid censoring his posts.[47] "The lack of an appeals system for individual users," Klonick writes,[48] "reveal that a fair opportunity to participate is not currently a prioritized part of platform moderation systems." This, she reminds us, hurts most because even though the media has always been dominated by elites, it seems to shatter the dreams we had for the internet, as a liberating force for free speech and democratic equality.

The lack of information about moderation that is available feeds anxiety about bias in the way that internet platforms make decisions about what content is permitted and what stories will filter to the top of news feeds and search results. It also goes some way to explaining our collective fascination when mistakes are made:

high-profile cases, like Kaur's, catch mainstream attention and give us a rare glimpse into how the system works. Part of the reason these stories become so popular is because platform companies closely guard information about how they moderate content, keeping both the rules and the data we would need to evaluate their performance secret.

The real rules of social media platforms are hidden, in part, because they are so messy and contested. For online social spaces to be useful to us, they have to be moderated in some way. There are always choices to be made about what counts as acceptable conduct and content. The great difficulty that platforms face, of course, is that deciding what is acceptable or not is highly subjective. In any community of more than a few people there's no easy way to articulate a set of rules that everyone agrees with, and, even if we could agree, there will inevitably be disagreements about how those rules should be interpreted in particular contexts.

Gillespie warns about the dangers of focusing on individual mistakes. Moderating is hard, Gillespie points out, and taking on the challenge of moderating

> means wading into some thorny questions: not just determining what should count as unacceptable, but balancing offense and importance; reconciling competing value systems; mediating when people harm one another, intentionally or otherwise; honoring the contours of political discourse and cultural taste; grappling with issues of gender, sexuality, race, and class; extending an ethical obligation across national, cultural, and linguistic boundaries; and being called to account for the hottest hot-button issues of the day.[49]

Rather than focus on the inevitable individual mistakes or controversial choices, Gillespie points out that we should pay more attention to the structural problems. The big question we face, as a society coming to grips with the digital age, is what role we want platforms to play in governing our lives – and what we might do to make sure this power is exercised in a way that is legitimate and fair.

One of the most pervasive complaints about content moderation is that the rules are not applied fairly or consistently. At the massive scale involved – millions of complaints about content per week – mistakes are inevitable, and similar content is often treated differently. Many of these complaints are unreliable; people often flag content not because it breaks the rules, but because they don't agree with it or like the person who posted it. And because moderation relies on users to flag or complain about offensive content, the entire system is vulnerable to coordinated action by brigades of people unified behind particular causes who single out the posts of other users with thousands of complaints. The resulting system looks decidedly unfair to those who have been censored and those whose complaints have been ignored.

3

The Internet's Abuse Problem

The rules that different internet companies put in place about what content they allow are complicated and often controversial. All types of intermediaries are coming under pressure from many different directions to change their rules in different and often conflicting ways. Nowhere is this more visible than in the growing attention to the abuse, harassment, and hatred that has become so commonplace on the internet. Over the past decade, sustained media attention has driven a recognition that the rules and technical design of the internet's social spaces have enabled hatred to flourish in a way that is harmful to individuals and to the quality of our shared media and debates. Internet companies are under a great deal of pressure to do more to limit abuse and to ensure that vulnerable people are not exposed to harm or driven off and silenced. Making real change, though, requires not only difficult debates about where to draw the lines, but also a rethinking and retrofitting of the core assumptions built into many of the services that enable us to communicate online. In this chapter, we will address how society is turning to internet intermediaries to help tackle the abuse problem and why this is such a complicated problem to address.

For a long time, the reverse side of British banknotes primarily featured pictures of white men like Isaac Newton, Adam Smith, and Charles Darwin. When the Bank of England announced in 2013 that it would issue a new £5 note, replacing Elizabeth Fry – the only female figure to feature on the reverse of a current note – with Winston Churchill, it sparked a major debate about the representation of women in British culture. Caroline Criado-Perez led a campaign to feature more women on banknotes, collecting 35,000 signatures on a petition that would eventually see Jane Austen replace Charles Darwin on the £10 note. But the campaign came at great cost for Criado-Perez and others, who suddenly found themselves at the center of a violent storm of abuse and threats of murder and rape.

Emma Jane is a researcher who has spent several decades cataloging and documenting the abuse that women receive just for being visible on the internet. Jane explains that there has been a vast expansion in the severity and volume of abuse since approximately 2010; over the past decade, online abuse has become more widespread and more organized, and has started to target a much broader range of people. The mobs of people that carry out coordinated attacks have also grown much larger and long-lived. She recounts the story of Catherine Mayer, a journalist for *Time* who was covering the campaign. One day Mayer received a tweet that read "A BOMB HAS BEEN PLACED OUTSIDE YOUR HOME. IT WILL GO OFF AT EXACTLY 10:47PM ON A TIMER AND TRIGGER DESTROYING EVERY-THING."[1] Like many others before and since, Mayer received no help from the authorities – as Jane puts it, the police Mayer encountered "thought the best solution was for Mayer to unplug and avoid the whole cyberweb IP secret code-name spy thing altogether."[2]

These types of threats are a common experience for women and minorities who dare to be publicly visible online. Amanda Hess, a prominent journalist who writes about culture and sex, reports her experience after receiving a threat that seemed worryingly specific on Twitter:

> I am 36 years old, I did 12 years for 'manslaughter', I killed a woman, like you, who decided to make fun of guys cocks; Happy to say we live in the same state. Im looking you up, and when I find you, im going to rape you and remove your head; and You are going to die and I am the one who is going to kill you. I promise you this.[3]

Terrified, Hess called 911 and waited. When a police officer finally arrived two hours later, she had to explain to him what Twitter was. Like every other time she had reported threats to the authorities, and like the experience of so many others, the police were of little help. These are not isolated experiences. While there have been some arrests of people who threaten and stalk women online, Jane points out that abuse and harassment is still "profoundly underreported," and "those targets who do go to police rarely receive a satisfactory response."[4] One of the major persistent problems victims of online abuse face is that threats made against them are not taken seriously by law enforcement authorities – police still commonly view technology-facilitated abuse and stalking as less serious than or separate from "traditional" violence.[5] Too often, women and members of minority groups who try to get the police to help when they are being harassed are told they can avoid the problem by simply turning off their phones, choosing not to log in to Facebook, and getting off Twitter.

Abuse and harassment is rampant online. For women and minorities, merely being visible online makes you a target for abuse and threats hurled by strangers. In a recent survey of women aged 18–55 in eight Western countries conducted by Amnesty International, nearly a quarter (23 percent) reported that they had experienced online abuse, and 41 percent of those reported feeling that their physical safety was at risk.[6] Nearly 60 percent of the participants who reported experiencing abuse online said it included racism, sexism, homophobia, or transphobia. A 2017 report by the Pew Research Center found that about 40 percent of Americans had experienced some form of harassment online, and 18 percent had experienced serious threats, sustained harassment, stalking, and sexual harassment.[7] The same report showed that approximately 1 in 10 Americans had experienced abuse on social media because of their physical appearance, race, ethnicity, or gender. Nearly 80 percent of Americans surveyed believe that internet companies have a responsibility to step in when harassment happens on their networks. Women and people of color who work to fight inequality are often more exposed to abuse and harassment. Journalists, politicians, and activists are particularly targeted for abuse, and the abuse is worse for people who experience multiple intersecting forms of discrimination.[8] In a survey of feminist and LGBTIQ activists around the world, 75 percent responded that they had experienced online harassment, and 63 percent said that they had received comments designed to intimidate them.[9] For marginalized people, merely having an online presence or speaking out is often enough to trigger floods of abuse from strangers. Often, attacks are coordinated or amplified by influential figures who seek to silence minority voices and can marshal their large audiences to direct an overwhelming tide of abuse at their targets.

These tactics work. Widespread, routine abuse silences minority voices. People who experience abuse often change the way they communicate online by locking down their accounts and posting less. One of the major problems the internet faces today is that many of its open spaces, from social media platforms to online games, are becoming toxic. The rules of most major social media networks prohibit abuse, but there is a great deal of frustration by victims of abuse who continually see their complaints rejected. Even when abusers have their accounts suspended, they typically reappear quickly after their suspension period is over – or even beforehand, under a new alias. The sheer size of the problem – in many attacks, thousands of people might send abusive messages – means that reporting individual users also has little effect on overall levels of abuse. Abuse has become a massive social problem that can only really be addressed through changes in the culture and the architecture of the internet.

It's well acknowledged that today's internet has a harassment problem. In late 2016, the editorial staff at *Wired Magazine*, one of the longest running outlets and supporters of tech culture,[10] wrote an open letter to the internet that explicitly recognized how abuse and harassment had grown out of tech culture. *Wired's* editorial explicitly contrasts the dreams that many had for the internet at its birth twenty-five years ago with the rampant harassment we see today:

> You were supposed to be the blossoming of a million voices. We were all going to democratize access to information together. But some of your users have taken that freedom as a license to victimize others. This is not fine. . . . As you got bigger and stronger, more people wanted to talk – but some of them were jerks, or worse. . . . You had no immune system, and you started to rot. Now that rot has turned to blight. And here we are.[11]

Most importantly, *Wired*'s editors put the responsibility for rampant harassment squarely on the people in charge of internet infrastructure and services:

> Internet, it has to stop. And since you are this enormous, limitless beast with many heads and hearts and faces, the best way we know to get your attention is to talk to the companies and people who form your backbone and your bloodstream.[12]

Wired called out the inaction of companies who spent resources developing sophisticated spam filters and tools to automatically detect copyright infringement but appeared powerless to respond to abuse occurring on their networks.

This is a deeply controversial position among the engineers of the internet. For a long time, the engineers who create internet protocols and the systems administrators who run platforms have refused to deal with harassment. It's not necessarily that they couldn't see that it exists – although, as an industry dominated by educated, well-off white males, they certainly were not exposed to the same harassment that others suffer on a daily basis. It's mainly because they couldn't agree that it was the role of technology providers to tackle issues that they view as purely social, not technical, problems.

One of the core points to remember here is that even if a moderation system is working well, it is never neutral. The posts that people make online reflect deep structural inequalities in society and, without careful attention, the moderation systems that platforms implement will replicate and reinforce these biases. One of the most dangerous design choices built into the architecture of the commercial internet over the past few decades is the assumption that the technology should try to be neutral. *Wired*'s editorial is powerful because it marks a potential turning point in how those most in the center of tech culture view their responsibilities for how technology is used. The liberal ideology that dominates Silicon Valley has for a long time prioritized individual responsibility and technology neutrality.

The idea that technology is neutral suggests that its developers cannot be held responsible for how people choose to use it. But technology is not at all neutral. Melvin Kranzberg, historian of technology, famously articulated this as one of his six laws in 1986: "technology is neither good nor bad; nor is it neutral."[13] By this, he meant to draw attention to the effect of design choices in influencing how technology is used. The protocols at the heart of modern internet infrastructure were designed to avoid discriminating between different types of content or different speakers. The decentralized design of core internet protocols reflects a dream of equality and liberty: the brave new world of cyberspace would be a place where everyone is free to speak and to seek out information. This was a deliberate choice, and it is continuously remade in the new applications that build on top of internet infrastructure to help people communicate.

These decisions always have ramifications. We should be grateful to the engineers of decades ago who designed the core foundations of the internet to be resilient and decentralized – it was a farsighted move that makes it extremely difficult for one company or government to seize technical control of the internet. The decentralized ideal of the internet is fundamentally libertarian, in the sense that it is designed to be difficult to control and, therefore, resilient to attack and failure. It's a decision designed to maximize freedom of speech and limit censorship. But it's also a decision that enables the worst of human nature to flourish. When social media platforms themselves try to adopt these principles and make their networks neutral, they often end up creating systems that reflect and amplify existing inequalities and drown out the voices of the most disadvantaged members of society.

Adrienne Massanari writes about how Reddit's apparently neutral design encourages a toxic culture among its users. The features of Reddit look neutral enough on the surface – the platform allows anyone to post and uses a voting mechanism to allow the community to make decisions about which posts and comments are most visible and to hide less valued posts. But Massanari points out that "the culture and design politics of Reddit implicitly allows anti-feminist and racist activist communities to take hold."[14] Reddit is made up of a large number of different communities dedicated to particular topics, and each of these sub-Reddits have their own community moderation teams to enforce their own rules. The operators of Reddit try to remain neutral and generally only intervene to enforce a small set of global rules. Other than that, the work of moderation is generally left up to the communities themselves. What ends up happening, though, is that many sub-Reddits become a breeding ground for toxicity.[15] Reddit is a hub of geek culture that skews toward the white and male and is often criticized for insensitivity and hostility along gender and racial lines.[16] The voting system rewards content that appeals to this dominant culture and makes it more visible in a cyclic way that often makes others feel less welcome on the platform. The result is a platform that in part is often actively and openly hostile to women and people of color.

Tools designed to help people connect will inevitably be used to amplify hatred and abuse. In an open letter in late 2017, a coalition of nineteen civil rights organizations representing African American, LGBTIQ, and Muslim communities wrote to Facebook to complain about how the platform was being used to promote bigotry.[17] The organizations expressed a deep frustration that they had been raising concerns about the pervasive presence and organizing of hate groups on Facebook for many years to little effect. The letter was prompted by revelations that Russian operatives were impersonating hate groups as well as the Black Lives Matter movement and organizations promoting tolerance and discourse in order to amplify bigoted messages. Facebook's advertising tools, which enable advertisers to target potential customers on very specific characteristics, were being used to incite hatred and directly target and mobilize groups of people in the lead-up to the 2016 election.

This was not the first time that advertising systems had been abused to spread hatred. Another high-profile example was in 2015, when someone impersonated a prominent feminist and used Twitter's advertising system to directly target people who identified as transgender with hateful messages that encouraged them to commit suicide.[18] *ProPublica* has reported about how Facebook's advertisement system allows advertisers to target people on the basis of race, gender, religion, age, and other characteristics, and companies have been using these systems to unlawfully discriminate in employment advertisements.[19] Advertising tools are designed to provide sophisticated mechanisms for businesses to better connect with audiences, not to help people discriminate or send targeted messages of hate, but tools are never neutral. Technical systems that are deployed within societies that are fundamentally unequal will always be used in ways that reflect and perpetuate those underlying social inequalities.

Platforms face many similar challenges. Twitter used to boast of its style of management as "the free speech wing of the free speech party."[20] For many years, however, the platform has struggled to deal with rampant abuse. Twitter was designed to be fast and open and difficult to control. Twitter makes it easy to register new accounts and defaults to a system that allows any person to publicly talk to any other. When it works well, it's a beautiful network of fast-traveling news and opinion. But it's also a network full of abuse that has been steadily driving people away for years.

Twitter has repeatedly iterated its commitment to tackling abuse after every major scandal, but these efforts have so far not been successful. By the end of 2016, the struggling company's inability to deal with abuse effectively had started to trouble potential investors like Disney, as discussions about the sale of the platform reportedly failed.[21] Even when the platform's future looks to depend on it, changing culture (of both the company and its users) is tough. In an internal memo in 2015, Twitter CEO Dick Costolo had to admit to the failure of the company to address the problem of abuse on the platform:

> We suck at dealing with abuse and trolls on the platform and we've sucked at it for years. It's no secret and the rest of the world talks about it every day. We lose core user after core user by not addressing simple trolling issues that they face every day.
>
> I'm frankly ashamed of how poorly we've dealt with this issue during my tenure as CEO. It's absurd. There's no excuse for it. I take full responsibility for not being more aggressive on this front. It's nobody else's fault but mine, and it's embarrassing.[22]

The major social media platforms are starting to recognize that their systems do not deal well with abuse, but, so far, none of them have been able to find effective ways to address the problem. The core challenge is that abuse is a systemic problem that has become normalized. These types of problems can't be fixed through the normal tools of content moderation via the flagging and removal of individual posts. Making a real change in the culture of modern social media platforms will require a broader, collaborative social movement, new tools, and careful attention to how the rules and designs of online spaces work to encourage and amplify underlying inequalities.

ABUSE REFLECTS AND REINFORCES SYSTEMIC INEQUALITIES

Online hate, harassment, and abuse are extensions of hate and discrimination that already exist in all societies. Because the internet makes it possible for everyone to communicate to much larger audiences and to more easily target strangers, though, it amplifies abuse in new ways. Victims of hate online report receiving much more abuse than they typically experience in the physical world.[23] Online hate and abuse is a growing problem that is disproportionately harmful to the mental and physical well-being of vulnerable and disadvantaged groups, and it is working to exclude people from the essential opportunities the internet has to offer for everyday life.

Online abuse has become normal. Emma Jane's work explains how everyday abuse has become accepted online. She calls it "e-bile": "extravagant invective, the sexualized threats of violence, and the recreational nastiness that have come to constitute a dominant tenor of Internet discourse."[24] The fact that threats and abuse have become so commonplace means that it has become routine and expected, to the extent that people have grown to be desensitized or tolerant to harassment.[25]

If police are slow to act on rape and death threats, they are almost completely powerless against the tide of abuse that is constantly hurled at people who are visible online but are not white men. Criminal laws around the world prohibit credible threats and prolonged stalking, but most of the abuse that makes up the broad waves of harassment aimed at women, minorities, and other marginalized groups does not individually raise to the standard that we would expect police to lay charges.[26]

The cumulative weight of widespread and ongoing online abuse is incredibly harmful to the people on the receiving end. This harm is often hard to recognize because powerful people who don't experience it on a daily basis often dismiss online abuse as "just speech." The libertarian streak that runs through much of dominant tech culture minimizes the harm that comes from sustained and pervasive toxic environments. Even where there is recognizable harm, the libertarian presumption is that the answer to bad speech is more speech. The underlying idea is that mere abusive words, without an associated credible threat or other directly harmful consequence, do not cause harm. Taking offense, this line of reasoning argues, is wholly within the power of the target: she can either choose not to listen or choose to be a victim. The old adage, taught early on to children, "sticks and stones may break my bones, but words will never hurt me" still has a great deal of weight in how we think about hate and abuse online.

The internet, a network of networks for transmitting bits, is all about the flow of information. This much is true. But at some point it became embedded in the public consciousness that the internet is *only* information. That speech in the digital world is only speech and it therefore cannot directly cause harm in the physical world. This part is not just false, it is dangerous.

Online abuse takes many forms, including name-calling, bullying, threats, impersonation, and doxxing (releasing personal information about a person).[27] A great deal of online abuse grows out of domestic violence started by perpetrators that the victim knows personally.[28] Digital technologies are routinely used by current and former intimate partners as tools to coerce and control women. A recent survey on online harassment in the United States found that the most common perpetrators of online stalking are current and former partners.[29] Abusive partners use social media to harass their victims, as well as stalking them through GPS data, recording their activities through internet-connected devices, monitoring their email and instant messaging, using their victim's accounts to impersonate them to others, and publishing their private information online.[30] Digital technologies allow abusers to expand their ability to control their victims – they make abuse and stalking easier, more pervasive, more immediate, and more difficult to escape.[31] The public nature of many online networks also creates new opportunities for humiliation, like threats to release intimate images or embarrassing or defamatory content to the victim's social and professional contacts.[32] Abusive partners are learning to leverage the internet to enlist strangers to amplify and pile on campaigns of harassment that can quickly grow and amplify abuse at a massive and unmanageable scale.[33]

In order to understand online abuse and harassment against people in disadvantaged groups, we have to first understand how normalized, everyday acts of abuse take place in the context of a broader landscape of inequality and harm.[34] The "ceaseless flickering hum of low-level emotional violence"[35] that has become part of everyday life online comes out of a culture of misogyny and sexism, and it makes abuse more normal and acceptable. Criminologists who study domestic violence have warned for a long time that we should not try to draw a sharp distinction between the types of aberrant behavior that are clearly recognized as criminal or deviant (stalking, coercive control, rape, and physical violence) and the more ordinary incidents of everyday harassment and abuse that feed and reflect a culture of sexualized violence.[36] This means that the more typical manifestations of online abuse cannot be divorced from acts that are more widely recognized as causing harm.[37] Different types of gender-based violence are all profoundly shaped by gender inequality and underpinned by common social attitudes that minimize and excuse violence against women.

Online abuse and harassment is both a cause and effect of inequality. The widespread abuse and harassment that has become common online presents real threats to the participation of women in social life. This is the intent; abusers aim to objectify, to subject the dignity of the victim to the will of the abuser. The reason abuse is so powerful is that it disempowers the victim; it seeks to reduce their autonomy, to make the victim feel as though they are not worthy, and to deny the subjectivity of their experience.[38] Online abuse is designed to shame and intimidate, and it often has a serious impact on the victim's daily life. Martha Nussbaum, a law professor and philosopher at the University of Chicago, explains abuse in terms of "objectification." When someone posts on social media, for example, that a woman should "sit on a butcher's knife so that you may never be able to reproduce,"[39] they're treating the target as "a mere thing, a tool of the purposes of the objectifier, an entity whose subjective feelings need not be taken into account, or whose feelings, like her autonomy, may be willfully violated."[40] When a target is continuously told that she has no worth, the aim is to objectify – the "achievement" of the abusers is measured in their success "to take over her mind, make it impossible for her to think happy thoughts, to do her work in the normal way, to pursue friendships and sexual relationships with confidence."[41] Ordinary, everyday abuse and harassment is inextricably linked with structural inequalities in society, and feeds off and reinforces experiences of coercion and threats of violence perpetrated "offline."[42]

DEALING WITH ABUSE NEEDS THE INVOLVEMENT OF PLATFORMS

Because online abuse and harassment is a manifestation of deep social inequality, it is a complex problem that requires attention at many levels by many different types of actors. For the victims of abuse, tracking down the individuals responsible is only useful in the most serious cases. Where there are specific, credible threats of physical violence, it is possible to seek help from law enforcement agencies. Law enforcement are more likely to respond to prolonged and focused harassment than individual incidents, and some agencies are developing specialist capabilities to respond to online abuse, but state responses remain inconsistent at best. There are some positive signs that this is improving with greater education for police, but without dedicated resourcing this is likely to continue to be a problem.[43]

Criminal law is not an appropriate response to the more ordinary types of abuse and harassment that people experience every day online. Legal tools can't solve the underlying problem of hatred and inequality,[44] and criminal remedies often have unintended consequences.[45] Criminal sanctions and police resources should be reserved for the most directly harmful acts of violence and incitement.

Tackling normalized abuse requires a range of different approaches. Currently, targets of the type of abuse that has become ordinary online often have no real recourse. Most platforms have rules against harassment and abuse, and they try to set out standards of acceptable behavior and inappropriate conduct. But one of the longer-running controversies over content moderation concerns the lack of enforcement of these rules and the apparent bias and double standards that victims experience when reporting harassment and abuse to platforms. Generally speaking, the reporting systems that social media platforms use to remove hate speech and abuse are not working well. Targets of abuse often express a deep frustration with the major social media platforms that constantly promise they will do more to tackle abuse and repeatedly fail to deliver. Reporting systems place the burden of reporting on the victims – and navigating these systems often requires the user to collate and provide detailed evidence, including links and screenshots, to document the abuse.[46] Amnesty International's recent report about abuse on Twitter criticizes the company's inadequate enforcement mechanisms when women report violence and abuse:

> Twitter's inconsistency and inaction on its own rules not only creates a level of mistrust and lack of confidence in the company's reporting process, it also sends the message that Twitter does not take violence and abuse against women seriously – a failure which is likely to deter women from reporting in the future.[47]

One of the major challenges of reporting systems is that they don't deal with context very well. Most platforms use simple web forms with check boxes and preset categories to allow people to complain about a specific piece of content. Victims of abuse have no easy way to talk about the context of abuse, and the platform does not follow up with users for more detail about their experiences. This makes it very difficult to understand how people are being harassed – something that is not obvious just by looking at a post or series of posts. Sometimes, abusers can delete threats and abusive posts after they have been read, but before a moderator has time to even look at them. A research report for Women, Action, & the Media (WAM!) worked with people experiencing abuse on Twitter and acted as an "authorized reporter" to report harassment to Twitter on their behalf. One of its key findings was that dealing effectively with harassment requires in-depth communication because "People experiencing harassment often have complex situations with needs that only become clear through multiple exchanges."[48] But because the content moderation systems of platforms need to deal with a great many complaints very quickly, they are not designed to deal with complexity and nuance.

A lot of abusive material on social media slips through disguised as humor. Ariadna Matamoros-Fernández, a lecturer at Queensland University of Technology in Brisbane, Australia, studies the spread of racism on social media. Her research shows how racist memes spread on Twitter, YouTube, and Facebook. She found that overtly racist memes, videos, and comments circulated widely, often framed as jokes. Much of the racist content she looked at was not removed by platforms when it was reported, largely because of the explicit exceptions in their rules for humorous content.[49] While major platforms have policies against racist speech, they are still reluctant to enforce their policies in a way that requires them to exercise a value judgment about content that some audiences find humorous while others find deeply offensive.[50]

Platforms often take a view that tries to err on the side of protecting freedom of speech, but what this means in practice is that racist and sexist commentary flow freely online disguised as satire and irony.[51] Activists working to fight racism, sexism, and religious vilification are particularly concerned that the decisions of platforms to tolerate abusive humor signals that it continues to be acceptable to hold bigoted opinions.[52] Their point is that normalizing hate speech, even disguised as humor, reinforces a culture of hate that tolerates abuse and violence.[53] They point to examples like the genocide in Rwanda in the 1990s, which was preceded by a wave of populist media that dehumanized the Tutsi people, painting them as cockroaches, allowing the justification of widespread violence against them. Some free speech activists, in contrast, worry that policing the expression of racist content is likely to stifle legitimate debate and discussion and not likely to be helpful in changing behavior. For the most part, the free speech arguments have been winning out on major platforms, but the result has been that many of our shared online spaces have become toxic – flooded with abuse that, even from the perspective of freedom of speech, works to silence the voices of disadvantaged groups and minorities.

Some campaigns have been able to drive change in the policies of major platforms. In an open letter to Facebook in 2013, the activist group WAM! demanded "swift, comprehensive and effective action addressing the representation of rape and domestic violence on Facebook."[54] The group explained that the types of content it was concerned with reflected a double standard by Facebook:

> Specifically, we are referring to groups, pages and images that explicitly condone or encourage rape or domestic violence or suggest that they are something to laugh or boast about. Pages currently appearing on Facebook include Fly Kicking Sluts in the Uterus, Kicking your Girlfriend in the Fanny because she won't make you a Sandwich, Violently Raping Your Friend Just for Laughs, Raping your Girlfriend and many, many more. Images appearing on Facebook include photographs of women beaten, bruised, tied up, drugged, and bleeding, with captions such as "This bitch didn't know when to shut up" and "Next time don't get pregnant."
>
> These pages and images are approved by your moderators, while you regularly remove content such as pictures of women breastfeeding, women post-mastectomy and artistic representations of women's bodies. In addition, women's political speech, involving the use of their nude bodies in non-sexualized ways for protest, is regularly banned as pornographic, while pornographic content – prohibited by your own guidelines – remains. It appears that Facebook considers violence against women to be less offensive than non-violent images of women's bodies, and that the only acceptable representation of women's nudity are those in which women appear as sex objects or the victims of abuse. Your common practice of allowing this content by appending a [humor] disclaimer to said content literally treats violence targeting women as a joke.[55]

Survivors of domestic violence and sexual abuse have been complaining for a long time that the permissive stance of major social media platforms about abuse cloaked in humor works to normalize sexual violence. Facebook's response to campaigns by activists had in the past been dismissive of their concerns. Jane gives the example of a campaign in 2011 against some highly visible pages that promoted rape, with titles like "You know she's playing hard to get when your [sic] chasing her down an alleyway."[56] Facebook's initial response was that it wasn't willing to act as the arbiter of taste in what it saw as risqué jokes: "It is very important to point out that what one person finds offensive another can find entertaining. Just as telling a rude joke won't get you thrown out of your local pub, it won't get you thrown off Facebook."[57]

WAM!'s open letter marked a turning point in how platforms respond to criticism about their policies. One of the reasons it was successful was that WAM! was able to build a coalition of more than 100 women's movement and social justice organizations and run a coordinated campaign that exerted real pressure on Facebook. The campaign enlisted people to send over 60,000 tweets and 5,000 emails to companies whose advertisements appeared on pages that promote rape or treat sexual violence as a joke. This tactic was finally able to get Facebook's attention after years of campaigning by convincing fifteen companies to start to pull their advertisements from Facebook.

In response to WAM!'s open letter, Marne Levine, Facebook's vice president of global public policy, announced the platform would make immediate changes to its policies and procedures:

> In recent days, it has become clear that our systems to identify and remove hate speech have failed to work as effectively as we would like, particularly around issues of gender-based hate. In some cases, content is not being removed as quickly as we want. In other cases, content that should be removed has not been or has been evaluated using outdated criteria. We have been working over the past several months to improve our systems to respond to reports of violations, but the guidelines used by these systems have failed to capture all the content that violates our standards. We need to do better – and we will.[58]

Facebook's 2013 response appeared to result in some changes, but many people think that these changes did not go nearly far enough. A 2017 report by the Association for Progressive Communications, which works closely with feminist activists, complains that major platforms are still too often unresponsive: "when women report the dozens to hundreds of comments attacking them and burying their message on platforms, they are told that threats and other violent content are not against community standards."[59] Four years after Facebook promised to do better, the Association for Progressive Communications and other groups published a joint statement on Facebook's internal guidelines for content moderation that expressed frustration about the slow pace of change:

> Although Facebook has made some improvements, these documents confirm that it's often one step forward, one step back, as the platform continues to censor women's agency, especially women of colour and especially in relation to activism, while letting harassment flourish. . . . Clearly, Facebook's limited consultation with women's rights groups and activists has not been meaningful enough to create real change.[60]

Not only are reporting systems not working particularly well for people who experience abuse, but these same systems are also being gamed and misused by abusers as a tool to further silence marginal voices. The same activists who are unable to get platforms to deal with the abuse they receive often find that their own accounts are suspended or banned. A lot of this is a numbers game – people who spread hate and abuse against minorities can form large, loosely organized mobs that use the reporting features of social media platforms as weapons in their tactics of harassment. When a small number of outspoken activists are the highly visible targets of large, amorphous groups of haters, the haters are often better at using the flagging systems that platforms provide to complain about their targets.[61] Activists, therefore, frequently find themselves on the wrong side of the enforcement of the platforms rules; they end up banned and are unable to get their messages out, while their abusers run wild. More than a frustration, this is a double standard that begins to look like a deeply entrenched bias.

Even when policies against hate speech and abuse are enforced, abusers have proved to be very resilient. The great liberating potential of the internet is that it massively reduces the costs of communication and enables everyone to have a voice. When some of those voices are drowning out those of their victims, it is difficult to deal with them in a way that does not impose substantial costs on the rest of us. This is a problem as old as the commercial internet. Journalist Julian Dibbell, in his famous report on "A Rape in Cyberspace" for *The Village Voice* in 1993,[62] explains how features designed to facilitate communication can be repurposed in unexpected ways by abusers. In the story Dibbell tells, in the text-based virtual environment LambdaMOO, a persistent abuser was able to turn an innocent-enough feature into a tool that allowed him to control the acts of the avatars of other users. The abuser, who went by the name Mr. Bungle, sparked outrage in the community and very real feelings of harm and shame among his victims by making them appear to perform violent sexual acts in the public chat rooms. The incident is noteworthy both because it prompted the community to try to develop rules of acceptable behavior and because it showed the futility of all of the enforcement mechanisms available to the community. Mr Bungle's account was eventually banned, but the person behind the avatar was able to simply create a new account and continue abusing people as if nothing had happened. As anyone who has been abused on Twitter by someone with a faceless egg avatar that denotes new users knows, things have not changed much in twenty-five years. Not only can individuals create new accounts, but entire groups can even coordinate to move around and avoid bans relatively easily. When Reddit banned the subreddit /r/creepshots (which specialized in sharing sexualized images of women taken without their knowledge), for example, it was reborn relatively quickly on the same platform as /r/CandidFashionPolice.[63] Sometimes, the groups have to go to different platforms – like when Reddit shut down a raft of communities dedicated to harassment, instigating a sizeable migration to the alt-right Reddit clone, Voat.[64]

Some platforms, like Facebook and the short-lived Google+, try to deal with abuse by requiring users to register with their full names, on the reasoning that people may be less likely to engage in abusive behavior with strangers if their reputations are on the line. This is still a matter of debate; there have been few reliable studies, and there is little consensus about whether requiring real names reduces abuse. Importantly, though, it is clear that real name policies can have negative consequences for users who are most vulnerable.[65] Dissidents using social media to resist authoritarian states are put at increased risk,[66] and people who want to segregate different aspects of their identity for different audiences are disempowered.[67] Google+ sparked controversy when its decision to merge the different accounts of its users unwittingly collapsed the walls that some people had built around their separate identities – outing people to all of their connections without their control.

The lack of good responses from platforms has led some people who receive a lot of abuse to develop alternate strategies for calling out abusers. Games journalist Alanah Pearce receives a lot of abuse from young people; in late 2014, she caused a small sensation when she started writing to the mothers of young boys who were sending her abuse on Facebook. She posted to Twitter a conversation she had with the mother of a young boy who she didn't know, where she let his mother know that he had left her the message "i'll rape u if I ever see u cunt." His mother was shocked, but her reaction was exactly what Pearce was hoping for: a commitment to talk to her child about his behavior.

While this can be effective, this is not a strategy that scales well. It takes time to find out whether an abuser is a child, to track down their parents, and to engage in a conversation with them. It is of little assistance against adults or users whose personal information is not easily discoverable, and it can also generate a great deal more abuse from others in return.[68]

One of the tactics employed by Clementine Ford, a writer and feminist commentator, is to amplify abuse that she and others receive in order to raise awareness about how common and violent online harassment really is.[69] She tells the story of a time that a stranger left an abusive comment on her Facebook page, which she then sent to his employer. Ford describes the comment – he had called her a slut – as relatively minor, by her standards, but she was annoyed enough to take screenshots of his post and his public profile, which "happened to be chock-full of incredibly racist 'jokes.'" She took advantage of the fact that he had listed his employer on his Facebook profile and sent the screenshots to the company (a construction firm), which ended up terminating his employment contract.[70]

In an age where employers are exceptionally sensitive to viral negative publicity on social media, this can be a simple and effective mechanism to hold abusers accountable for their actions. Others see this tactic as mob justice, and it's not hard to imagine how it could go terribly wrong. Certainly, there are questions of proportionality: does someone who posts an abusive message deserve to lose their job? There are dangerous consequences to relying on companies to police the social media posts of their employees: the social media policies of many companies can be incredibly restrictive, and it is becoming more common to hear stories of people who have been fired for their political opinions or for criticizing the company and its commercial partners. Sometimes this seems justifiable, but there is little due process in these decisions, and we might worry about cases where the punishment does not seem to fit the crime. Author Jon Ronson writes about the dangers of vigilantism in his book, *So You've Been Publicly Shamed*.[71] He tells the story of Justine Sacco, who wrote a tongue-in-cheek tweet to her 174 followers: "Going to Africa. Hope I don't get AIDS. Just kidding. I'm white!" Sacco later explained to Ronson her motivations for writing the tweet: "Living in America puts us in a bit of a bubble when it comes to what is going on in the third world. I was making fun of that bubble." But this was certainly not the way the tweet was received. By the time she had touched down in Cape Town, South Africa, Sacco was the center of an international Twitter storm of angry users who read her tweet as disgustingly racist and ignorant. She lost her job, and her life was upended in the face of overwhelming humiliation that would follow her around wherever people searched her name.

For activists like Ford, social media can empower those who are on the receiving side of abuse. There is some poetic justice in giving back to abusers in-kind. But Sacco's tale, like others in Ronson's book, is a caution against relying on the power of social media to shame transgressors. It's unclear whether this type of shaming helps to change behavior over the long run. What is clear is that shaming is not a precise form of punishment – its effects are often unpredictable, and it is not very accurate as to who it punishes.[72]

The fact that targets of abuse turn to shaming reflects the difficult truth that they have so few other remedies. When neither the police nor the social media platforms take action, vigilantism certainly looks attractive. If there were better ways to enforce social norms of acceptable behavior online, victims of abuse might not need to resort to this kind of vigilantism. So far, though, despite years of promises from platforms to do better, many of these problems persist.

NO IMMUNE SYSTEM

Wired's editorial points out that the internet has no "immune system" to protect it from abuse. Speaking about how technology that is designed to be neutral can have deeply discriminatory effects, social media scholar danah boyd explains the problem: "We didn't architect for prejudice, but we didn't design systems to combat it either."[73] The tools we have created to allow people to communicate can be used to abuse others, and by designing the technology to be ambivalent about content we have created environments where abusers can thrive and their messages of hate can be amplified. This is a challenge that will take some fundamental reworking of parts of the technological infrastructure that supports our shared online social spaces to address.

One of the first challenges here is that platforms often think they are operating in a way that is neutral. They would prefer not to get into messy debates about the acceptable limits of freedom of speech, the lines between abuse and humor, and the lines between legitimate political speech and vilification. This is an important point, and we should be wary of how platforms draw these lines; they are often as likely as not to choose a position that harms legitimate expression and disproportionately hurts marginalized groups.

Addressing abuse and harassment is rapidly becoming a problem that platforms can no longer avoid. In response to repeated complaints over the past few years, most major platforms have made incremental improvements to their content moderation practices. They have hired many more moderators and introduced new training and tools to help those moderators make more consistent decisions. They also use the millions of decisions that moderators make to train machine-learning classifiers to identify harmful material more quickly and more regularly. These investments are paying off, and these systems are definitely getting better; they are getting more accurate and more consistent. These efforts should be encouraged and applauded. But still, platforms have been unable to really address the core problems of hatred and discrimination coursing through their networks.

The big problem is that there are no easy technical answers to the problem of abuse. Content moderation processes are not well suited to dealing with the underlying cultural problems that lead to hateful and abusive behavior. Platforms have tried to use flagging systems and moderation teams to enforce the rules against particular pieces of content, but this targets the symptoms and not the disease.

Content moderation is a system of classifying individual pieces of content according to a set of explicit rules. Because moderation systems rely on flagging and manual review, they are not set up to catch ordinary, widespread, low-level hate. They are better suited to dealing with content that can be clearly and quickly identified as prohibited – material that is sexually explicit, violent, or gory, or uses slurs that easily be listed. Hiring more moderators and building better machines to identify prohibited content is a necessary step in improving the moderation of explicitly offensive and vulgar material that is often a part of abuse and harassment. But the problem goes much deeper.

Ultimately, abuse and harassment are not just problems of content classification. It is not always possible to tell from just looking at the content of a single post, whether it is likely to cause distress or harm. The internet's major abuse problem is the mass of ordinary and pervasive posts that express discriminatory sentiments in ways that threaten and silence marginalized groups. These posts both reflect and fuel a culture of discrimination. A content moderation system can reliably deal with posts that are explicitly abusive, but the more ordinary, everyday manifestations of abuse are much more difficult to reliably and routinely catch and remove.

A system focused on classification is always going to struggle to work out nuances of intent and context. These systems are not set up to differentiate between self-deprecating humor, satire, and offensive humor. They can't effectively deal with false or poorly argued statements that advance fundamentally discriminatory ideas. They are not well suited to handling politely worded repeated interjections that are designed to wear down and eventually silence dissenting voices.[74]

Content moderation systems can filter out the most offensive content, but by themselves they can't set expectations for what a healthy discourse looks like. Changing the cultural norms on social media platforms will require a much greater emphasis on what sort of behavior is appropriate and acceptable. Part of this necessarily involves more education and better consultation with groups of users. New tools, too, will be required to empower people to manage their own communities, helping them to create and enforce their own standards of acceptable conduct. These steps are underway, but they will not be sufficient.

The biggest challenge platforms face is the need to develop ways to avoid amplifying hateful and abusive ideas. This is not something that the systems of most internet services are built to do. The basic assumption of neutrality that is baked into modern platforms makes it difficult to discriminate between different types of ideas. Content moderation systems are only set up to distinguish between prohibited and permissible content. The major platforms have no real way of dealing with the influential people who set out to incubate a toxic culture but who are always careful to skirt the rules on content. The do not have processes in place that allow them to articulate a set of principles that can justify excluding people based on the incendiary values that they hold and the hateful ideas they spread, rather than the individual pieces of content that they post.

The idea that a social media platform may make a call about what types of ideas are acceptable seems deeply troubling. I myself have trouble suggesting it, because I find it hard to imagine how these decisions could ever be legitimate. But the fact is that platforms can never be neutral. When they choose not to address abusive speech, they make a decision to tolerate it. Inevitably, this manifests in a culture that reflects and reinforces existing structural inequalities. It allows a culture of abuse to thrive, amplifies the voices of abusers, reinforces a norm that abusive speech is permissible, and forces out and silences minorities. By trying not to interfere with the diversity of permissible expression, platforms are supporting more polarized, less tolerant, and ultimately less diverse environments.

Whether they like it or not, platforms are in the game of drawing lines about acceptable behavior and speech. Drawing these lines is difficult, and politically loaded. Platforms often find themselves criticized no matter what they do – for every decision, they will always upset either the person whose content or account is restricted or the person whose complaints go unanswered. This is a tricky position to be in, and it's not surprising that platforms have been reluctant to take on more responsibility to actively enforce their rules. But if we are collectively going to address the problem of pervasive hate and abuse on the internet, we will need the cooperation of platforms. Fundamentally, the hard work that is yet to come in dealing with abuse centers around rethinking the basic assumptions that inform the design of modern communications technologies. If we are going to ask internet intermediaries to help to make our cultures less toxic, we are going to have to figure out how they might be able to intervene without making things much worse.

4

Legal Immunity

Technology companies are the sheriffs of what used to be the wild west of the internet. In the 1990s, when the internet was young, the imagery of the western frontier really seemed like a good analogy. The internet seemed to radically decentralize power: no longer could massive publishers or broadcasters control the media; anyone could be a publisher and get their message out.[1] The internet seemed inherently designed to preserve the freedom of individuals. It seemed impossible to enforce laws against the apparently anonymous masses of internet users distributed around the world. The commercial internet grew out of a military design that avoided single points of failure and was resilient against both nuclear attack and interference by hostile governments.[2]

The wilderness was eventually tamed, at least in the mainstream parts of the commercial internet we know today. The dominance of the old publishers of the mass media era has given way to the rise of new, even larger and more powerful publishers of the internet age. Companies like Google, Facebook, Amazon, and eBay all benefit from network effects: the principle that communications networks become exponentially more useful as the number of users grow.[3] A single telephone or fax machine is useless on its own; two can be handy in some situations, but the real value comes when many people have access to the same network.

The massive tech platforms we know today are built on a fundamental principle: they don't screen content. This means they don't exercise control over who gets to participate, and they don't try to decide in advance what their users will find relevant or interesting. The old mass media publishers helped us find information by deciding who and what gets published – they guaranteed quality. The new internet intermediaries don't focus on gatekeeping;[4] instead, they bring order to the sprawling mess of the internet by helping people search for information and connect with others. Google grew to be a giant because it helped people easily find relevant but obscure content – unlike Yahoo!, which tried to use an old media idea to categorize lists of what it thought was the best content on the internet.[5] This was a big change: a broadcaster can be expected to know what is in the television programs it broadcasts, and governments can easily impose content standards on the broadcaster. But YouTube doesn't work if Google has to watch videos in advance – users upload more than 300 hours of video content to YouTube every minute, or 432,000 hours per day.[6] If we want users to have the freedom to communicate this easily, the rule that platforms don't select content in advance is fundamentally important.

These commercial platforms provide value by connecting people together, within a single marketplace or social network. Each platform sets and enforces its own rules and tries to make the network useful for its users. So eBay doesn't just help us find other individuals who happen to be selling something we want; it uses star ratings, review systems, spam and fraud detection algorithms, and a dispute resolution team all working together to create a platform that lets us trust strangers on the internet to deliver the goods we pay for. YouTube, too, must make sure the videos people upload are acceptable – or risk losing its users in a torrent of smut and spam. Like most other social media platforms, YouTube relies on complaints mechanisms that get users to do the bulk of the work involved in finding offensive videos. The flagging system is an ingenious invention: rather than moderate all content in advance, flagging lets YouTube wait and see which of the millions of videos on its network other users think are inappropriate.[7] Only once a video has received enough complaints does it go into a queue where a human moderator might look at it. Most social media sites have similar systems – and they rely not only on complaints to flag content that breaks the rules, but on other triggers, such as Facebook's "Like" or Reddit's "upvote" and "downvote," to help sort posts into an order that other users are likely to want to see. Facebook's business model is based on how well it can design algorithms that sort massive amounts of content – posted by friends, injected by advertisers, or drawn from the web – into an engaging feed that keeps us scrolling and coming back. Facebook has been so successful because its personalized algorithms are much better at picking what individual users want to see than a network executive or editor could ever be.

US law provides these platforms with almost complete autonomy to make and enforce their own rules. Except in a few cases – mostly child pornography and copyright infringement – US platforms are never liable for what people post or do on their networks. Generally, the law provides almost no oversight of the decisions these commercial giants make. They are immune from legal requests to remove content, and the contractual terms of service that users agree to when joining give them absolute discretion over what they choose to remove.

This can be confusing, so it's worth going back two decades to understand how we got here. In the 1990s, the US Congress was worried about children using the internet to access pornography and other indecent or obscene content. It introduced the Communications Decency Act (CDA), which would have required internet content hosts and others to ensure that children could not access inappropriate content on their networks. The penalties were steep: up to two years imprisonment for anyone who permits the use of their systems to host or transmit offensive content in a way that might be accessible to children. The Supreme Court struck down the law as unconstitutional because it imposed far too great a burden on websites that adults were lawfully entitled to access – in trying to make the internet safe for children, the law would have unacceptably restricted the liberty of adults.

The most important thing to come out of this Act was one clause the Supreme Court did not strike down: Section 230. Section 230 of the CDA is an extremely powerful "safe harbor" that protects internet providers from liability for content posted by others. The only exceptions are for intellectual property law and for US federal criminal law. For all other breaches of state law, CDA 230 became an incredibly strong shield for online intermediaries. It firmly establishes the ground rules for lawsuits over internet content: a victim can sue the person who is directly responsible for causing harm online, but can almost never sue the service providers who host the content or facilitate communications.

It is hard to overstate the significance of CDA 230. The safe harbor that it provides is very generous: it gives platforms the right, but not the responsibility, to remove content as they see fit.[8] This protection that has proved vital to the success of platforms that host user-generated content or allow users to talk directly to each other. From Craigslist to Facebook, it ensures that platforms do not have to monitor content that users post in advance and will not be held liable just because they provide the services that third parties use to harm others.

Without CDA 230 many sites would be inundated with requests for them to remove content. If it did not exist, the web as we know it would be very different. It is not exaggerating to say that CDA 230 has been absolutely vital to the boom in Web 2.0 sites and social media – it removes the uncertainty and legal risk that would discourage investors and innovators from providing new ways for us to communicate. It is also a massive win for freedom of expression. Without CDA 230, review sites like Yelp could be liable for false reviews of businesses, even though it would be almost impossible for it to distinguish a review by a legitimately disgruntled customer from a false one by a vicious competitor. Discussion sites, from Reddit to Twitter to small bulletin boards and mailing list providers, would be potentially liable when people made false defamatory statements, even though it would be almost impossible for the provider to work out whether the claims they made were true. Service providers would have to worry about potentially losing a lawsuit and being faced with crippling damages awards. Without CDA 230, the threat of a lawsuit alone would be likely to force many providers to remove content. If a person claims that a post is defamatory or a review is fraudulent, and the site has no way to check whether it is true, the rational move is to remove the content. The internet as we know relies on CDA 230; without it, we would lose many of the benefits of a diverse internet where people can communicate to the world without their posts being vetted and controlled in advance.

REVENGE PORN AND THE CRACKS IN CDA 230

But, if you're a victim, CDA 230 can seem like a harsh denial of justice. The protection it gives to providers that host user reviews is the same protection that immunizes hosts of the most vile and repulsive content on the open web. The controversial (and now defunct) website Is Anyone Up? started by Hunter Moore (who was later sentenced to two and a half years in prison for identity theft and hacking) is a prime example. The site was dedicated to posting nude pictures of women, often alongside screenshots of their social media profiles, and encouraging people to post misogynist and abusive comments underneath. The images were sometimes submitted by abusive partners trying to control and intimidate women, uploaded by ex-lovers who could not deal with being dumped, and sometimes stolen from hacked accounts and devices.[9]

For the women whose most intimate images now appeared next to their names and social media profiles at the top of Google search results the effect was devastating.[10] They were often subject to abuse and harassment,[11] as complete strangers hurled bile at them for their imaginary crimes.[12] As images are posted, the primary invasion of privacy often cascades into severe ongoing shaming of women's bodies and sexuality by those who comment upon and spread the images across networks.[13] Where victims are easily identifiable (and the images show up in search results for their names), victims have also reported significant abuse online and offline, the loss of professional and educational opportunities, and exposure to stalking, as well as increased risk of harm and violence when they speak out.[14] More than one young woman has been driven to suicide after the images were distributed without her consent.

More generally, the problem of nonconsensual sharing of intimate images occurs within a broader context of sexual and domestic violence. As criminologists Nicola Henry and Anastasia Powell found in their research, explicit images are increasingly used by sexual partners "as a tool to threaten, harass and/or control both current and former partners."[15] Abusers deploy the threat of releasing images, either broadly or directly, to the victim's employers or immediate or extended family in order to intimidate their victims – including, in some cases, to prevent the victim from bringing formal complaints of domestic violence against the abuser. When images are circulated by partners on social networks and through sites made up of people the victim knows, the material not only has the capacity to quickly reach a large audience, but the harms are also direct and more personalized. The reputational effects, in these cases, are not the abstract fear that images are indexed and searchable on the internet, but rather the direct and certain knowledge that they are accessible to acquaintances of the victim. The shame that is frequently attached to women's bodies and sexuality can cause immense harm for victims.

The law is often of little help. Victims who go to the police are often told that they should have been more careful – if they did not want intimate images circulated, they should not take them at all, should not store them on insecure personal computers or on cloud storage providers, and should certainly not send them to others. There is a great deal of victim blaming at play here, which is made much worse by a deep gender imbalance: women who take intimate photos, by themselves or with their sexual partners, are derided as promiscuous, while men are more often able to escape moral condemnation and may even be celebrated for their sexual prowess. Victims of this type of abuse are disproportionately women and girls; when men are targets, they are rarely abused and humiliated in the same way that women often experience. As Danielle Keats Citron and Mary Anne Frank put it, "women would be seen as immoral sluts for engaging in sexual activity, whereas men's sexual activity is generally a point of pride."[16]

Hunter Moore eventually shut down Is Anyone Up? by selling it to an anti-bullying activist. But the law had little to do with it. Under the protection of CDA 230 Moore could not be held responsible for what his users posted, even if he encouraged their behavior.[17] Moore apparently made around $150,000 a year from the website. When asked by *Gawker* journalist Adrian Chen why he was shuttering the site, he mainly pointed to how tiring it was to screen child pornography out of the submissions: "I'd get at least 50 or 60 underage kids a day. It wasn't just 17-year-old girls. It was 12-year-olds and 9-year-olds. It definitely got old looking at that stuff every day."[18] It is hard to see Moore as suddenly coming to empathize with the victims whose lives he was helping to destroy. Only two weeks before shutting down the site, he was quoted in an interview with *The Village Voice* talking about how he would financially benefit from the publicity if one of his victims committed suicide. "I do not want anybody to ever be hurt by my site – physically," he says. But "I don't give a fuck about emotionally. Deal with it. Obviously, I'd get a ton of heat for it. But – I'm gonna sound like the most evil motherfucker – let's be real for a second: If somebody killed themselves over that? Do you know how much money I'd make? At the end of the day, I do not want anybody to hurt themselves. But if they do? Thank you for the money."[19]

While the site was up, dozens or hundreds of people wrote to Moore every day asking for their pictures to be removed. Moore refused each one, and CDA 230 supported him. The logic behind CDA 230 is that victims of harm online should address their complaints to the source – the abusive ex-lover or the hacker who stole the images. This is obviously of little help to victims once the images have been posted and made available to the world.

If victims of leaked intimate media are to have an effective remedy, the intermediaries who host, index, and make available content are the most effective points of control. Like all internet enforcement problems, the search engines, social media platforms, and content hosts are the most efficient means of policing content available. While it is generally not possible to completely eradicate material that has been posted online, it is possible to mitigate the harm by reducing its visibility. Effectively, this means ensuring that intimate images do not prominently feature in search results for a victim's name, ensuring that the material is not spread within the most popular or relevant social networks, and, as far as possible, attempting to regulate the most influential sites that host and distribute content online.

It's not just rogue websites like Is Anyone Up? that make harmful content available. Mainstream discussion sites like Reddit have to figure out how to deal with abusive content that their users post. In 2014, the actress Jennifer Lawrence was among hundreds who had their iCloud accounts hacked and their nude photos posted online. Reddit became a hub for people to post and seek links to the images. The site suddenly had to deal with massive public outrage as well as competing demands from some of its users to stand up for what they saw as their freedom of speech rights to share the leaked photos. The event shifted public debate about what role online platforms should play in responding to abuse. Jennifer Lawrence's outrage reverberated through mainstream media and public consciousness. Speaking of the attack that compromised her iCloud account, Lawrence told *Vanity Fair*: "It is not a scandal. It is a sex crime. It is a sexual violation. It's disgusting. The law needs to be changed, and we need to change."[20]

Reddit shut down the sub-Reddit that was primarily responsible for sharing links to "the fappening," as it became known, and it introduced new rules against sharing intimate images without the consent of the subject. Public outrage was so strong and focused that "revenge porn" has become one of the few categories where major internet providers will act quickly to remove content and links from their networks. Google, Bing, and Yahoo have created specialist simple web forms to handle complaints from victims who ask to remove links to intimate images from search results. Facebook, Twitter, and Reddit now have streamlined complaints and removal processes for victims who have their intimate images distributed without their consent.

Revenge porn has become one of the few areas where the tech industry has clearly stepped in to empower victims to complain about internet content without being compelled by law to do so. There are only a few situations where platforms routinely cooperate to remove content from the internet in an organized, efficient way. Most providers respond to valid court orders to block content in a particular jurisdiction, although this is usually done on a case-by-case basis. Some platforms give enhanced moderation powers to certain governments and other organizations that allow them to flag content for review much more quickly and efficiently.[21] All major platforms also abide by copyright notice and takedown rules and will routinely remove content that is alleged to infringe copyright (find more on this in Chapter 5). Most commercial providers cooperate fully with law enforcement agencies around the world, working to remove child pornography from the internet and bringing to justice those who make and post it. Many also work closely with national law enforcement and security agencies to tackle extremist content that seeks to radicalize people or encourage terrorism. And all major providers use sophisticated algorithmic techniques to combat spam. But in almost no other situation do platforms voluntarily provide a system where victims of harm online can file a complaint and have links to the offending material quickly and efficiently removed from search engines and discussion forums.

The streamlined revenge porn complaints systems are an exception to the US-based tech industry's extremely vocal support for CDA 230. It's actually not surprising to see the industry move in this way – collectively, tech firms cannot be seen to be sitting idly by when there is so much high-profile public attention to a problem that is almost universally condemned. Once Jennifer Lawrence and other celebrities had been attacked and stories of the terrible harm suffered by others began to gain visibility, social media platforms and search engines had to take action. Not only would resisting this pressure have been highly damaging in public relations terms, but it would threaten the ongoing stability of the CDA 230 safe harbor. By cutting out revenge porn as an issue, service providers defused some of the political pressure that was building to radically reshape or repeal CDA 230. There are still many groups that are upset with how difficult it is to get service providers to respond to harm facilitated through their networks and would like to see their immunity curtailed, but none of these issues are able to capture the attention of the public and of legislators as revenge porn.

For many, though, the questions still remain: why *only* revenge porn? Why *shouldn't* service providers do more to respond to the harmful content that disseminates through their networks? And why should we really on platforms choosing to do the right thing – what about the sites like Is Anyone Up? that will inevitably come in the future: if they don't voluntarily comply with social standards of decency, should the law compel them to act?

LOCAL LAWS AND GLOBAL NORMS

The protection that CDA 230 provides is almost unique to the United States. For the past two decades it has shaped the law and debates over how the world regulates internet content. For the massive service providers that are based primarily in the United States, it is seen as absolutely vital. But around the world, it looks like US free speech extremism gone too far. Other countries have much stronger rules than the United States does concerning defamation, privacy, and offensive content. Courts and legislatures in these countries have frequently held service providers responsible for material on their networks posted by their users. Some providers can afford to be completely based within the United States and mostly ignore requests from other countries, but most large commercial providers want to do business in other countries and have to work out how to deal with legal standards that differ from place to place.

There are plenty of examples of cases where foreign courts have ordered service providers to restrict what people can do on their networks. Some of the earliest were about Nazi memorabilia and hate speech. Strong First Amendment protections over speech don't apply in other countries, and both Germany and France have laws that prohibit the public use of Nazi war symbols and anti-Semitic hate speech.[22] When Yahoo was sued in France for allowing users to post auctions for Nazi memorabilia, it argued that US law protected it, and that since all of its servers were based in the United States, it should not be subject to French law. The French High Court rejected Yahoo's arguments under the reasoning that Yahoo's auctions were designed to be accessible to the world, and ordered the company to do what it could to prevent access to auctions of Nazi memorabilia to French residents.

For a long time, Yahoo and other tech companies had argued that it would be impossible to comply with the different rules of every country. They preferred a system where they could operate from the United States, under the safety of the First Amendment and CDA 230, and not have to worry about the rules of other countries. Unsurprisingly, courts in other countries weren't impressed. The Australian High Court warned about the need to avoid "American legal hegemony,"[23] where US laws would effectively apply to the world. This, some courts thought, would rob citizens of other nations of their democratic rights to choose the laws they lived under. The Australian case arose when the *Wall Street Journal* published a story warning about the alleged shadiness of an Australian business man. The article was clearly legal under US law, but contravened Australian defamation laws at the time. Dow Jones, the publisher, worried that if it lost the case, it would have to worry about too many different laws around the world – "from Afghanistan to Zimbabwe."[24] The result would be a lowest-common-denominator approach to speech: if everything they published had to be acceptable to everyone, then only the most banal commentary, which was not prohibited anywhere, would be permissible to print.

Neither the French nor the Australian courts accepted the concerns of the US tech firms. From their perspective, domestic laws provided protection for their citizens and it would be wrong to allow US companies to breach those laws just because they weren't primarily based in the country. In both cases, as well as in many similar later cases in other countries, the courts noted that the internet was global, and the international service provider was targeting users and doing business in the local jurisdiction. Ultimately, it was Yahoo's desire to show French advertisements to French viewers that first broke its attempts to avoid French law. If Yahoo was able to identify that its users were visiting from Paris to show them advertisements for florists in Paris, then it could use the same technology to block French users from accessing auctions for Nazi memorabilia. The blocks didn't have to be perfect – geolocation technology can often be fooled and can be easily circumvented – but they worked well enough in most cases.

Geolocation technology has improved, and it is now common for platforms to block content in various jurisdictions. YouTube, for example, blocks videos that criticize the King of Thailand, which is a criminal offense under Thailand's lèse-majesté rules.[25] (Those laws were a lot less controversial before the passing of the deeply beloved late previous King Bhumibol Adulyadej.) Turkey routinely requires Twitter to block access to tweets that are critical of Turkish President Erdogan or advance Kurdish political views.[26] In most cases, providers choose only to enforce these rules in a way that affects people within those countries. Users that appear to be based in one of these countries will see an error message, but the content will still be visible to viewers from other countries (or people who can use a virtual private network or other tool to mask their location).

Even though the technology exists to treat users who appear to access a service from different countries differently, this type of blocking raises very difficult contested questions about human rights. Google was heavily criticized when it launched operations in China because it would have to agree to demands by the Chinese government to censor content that might stoke democratic resistance. At the time, Google argued that it was better to provide the Chinese people with some services rather than none at all.[27] But a few years later, when Google's mail servers were apparently hacked by people working with the Chinese government and the private emails and details of Chinese human rights[28] activists were leaked, Google pulled out of China and moved its operations to Hong Kong.[29] This hacking posed serious threats to the safety of the activists and their families and contacts – those who mobilize dissent against the Chinese government are often targeted and detained by Chinese police. The controversy renewed a lot of discussion about when US tech giants should obey the rules of foreign countries and when they should be expected to stand up for basic rights like freedom of speech and privacy.

US courts have generally not required tech firms to remove objectionable content, but this brings its own problems. After most of the CDA was struck down by the Supreme Court, the law has largely left it to commercial firms to clean up their own parts of the internet. The Daily Stormer example (discussed in Chapter 1) shows that US companies are definitely enforcing rules against Nazi speech – unlike in France and Germany, though, these rules are not being enforced by courts. When a court makes a decision to block content, it has to weigh the competing interests – it balances the harmful content against the impact of blocking access on freedom of speech. When a court makes mistakes, its decisions are publicly available and can be appealed. When Google, or Cloudflare, or Digital Ocean, or GoDaddy make decisions to keep Nazi sites off the public web, the effect might be the same, but the process is much different.

THE RIGHT TO BE FORGOTTEN

The problem of jurisdiction is not just a problem of authoritarian regimes imposing restrictions on speech. One of the best examples of intermediaries caught in real conflicts between different Western democratic systems is the European "right to be forgotten." In Europe, protections for individual privacy are far stronger than they are in the United States. This creates major headaches for US internet providers whose major source of income is trading in user data and targeted advertisements. In one of the major conflicts between Europe and US tech companies, the European Court of Justice ruled that search engines had an obligation to remove links to personal information on the internet that were inaccurate, inadequate, irrelevant, or excessive.[30] Dubbed the "right to be forgotten" (or RTBF), the ruling empowers individuals in European states to request information be scrubbed from the indexes of major search engines. It does not remove the content from the open web, but it can significantly limit the visibility of the information.

The costs of the RTBF are substantial. The Court of Justice's decision requires search providers to balance rights of privacy with freedom of expression. Major search engines Google and Bing have implemented a web form to allow people to request removal of a particular URL from their index. These URLs are manually reviewed, and so far Google has approved 43 percent of requests.[31] Many people worry not just about the financial costs, but also about the imposition on freedom of speech, access to information, and the archive of recorded history. The requests made to Google often come from people who want to remove links to their criminal past from present-day searches for their names, and opinion is fiercely split over whether the public has an ongoing right to know about past wrongdoings or whether those who have served their time and repaid their debts should be able to get on with their lives without their pasts overshadowing their present job opportunities and personal relationships. Other requests often come from politicians and public figures who want critical news reports scrubbed from the internet, and there is much less disagreement here; this is clearly the kind of information that many think should be available for the public interest.

The challenge is that a company has to make the decision about whether a piece of information is in the public interest to know or not. This is not something that is done in public or by an independent judiciary according to the rule of law. It is a decision made by Google's employees, with little oversight and accountability. As a private company, Google is spectacularly badly placed to make these sorts of decisions. In easy cases, it may have no trouble, but where there is a real potential impact on freedom of speech it gets much more difficult. Faced with a claim by a politician that a negative news report is fabricated, should Google remove links to it? Google has no fact-finding powers to compel people to give evidence and so will often not be able to tell whether a report is true. Unlike when a court censors content, there is no public hearing and no real mechanisms for review if a mistake is made.

The introduction of the RTBF may signal the start of more efforts worldwide to have Google and other tech giants take a more active role in restricting access to different types of content. Google resisted the decision initially but has since cooperated by adding a simple request form for its users. It publishes regular statistics showing the number of requests it receives – nearly 600,000 requests complaining of more than 2 million URLs since 2014.[32] The simple web form it has provided appears to demonstrate to regulators that the system works effectively and efficiently, and it will be tempting for governments to request similar systems for dealing with other types of content, like bullying and hate speech. It may not be long before courts in other places around the world look to the European Court of Justice's RTBF precedent to try to get tech firms to introduce more tools to protect their residents. This is exactly what those who advocate for free speech worry about: it is easy to imagine a future where a handful of powerful tech companies are continuously making decisions about whether information should be available to their users. As we have already seen, clearly, tech companies are already doing this in the way that they rank results and remove content that violates their terms of service. But the more routine this becomes, the free speech advocates worry, the further we drift from the freedom of the open web, where everyone can have a voice and the wealth of human history and knowledge is available to all.

ONGOING INTERNATIONAL PRESSURE

Technology companies continue to fight ongoing battles over liability all over the world. The case against Dow Jones back at the turn of the century opened the door to lawsuits by people around the world to try to get internet intermediaries to remove defamatory posts about them from their networks. Plaintiffs have a tough time suing the people who post defamatory information themselves; they might be hard to track down, or they might live in a country, like the United States, that has strong protections for freedom of speech that make them impossible to sue. Even if the original poster can be tracked down, the "Streisand effect" practically ensures that the information will be available somewhere. Coined by journalist Mike Masnick, the "Streisand effect" is used to explain why it is often counterproductive to try to use the law to restrict the flow of information online. When Barbara Streisand complained about pictures of her private residence that were posted on the website of the California Coastal Records Project, among some 80,000 other photos documenting erosion along the Californian coastline,[33] they were immediately copied and reuploaded on hundreds of different sites. Before the complaint, the photo had only been accessed six times, including twice by her lawyers.[34] Merely trying to get information taken down often spurs others to make sure it remains available. The US motion picture industry learned this when they tried to get the internet to forget the decryption key that a young Norwegian discovered would allow anyone to break the digital locks on the newly released DVD format discs.[35] With this key, consumers could rip DVDs into digital files, allowing them to play back films that were previously locked to only work in complying devices. This breakthrough opened the possibility for the widespread file sharing of films – once the files were available in an unlocked digital format, they could then be shared over peer-to-peer networks. Within days, the 128-digit string found its way to thousands of websites and T-shirts and was even recreated as instructions contained within a very long series of Haiku poems that, when followed, allowed programmers to recreate the sequence.[36]

But victims of defamation have learned that they don't need to have the material completely removed from the internet. Instead, what they often want is for it not to be easily accessible to their social circles and people they know who might search for their names. So their primary targets are the search engines and social media providers, not the people who originally post the content or the smaller websites they post to.

Janice Duffy is an Australian health researcher who is taking on Google to take control of search results for her name. Dr. Duffy had consulted with a range of psychics about her romantic attachment to a man she had met in New York. All of the psychics she spoke to predicted a positive relationship and Dr. Duffy was devastated when the man dashed her hopes in favor of another woman. Disillusioned with the quality of the psychic predictions she had received, Dr. Duffy started writing reviews, complaining about the psychic services she had received. She posted these reviews to the Ripoff Report, a site that aims to warn others about scams and frauds and allows users to submit reviews about any organization or individual. She went further and started making new appointments with psychics, creating fake identities and backstories. One of the alter egos she created was Oswald Billet, whose wife committed suicide after a psychic raised her hopes of a romantic relationship that was later dashed. She created a range of different pseudonyms to talk to psychics and then post complaints about them to the Ripoff Report.

The psychics fought back in response to Dr. Duffy's actions. Other people started posting to the Ripoff Report that she was a "psychic stalker," warning other psychics not to deal with her. These are the posts that led Dr. Duffy to take legal action. When she searched for her name through the Google search engine, she found that some of the first search results were links to forum posts that she found hurtful and damaging. She asked the Ripoff Report to remove the claims against her, but the site usually refuses to remove reviews.

Frustrated, Dr. Duffy asked Google to remove the links to the reviews on the Ripoff Report from its search results. If she couldn't get the content removed from the review site, she reasoned, at least she could stop the results from showing up when people she knew searched for her name. Google refused to remove the links. It argued that searchers have a right to know about the experiences of other people and that it was important for people to be able to share reviews without being silenced by the target if the review is negative. Google has a point here: we now rely heavily on information on the web to inform us about people and businesses we interact with, and reviews provide valuable information in an age where we are often dealing with strangers. "On the internet," the famous *New Yorker* cartoon goes, "nobody knows you're a dog." Reviews fixed that problem, at least in part: by and large, consumers can trust eBay sellers, Amazon merchants, Lyft drivers, and Airbnb hosts because other people have posted good reviews of their experiences. The system isn't perfect, but it depends on people being able to be honest in their reviews without having negative reviews removed.

Dr. Duffy sued Google in Australia. The negative reviews about Dr. Duffy are almost certainly lawful in the United States, where defamation laws are not as strict as in other countries. In Australia, where Dr. Duffy lives, the reviews were held to be defamatory.[37] The Court found that Dr. Duffy's behavior was "reprehensible" and "offensive," but did not amount to "stalking" – she didn't try to invade the privacy of the psychics, and she wasn't carrying on an obsessive and persistent campaign to harass a particular psychic over a period of time. Because Google wasn't able to prove that the negative reviews were true in the strictest sense, the Australian Court found that they were defamatory, as were the snippets that Google extracted in its search results. Google was held liable for publishing both the snippets and the links to defamatory material, and Dr. Duffy was awarded $100,000 in damages.

The lawsuit is one example of many different cases that Google is currently facing around the world. Under US law, not only is defamation harder to prove, but both the Ripoff Report and Google are clearly protected by CDA 230. Lawsuits like these are still filed in the United States, but they don't last very long. Generally, a website like the Ripoff Report does not have to worry about foreign law – its operators can safely ignore the laws of Australia and other countries if they don't have assets overseas. Unfortunately, for people like Dr. Duffy, it is impossible to enforce an Australian defamation judgment against a US company, since the reviews do not breach US law. The reasoning here makes sense: US residents have a constitutionally protected right to freedom of speech, and allowing foreign countries to impose more restrictive standards would harm their interests. But the Australian Court's reasoning also makes sense: Australians have a recognized legal right to object to defamatory statements that are not true or honest, and if the courts do nothing to enforce those rights, then Australians will inevitably be harmed by people in other countries.

The major problem here is that there is no way to tell if someone is being honest in their reviews. The approach favored in the United States is to err on the side of free speech: unless the review is clearly malicious, it will usually be permitted.[38] The approach in other countries, however, lets individuals (but not businesses) who think that a review is false clear their name through a claim in defamation. This matters a lot in borderline cases: US law is more favorable to reviewers; Australian law is more favorable to people who have been defamed. This difference causes a massive problem for service providers that need to know what law they should apply and whose interests they should protect.

Google's concern is that defamation law might be abused to remove negative reviews. It does not want to be in the difficult position of having to decide whether a review is real or fake. Because courts sometimes award massive damages in defamation claims, a firm like Google would be smart to remove content that people complain about, unless it can be very sure that it wasn't clearly false, malicious, or negligent. If Google had to evaluate each claim, it would likely end up removing links to many negative reviews that may well be real.

Dr. Duffy is one of a growing number of people around the world who want to see companies like Google take more responsibility for harmful online content. They are trying to achieve through defamation law similar results to the RTBF. Their argument is based on the pragmatic recognition that search engines and major social media providers represent the most efficient points of control for limiting the spread of harmful information when the source itself is difficult to take legal against against. Courts around the world are split on this question at the moment. Some courts consider the search engines to be neutral indexes and, as such, not in a good position to determine whether content should be removed or not. But increasingly, it seems like courts outside of the United States are sometimes willing to make orders that require Google and other search engines to remove links to defamatory content. Plaintiffs like Dr. Duffy have spent years litigating these questions, at times representing themselves in extremely difficult conditions. Some of these cases fail, but, as more and more are successful, we can expect an increase in the number of people willing to take search engines and social media platforms to court.

SPEECH TRADE-OFFS AND THE PROBLEM WITH LITIGATION

There are an increasing number of judgments coming from all around the world trying to police content on the internet, dealing with issues like defamation, invasion of privacy, the disclosure of confidential information, and more. We should have some sympathy for foreign courts trying to deal with US companies to enforce their law. In cases where the plaintiff has a chance of succeeding, the court is already convinced that the material they are complaining about is unlawful. These courts are just looking for a way to enforce their local laws and not give in to "American legal hegemony." Within the confines of a particular case, it is easy to see why a court would want to find a way to protect the rights of the plaintiff that has clearly been wronged. For these courts, this is not a difficult question of protecting freedom of speech: the speech complained about is unlawful in these countries and removing content, therefore, is not an imposition on freedom of speech. Any problems at this stage are dealt with immediately by the court – if the claim has no merit, or the remedy the plaintiff seeks would impose too high a cost on freedom of expression, the court will choose not to make the order that content should be removed.

In common law adversarial systems, these are the main issues that matter. The court is not well placed to worry about what might happen in other, future cases, the potential plaintiffs of which may not have a valid defamation claim. But digital intermediaries, in contrast, contest these claims because they worry about the precedent. Once the law is settled that they are liable for defamatory content posted by others, then they expect that many more people will begin to file defamation cases. Certainly, this was Google's experience with the RTBF: once it became possible to ask Google to remove search results from its index, thousands of people flocked to the complaints form. All of a sudden, Google and companies like it are tasked with the unenviable job of trying to work out whether a particular claim is meritorious or not: is a review real or is it dishonest? Is a negative story about a politician accurate? Is information that was a matter of public record now no longer sufficiently relevant? Should the company obey an antidemocratic law that restricts information about another country's government, or criticism of their king?

We should worry about companies like Google making these decisions. These are questions that throughout the history of modern democracies have been made by courts. A great deal of our Western liberal theory warns about the potential for tyranny where decisions to censor information are made in secret, without a clear avenue for appeal, by people who are not accountable to the public. This is exactly the reason that free speech advocates worry so much about the weakening of CDA 230: when private companies have to make decisions to censor speech, they will inevitably make mistakes and we will lose some of our liberty.

At the same time, it is also important to recognize that the extremely strong protections for freedom of speech that CDA 230 provides are increasingly difficult to justify, particularly outside of the United States. The problems of revenge porn are an example of when freedom of speech seems to go too far, even in the United States. The quick procedures that internet intermediaries have developed to remove intimate images were developed in response to the rapid emergence of a generally agreed-upon social norm. The law does not require these responses, but there's a strong moral view that respectable companies should not tolerate this type of abuse. Within only a few years, and triggered by a relatively small number of high-profile cases, society became relatively united around a value judgment that technology companies should help out when people post nude pictures of others without their consent. This is hard to argue against, in a way that more difficult questions of defamation and privacy law are not. We don't have strong social agreement about whether people should be entitled to have their past criminal histories scrubbed from the web or whether they should be able to ask for negative reviews about themselves to be removed.

What we know is that CDA 230 is vital to innovation, but sometimes technological innovations result in real harms to real people. People who have been harmed by online content want intermediaries to take responsibility for helping to prevent that harm, and their claims are often sympathetic. But we know from the experiences of other countries that, without a strong immunity, service providers end up in a difficult position wherein they must evaluate the validity of complaints without the proper tools of the judicial system to help them. In borderline cases, they almost inevitably err on the side of appeasing the person who complains, because the alternative – going to court and potentially having to pay both legal fees and heavy damages – is too risky.

Intermediaries will ultimately adapt to what the law requires. Google fought the RTBF and continues to lobby against its extension, but the tech giant also developed a system to handle hundreds of thousands of requests per year relatively efficiently.[39] Many of the major commercial internet companies developed efficient schemes to handle requests to remove intimate images posted without consent. If the law settles outside of the United States that search engines and social media platforms are liable when they link to defamatory content, then they will also develop efficient systems to handle removal requests. Ultimately, those service providers that operate outside of the United States will find efficient ways to deal with the law, just as every company has ever since Yahoo started blocking auctions for Nazi memorabilia.

This is exactly what advocates of free speech worry about. The more complaints made, the more that service providers have an incentive to deal with them quickly and cheaply. When a service provider is liable only for failing to remove content, and never for removing the wrong content, it is always likely to censor more than it strictly has to. This lopsided incentive can be even worse than government censorship: for those who have been censored, there is no transparency, no avenue of appeal, and sometimes even no notice. Without legal oversight that ensures decisions are legitimately made and disputes are properly adjudicated, it is hard to have faith that the power that massive tech companies wield is being fairly exercised. Finding a way to regulate the internet quickly, cheaply, and in a way that is legitimate is the big challenge that will be discussed in the second half of the book.

5

How Copyright Shaped the Internet

To an extent that nobody else has managed, the copyright industries have been able to bake protection for their rights into the very infrastructure of the internet. The challenge of limiting illicit file sharing is similar to many of the other difficult issues – like addressing offensive content, removing defamatory posts, or limiting the flow of misinformation – in internet regulation. How do you control what users do online without directly going after individual users? Legal actions against individuals are expensive; they only really make sense in high value cases. Changing the behavior of many individuals on a large scale is much more difficult, whether it's users sharing copyrighted music and films or people using the internet to harass others. Any effective answer has to involve technology companies and internet intermediaries in some way, because they have the power to influence large numbers of users through their design choices and policies.

Copyright owners have spent more time and money trying to find an answer to this problem than any other group (except for maybe the surveillance and national security agencies of governments). Over the past two decades, the copyright industry has worked to enlist a broad range of technology companies and internet intermediaries to protect their interests. No other group has been so successful at influencing technology companies to regulate what internet users do online.

Copyright owners realized very early on that the key to regulating the internet in their interests was to exert pressure on the technology companies that make the tools and provide the services that people use every day. We have already seen how the extremely strong safe harbor in CDA 230 of the Communications Decency Act protects tech companies against liability for almost everything their users do online. This does not apply to copyright. The copyright industry negotiated a separate safe harbor, introduced as part of the Digital Millennium Copyright Act (known as the DMCA). Under the DMCA, tech companies are protected from potential liability for what their users post, but only if they agree to introduce a "notice and takedown" scheme that gives copyright owners a right to complain about content they host or link to. The copyright notice and takedown scheme has become a default standard among much of the commercial internet, and tech companies now process billions of requests to remove content on copyright grounds each year.

The control that copyright owners exercise over internet users extends much further than notice and takedown. Their biggest success has been working with internet companies to create new technical systems that proactively protect their interests. There are automated detection algorithms working constantly to check everything that people upload to platforms like YouTube, Facebook, SoundCloud, Twitch, and many others. Copyright owners have also ensured that the platforms that make films, television series, games, music, and books available to buy or stream are engineered in a way that provides them with control over how people access digital content. They have ensured that services like Netflix, Spotify, iTunes, Steam, and Amazon all use technical locks (known as digital rights management or DRM) to extend their control to the applications and devices that people use to consume media content.

Copyright owners have quite literally shaped the development of the internet to work in their favor. They have been able to tame the wild west of the early internet by creating new systems of enforcement that operate parallel to the law. These systems are made up of many different interacting components, including automated algorithmic tools that can detect copyrighted content as soon as it is uploaded and prevent it from being shared on major commercial platforms, notice and takedown schemes, and pervasive DRM. Many of these systems work almost invisibly to give copyright owners greater control over the commercial internet. They are not perfect, but they operate at a scale that is almost inconceivable for other groups that want more influence over what people do online. Some of these systems exist because the industry was able to get new laws passed, and others came about through extended negotiation with the technology companies around the world. All of them have something in common: they have tried, as much as possible, to get private companies to make decisions about what content people are allowed to search for, share, and see. Each of these systems is designed to increase corporate control over the flow of information while avoiding the expense of real oversight by judges.

At least as far as copyright is concerned, the lawlessness of the early internet has been replaced not by legitimate legal processes, but by corporate rule through algorithmic enforcement. As the control of copyright owners has increased, so too have complaints from people whose content has been removed, whose rights have been restricted, or whose accounts have been suspended with no real avenue of appeal because of a mistaken algorithm.

It has taken decades for the copyright industries to convince technology companies to develop automated tools to fight copyright infringement and to put policies in place to police what their users do. The algorithmic tools for detecting infringing content are still evolving, and the work to embed technical controls in the normal business processes and policies of a growing range of internet inter-mediaries is ongoing. The journey has been difficult, and the lessons that the copyright industry learned over this time are important for others who want technology companies to design their technologies in ways that promote their interests. We can also learn a lot from the problems that these schemes create about the limits of technical solutions and the dangers of handing over so much power to opaque and unaccountable systems.

THE TROUBLE WITH FILE SHARING: SUING USERS IS EXPENSIVE, SLOW, AND OFTEN COUNTERPRODUCTIVE

Twenty years ago, Napster changed everything. MP3 technology had been around for a few years, but Napster's peer-to-peer file sharing software made it possible to find music easily. Nearly overnight, the potential of the internet as a limitless digital library became clear to millions around the world. Almost any song ever recorded, no matter how obscure, was stored and shared by someone, somewhere in the world. For many, Napster was the first glimpse into how the internet could become much more than news groups, email, and telephone directories. It promised the abundance of culture, and the limitless choice was intoxicating. This turned out to be incredibly important in driving innovation in the record industry. It showed consumers what was possible in a way the industry could not afford to ignore.

For copyright owners, Napster was the first real manifestation of an existential threat to their businesses. In a world of physical distribution of music and other entertainment products, copyright owners could exercise a large degree of control over their supply chains. They were able to ensure that most retailers stocked only legitimate products, and they were able to keep industrial-scale counterfeiting mostly under control. Bootleg records still circulated, of course, but never really threatened copyright owners' legitimate markets. Napster changed this when it provided the tools for any person to upload and share illegitimate copies of music to the world. Suddenly, the number of people involved in large-scale copyright infringement grew exponentially. Left unchecked, the copyright industries worried that illicit peer-to-peer file sharing would utterly decimate their sales channels.

The copyright industries spent much of the time after Napster's introduction trying to put the genie back in the bottle. The technology had been developed that could radically disrupt these industries' lucrative physical distribution channels, and they were frantically trying to find a way to stamp it out. For the recording industry, this seemed like a life-or-death battle for control over the flow of information. The "copyright wars,"[1] as they are known, are an excellent example of how hard it is to regulate the internet. There are few lobby groups with the resources and persistence of the US recording and film industries faced with what they see as an existential threat. Their struggle to control the evolution of technology and the way that people communicate serve as a warning to others, and the lessons they are still learning can help pave the way for the development of more effective strategies in the future.

The first lesson the industry really learned was that trying to sue users directly was a very bad idea. Users loved the ability to access whatever music they wanted for free, and improvements in technology had also allowed people to share books, television shows, and movies just as easily. In 2003, the Recording Industry Association of America (RIAA) became desperate and launched a disastrous campaign to sue thousands of individual users who were sharing music online.[2] As a public relations move, the suits were a nightmare: the music industry looked like a dinosaur that refused to adapt to the digital age and preferred to sue its fans than find a way to serve their new needs. This was made much worse when it became clear that the techniques the industry was using to identify people to sue were deeply flawed. The headlines about the cases were dominated with examples of suits against grandmothers for downloading rap music they had never heard of, a man paralyzed by a stroke living on disability payments, a homeless man, and a woman who had passed away several months earlier.[3] All in all, the recording industry sued or threatened to sue more than 30,000 people, trying to settle most cases for a few thousand dollars at a time. As a strategy to stop file sharing, it was woefully ineffective. In the long term, the legal costs and the negative press proved to be far greater than the deterrent effect – particularly since the chances of any given individual being caught were still very low.

The low point of public relations problems for the copyright industry probably came with its bittersweet victory against Jammie Thomas-Rasset, a Native American mother of four living in Minnesota. It was the first file sharing copyright infringement case brought before a US jury by a major record label. Thomas-Rasset had been sued for sharing twenty-four songs on the now defunct file sharing network Kazaa. Capitol Records and five other record companies initially sought a settlement for $5,000, which she declined.[4] She fought the case in court, putting her trust in a jury of her peers. After three trials and an appeal, including one mistrial and one decision that would have awarded $1.92 million to the record companies in damages, Thomas-Rasset was finally ordered to pay $222,000. Unable to pay, she declared that she would file for bankruptcy.

This case is an excellent example of the challenges of using the legal system to try to deter wrongdoing on the internet by focusing on individual users. Copyright infringement is widespread – copyright owners were trying to address a behavior that had already become commonplace among a great many consumers. The recording industry tried to influence users directly by making an example out of people who illicitly downloaded music. Because the chances of getting caught were so low, the copyright industry tried in these cases to sue a great many people and, in some cases, seek extremely high damages awards, hoping people would think twice in future before they decided to illicitly download music files. Of course, Thomas-Rasset didn't have the money to pay such a massive damages award, but the case was designed to send a message to people who share files across the country. Instead, it galvanized opposition to the copyright owners' cause. The chances of getting caught are *still* very low, the consequences (if any) come too late to be really effective, and the unfairness of the system undermines the public's belief that the law should be obeyed. At some point, increasing the penalties does not actually increase the deterrent. The harsher copyright gets, the more it seems that people might view it as technically unlawful but not morally wrong.[5] By the time it was over, the tide of public opinion was firmly on the side of consumers – it was almost impossible to justify why an ordinary person should be expected to pay hundreds of thousands of dollars in compensation for sharing one or two albums.

This was a lesson copyright owners would learn well. Now, the idea of suing individual users is almost unthinkable, at least for the major players. Smaller copyright owners – independent film producers and porn distributors – still occasionally try, but the industry has been quick to distance itself from a massively unpopular and largely ineffective strategy.

DECENTRALIZED TECHNOLOGIES ARE RESILIENT

The first set of technology companies that copyright owners targeted were the software developers that had the closest connection to copyright infringement: the creators of peer-to-peer file sharing programs and websites. The people who create tools specifically designed to help people infringe copyright are relatively easy targets under copyright law, and the copyright industries have worked for many decades to ensure that these tools are kept out of the general commercial market. Even before the internet, the prime targets of copyright owners have been technology manufacturers – from the automated piano player at the start of the twentieth century to the videocassette recorder manufacturers of the 1980s. In the internet era, they have been fairly successful at shutting down some of the most popular networks, but they have not been able to prevent the technologies themselves from developing or really do anything about the dedicated pirates that operate from countries with weak copyright laws and no extradition treaties with the United States.

When Napster was launched, it inevitably became a massive target for the recording industry. In a high-profile case, backed by recording artists like Metallica and Dr. Dre, the RIAA was able to successfully sue the creators of Napster. By legal standards, the lawsuit was a huge success. Napster shutdown its entire network in 2001,[6] and promised to pay $26 million in compensation to copyright owners.

Suing the developers seemed to work initially, but it spurred an arms race as new services learned how to adapt to the limits of the law. In an effort to clamp down on new technologies that helped people to infringe copyright, the industry has targeted a constantly evolving group of players. Before the dust had even settled after the Napster case, Napster was being replaced by a new generation of file sharing networks, like Aimster and eDonkey and the FastTrack networks Kazaa, Grokster,

Morpheus, and iMesh. The music industry spent a great deal of time and money over the next decade suing each new file sharing network. After much effort, they managed to shutdown many networks in big legal victories around the world.

The strategy to sue software developers stopped working when the technology became decentralized. While these cases were underway, Bram Cohen quietly released the BitTorrent peer-to-peer protocol in 2001. By 2004, BitTorrent traffic was estimated to account for nearly one-third of all global internet traffic.[7] BitTorrent is now the dominant peer-to-peer file sharing protocol and still has hundreds of millions of monthly users worldwide.

Manufacturers and technology developers are usually not legally responsible for how people use their tools if they have no power to control those users. The general principle is that people who make tools that have lawful uses should not be punished just because others choose to use those tools in unlawful ways. This rule has been fundamentally important to the development of the modern internet. In a digital world, all transmission of information involves some degree of copying. When you send an email to a friend, the email exists as bits – ones and zeroes – that are copied temporarily by dozens of computer systems as the message is passed along the network. Any internet technology that helps people communicate can also help people to copy or send content in a way that infringes copyright. If technology developers were liable for everything users of their tools did wrong online, they would be much less likely to invest in creating innovative, new technologies that bring substantial benefits to us all.

This basic principle means that BitTorrent is so decentralized that legally it is almost unkillable. Cohen and the developers of the software tools that implement the protocol he designed have almost nothing to do with the users of the system. BitTorrent has many legitimate applications; it is an incredibly efficient protocol that is now used by many major companies to distribute software and media files. Unlike previous file sharing networks, the developers of the protocol and the tools are not setup to make money from the sharing of infringing content, and they legitimately have no control over how people use the systems they create.

Practically, too, BitTorrent's decentralization makes legal enforcement extremely difficult. The people who promote and profit from illicit file sharing on the BitTorrent protocol are also difficult to sue. The network relies on servers called indexers that allow people to find torrents, and trackers that coordinate the groups of users sharing those particular torrents. These servers have a much closer connection to the content that is being shared and can exercise greater control over their users – and, as a result, they are potentially liable when their users infringe copyright. Indeed, many of them have been sued and shutdown over the years. The trouble is that, with a decentralized network like BitTorrent, it is cheap and easy to create a torrent site and difficult to track down the operators.

Massive operations like The Pirate Bay have resisted legal efforts to shut them down for many years. Even after the site's founders were criminally prosecuted, others stepped forward to keep the site running on new hardware from hidden locations around the world.[8] It has become almost prohibitively expensive for the recorded music and film industries to track down those responsible for running illicit file sharing networks and bring lawsuits against them in their home countries. Even after long-running, expensive lawsuits are successful and file sharing sites get shutdown, there are new ones constantly taking their place.

The key lesson we can learn from the copyright wars here is that suing the developers of new technologies works only up to a point. The law can be effective against technologies that can only practically be used for illicit purposes. This means it is possible to suppress investments in high-profile commercial technologies aimed at the popular market, as long as those responsible live in a friendly jurisdiction. The strategy stops working when developers learn to make their software decentralized and multipurpose or when the technology is driven underground.

After BitTorrent became so popular, the copyright industry had to shift strategy again. The copyright wars were relatively effective at stopping local companies from investing in the promotion of peer-to-peer file sharing, but they weren't effective at stopping file sharing itself. Copyright owners had to find new ways to regulate the internet. This meant turning to enlist a broader group of internet intermediaries who could help police what users do online. This marks a fundamental shift in approach: instead of using the law to directly target wrongdoers, the industry started to experiment with how it could pressure other companies into doing its regulatory work.

NOTICE AND TAKEDOWN

Given the difficulties in policing infringing content online, the main game for copyright owners is now to focus on making it more difficult to find. The single biggest priority of the major copyright owners is to keep links to infringing material off of the first few pages of Google's search engine. Google processes more than 70 million requests to scrub links to copyrighted material from its search engine *every month*. The laws that enable copyright owners to make these requests have existed since the early days of the commercial internet, but it was only in the late 2000s that copyright owners started using it at a really substantial scale.

The notice and takedown regime that we have today grew out of a bargain between industries in the late 1990s. The copyright industries were quick to see the threat that the internet brought and wanted an effective way to police content people posted online. But the nascent internet industry was worried about being sued by the established giants of the copyright industries for content its users uploaded that they had no easy way to track or control. The deal that was struck in the DMCA in 1998 was a response to these fears. In order to provide safety and certainty for investors in the new technological economy, internet providers were granted a safe harbor that ensures that tech companies are not liable when their users use their services to infringe copyright. The DMCA includes the major operating principle that internet companies cannot be required to proactively monitor content posted by users of their services. In exchange for this immunity, tech companies had to introduce a notice and takedown scheme.

The DMCA's notice and takedown scheme allows copyright owners to send a notice to content hosts and search engines when they discover that their material has been shared unlawfully. The service provider then has an obligation to remove the content as soon as reasonably possible. For content hosts, this means deleting or disabling access to the files; for search engines, the link is removed from their index. Where possible, the service provider notifies the person who uploaded the content, and they have an opportunity to file a "counter-notice" if they think a mistake has been made. For tech companies, the formal takedown scheme has real benefits. The legal regulations provide clear guidelines about what exactly they must do in response to notices of infringement, and the scheme provides certainty that, if they follow these rules, they won't be liable for massive potential damages. The notice and takedown system is now commonly used throughout the world, and most major commercial sites that host user-generated content have implemented it in some form. The US exported the DMCA system to other countries through a series of trade agreements, and it is now in force in many jurisdictions worldwide. But even in countries without a formal notice and takedown scheme, US law has become a de facto standard, because so many of the major commercial tech firms that host content are based in the United States and have adopted its rules.

This deal was central to the growth of services like YouTube, which now sees its users uploading hundreds of hours of video content every minute. Some portion of that content will always include some copyrighted material. But with the sheer quantity of information being uploaded all the time, it would take an army of censors to screen it all before it was published. In the mass media era, newspapers and broadcasters could screen the material they published before they sent it out, and the law often expected that they do so to avoid publishing unlawful content. In the digital age, the job of screening content is many orders of magnitude larger. The balance the DMCA tries to strike ultimately seeks to preserve an internet where everyone has the chance to create and be heard, while providing copyright owners with a tool to request that infringing material be removed. Without the DMCA, the costs and delays involved in running large platforms would radically limit the vibrant, creative user-generated content the internet gives us today. YouTube, for example, has long argued that they simply wouldn't be able to function if they had to screen material in advance. Like many other major platforms that provide a home for user-generated content, the entire point is that they enable us all to post content to the world. Like CDA 230, the safe harbor in the DMCA ensures that the internet works with less friction, which is exactly what allows us to avoid the mass media model where only those selected by gatekeepers – record labels, publishers, news editors, etc. – get a shot at reaching a large audience.

The notice and takedown system for copyright infringement works on a scale that is unique on the internet. No other system of regulation exists with the capacity to police billions of allegations of infringement every year. But it only works at this scale because both copyright owners and the major tech companies have the cash to develop automated systems to send and receive notices, respectively.

Most of the work of finding infringing material on the internet is conducted by algorithms that scour the web for links to illicit downloads of movies and albums. The organizations tasked with protecting the rights of copyright owners scour the internet for new links to infringing material that are continuously being posted. These are usually links to torrent websites, file lockers, and streaming services. The people who post infringing content online know that copyright owners are always watching and that content, or links to content, may be removed at any time. Copyright infringement and enforcement has become a game of whack-a-mole.[9] Copyright owners race to find the material as it is uploaded, and uploaders race to put it back up.

The size of the job is so big that the copyright industries and Google have had to create new automated systems to issue and respond to millions of requests each day. An entire industry has grown out of agents who search the open web for copyright infringement and file takedown requests. These companies search for links to infringing content, often focusing on the most valuable content – prerelease or recently released albums and films. The links are aggregated into takedown notices and generally sent by the thousands to the websites that host them and to the major search engines. The entire process works with very little human oversight; Google uses its own automated system to evaluate notices as they come in and remove links from its index.

By automating notice and takedown, Google and the copyright industries have been able to develop a system that works relatively efficiently to police links to infringing content at a massive scale. The major problem with these notice and takedown systems, however, is that they are prone to mistakes, vulnerable to abuse, and have no effective system to resolve disputes.

The notice and takedown system is routinely abused by people filing false copyright claims to try to get all sorts of material they don't like removed from the web. For example, some companies use copyright notices to silence their critics and get negative reviews removed from websites or to try to harm their competitors. In other cases, copyright owners have been known to overreach and try to remove content that is perfectly legal. One example is Stephanie Lenz, who uploaded a thirty-second clip to YouTube of her adorable 13-month-old child dancing to Prince's *Let's Go Crazy* on the radio. Universal Music Group, who owns part of the copyright in the song, filed a takedown request, and the video was removed from YouTube. Universal explained that the decision was motivated by Prince's principles:

Prince believes it is wrong for YouTube, or any other user-generated site, to appropriate his music without his consent. That position has nothing to do with any particular video that uses his songs. It's simply a matter of principle. And legally, he has the right to have his music removed. We support him and this important principle. That is why, over the last few months, we have asked YouTube to remove thousands of different videos that use Prince music without his permission.[10]

Copyright law doesn't actually give Prince or his heirs the right to control all uses of his music. Videos like Lenz's are clearly fair use under US copyright law; they don't infringe copyright, primarily because they don't at all interfere with the market for the original song. Lenz sued, arguing that Universal abused the notice and takedown process by asking for the video to be removed when it had no legal right to do so. The Ninth Circuit Court of Appeals agreed, ruling that copyright owners must take the time to evaluate whether the content they complain about is actually likely to be infringing or not.[11] This is concerning for some copyright owners, who worry that it introduces extra costs and delays in the notice and takedown system.

Finding infringing content will always be an inexact science. People who try to avoid copyright regulations are used to obscuring links or putting them back up after they are removed. Catching more of these inevitably means making more mistakes as well. The automated systems that have been designed to detect infringing content look for keywords that suggest a website is hosting illicit copies of films and albums, but they misidentify a lot of material. Google's own figures show that it rejects just under 10 percent of the notices it receives because they appear to be invalid.[12] An independent study of copyright notices sent to Google in 2012 found that 8.3 percent of notices were invalid because they failed to specify the allegedly infringing material.[13] More than 90 percent of those were sent by large, sophisticated users of the takedown system. Another independent study found that 4.2 percent of take-down requests sent to Google were "fundamentally flawed because they targeted content that clearly did not match the identified infringed work."[14] These figures are conservative estimates; they count only notices that have obvious errors. They do not include substantive errors like the wrongful attempt to remove the dancing baby clip because these are much harder to detect. The rate of substantive problems, where the work is not actually infringing or the requester does not actually own the copyright, may actually be much higher. When researchers were going through the notices in one of these studies, they noted that 28 percent of the notices raised clear doubts about their validity, to the extent that they should not be automatically accepted without further human review.[15]

These error rates translate into millions of mistaken or invalid takedown notices every week. The key protection for users within the notice and takedown scheme is the "counter-notice" scheme. When a service provider receives a request to remove internet content, they are obliged to inform the user who originally posted it. The user has an opportunity to file a counter-notice where they think a mistake has been made or they have a legal right to post the material. At this point, the copyright owner has a choice to file a lawsuit directly against the user. When the copyright owner does not file a lawsuit within two weeks, the service provider must reinstate the content.

As a safety valve, the counter-notice system makes a lot of sense. If there is a genuine dispute about who owns a piece of content, whether the user has a valid license or whether the user can make a real claim that her use of the content is fair use (and therefore not infringing), the service provider is not in a good position to make a decision about whether it should be removed. This is a role that has otherwise always been played by courts, which have to weigh the evidence and make a ruling about whether a use really is infringing. The counter-notice system should, in theory, help to ensure that clearly infringing content is removed quickly and that users are protected from frivolous or incorrect claims.

Unfortunately, nobody is really satisfied with the counter-notice scheme. Copyright owners complain that it is abused by unscrupulous users who know that they are probably not worth suing. From the copyright industry's perspective, the counter-notice system is too easy to abuse – it is often as simple as checking a box on a web form to have your content reinstated. Those who worry about users' rights to freedom of speech, in contrast, think the counter-notice scheme is far too difficult to use. When people receive a notice that their content has been removed on the basis of a copyright notice, the language of the counter-notice scheme can seem very intimidating. A person who wishes to file a counter-notice must declare, under penalty of perjury, that they have "a good faith belief that the material was removed or disabled as a result of mistake or misidentification of the material to be removed or disabled."[16] The legislation makes it clear that they must give their complete contact details and be prepared to be sued if the copyright owner does not accept the counter-notice.

Even though many notices are likely to contain errors, users almost never file counter-notices.[17] Even for creators who are seasoned users of the counter-notice scheme, the process can be worrying and very time-consuming. For example, professional independent online video creators often have to argue with copyright owners that their use of existing footage is fair use when they are critiquing or reviewing the content. For these creators, filing a counter-notice is risky – they may actually be sued, and the court costs alone could bankrupt them, even if they win. It also takes several weeks for the counter-notice process to finish before content can be reinstated. Many internet videos are short-lived, and the window for viral content is short. If a video with good exposure is incorrectly removed early in its life and not reinstated for two or more weeks, it may never recover.

The impact of faulty notices on legitimate speech should not be underestimated. Many creators have learned to avoid using certain types of content where they know the owners are particularly aggressive, even if their uses are properly fair. A news organization, for example, may choose not to report on international sporting events because the broadcasters who own the rights will almost always complain about even very small clips used in a news show. Contesting the notices is often too risky and takes too long. Even if they can get the material reinstated, several weeks of having the story taken down is far too long in the news business.

Overall, the takedown regime is a mixed blessing. The compromise it reaches between service providers and rights holders is extremely important. Without it, today's internet would look much different, and it would be much harder for ordinary people to make their material available to the world. But users on the receiving end of notices that they think are incorrect often complain about how costly it is to navigate the system, contest the notices, and get their content reinstated.

AUTOMATED ENFORCEMENT

For the copyright industry, although the notice and takedown processes set out in copyright legislation around the world is extremely important, it is only a second-best solution. Copyright owners have been working closely with technology companies to build protection for their rights directly into the websites, software, and hardware devices we use every day. The idea is that prevention is better than cure – to ensure that the devices we use to communicate are designed to only work in ways that protect copyright owners. This is the objective of DRM, which uses encryption to try to keep copyrighted content within a tightly controlled environment that prevents users from doing things that might infringe on copyright.

The copyright industries have been very successful at building DRM into the most commonly used digital media services. For many years they have pursued a strategy of negotiating with device manufacturers, digital marketplaces, and streaming services to build encryption into their systems that would work to police what users could do.[18] Now, services like Netflix, Spotify, iTunes, Steam, and Amazon all have systems in place to limit what people can do with the films, television, music, games, and books that they rent or buy. The encryption that is applied to these systems means that we can only use approved apps and hardware devices to access digital content. These systems work much better than they did a few years ago, so many people never even notice that they exist – until they go wrong. Cory Doctorow, an author and longtime critic of DRM, warns about the dangers of building "computers designed to control their owners."[19] The control that DRM provides copyright owners gets in the way of anyone who wants to do more than just consume content in the way that the copyright owners and technology developers have decided. So, for example, where film students and critics might once have used VCRs to splice together clips from movies to make a review or a parody, the technical locks on Netflix and iTunes videos are designed to make this impossible.[20] Or in the case where a person with a print disability wants to use software to read a book that they have purchased aloud, DRM can prevent this unless the manufacturer has built the feature into the device (Apple's iBooks has a feature that will read a digital book aloud, but Amazon dropped the feature from its Kindle range after publishers complained it might hurt sales of audiobooks).[21] These types of activities are all perfectly legal under copyright law but get caught up in DRM that is designed to limit how people interact with digital content. By taming the services and devices that people use to access digital content, the copyright industries have created a set of rules that constrain what people can do that operates in parallel to the law – but without any of the protections for other peoples' interests that are built into democratically created copyright laws.

DRM is designed to control the *consumption* of commercial content, but copyright owners have also had to convince technology companies to build different systems to control how people *produce* content. Many of the major platforms for people to share content now have automated systems designed to detect and prevent copyright infringement at the time of posting.

YouTube is the star of automated copyright infringement detection. When YouTube launched, it quickly garnered a reputation as a business that attracted many viewers through the infringing content (usually music, but also TV episodes and feature films) that its users uploaded to the network. Before YouTube was sold to Google for $1.6 billion in 2006, part of the platform's popularity could be attributed to infringing content on the platform.[22] Copyright owners complained bitterly that the notice and takedown system did not provide YouTube with any incentive to proactively deal with infringing content. As long as YouTube followed the rules and removed content when a notice came in, it could rely on the protection of the safe harbors. Particularly, at a time before copyright owners developed automated systems to search for infringing content, this seemed unfair: YouTube knew that there was a lot of infringing material on its servers but seemed to turn a blind eye to it. YouTube's side of the story is somewhat different, of course. From YouTube's perspective, it was desperately trying to scale a video sharing system that was rapidly growing in demand, in the face of rising monthly bandwidth bills, with no real revenue stream. It could barely afford to keep its servers running, let alone employ people to watch videos as they were uploaded to try to enforce the rights of recording and film studios.

Once Google had bought the platform, it became clear that, if YouTube were to ever turn a profit, it would have to get the copyright industries on board. But, as long as it looked like they were ignoring the copyright infringement problem, that seemed unlikely. The answer was Content ID. Google spent more than $60 million developing a system that could automatically identify when clips were uploaded to YouTube that contained copyright material. The system works by developing digital fingerprints of copyrighted material provided directly by the copyright owners. Over the years and through continuous investment, it has become extremely good at spotting reuses of existing audio and video content within uploaded clips.[23] Once a clip is identified as containing copyrighted material, the copyright owner is given a choice by YouTube: the copyright owner could block the video completely, wait and see how popular the clip becomes, or choose to run advertisements with the video and take the revenue.

Content ID was a massive investment that has paid off spectacularly for Google – and for copyright owners. Since its introduction, Google has paid out more than $2 billion in advertising revenue to copyright owners who have chosen to monetize videos uploaded by users.[24] More than 8,000 copyright owners are registered for the system, which has flagged more than 400 million videos.[25]

Of course, not everybody is happy with Content ID. The system provides no reliable way to resolve disputes about fair use, which upsets both copyright owners and video creators. In modern equivalents to Stephanie Lenz's dancing baby case, the YouTube algorithm will automatically flag music and other copyrighted material that is caught in the background of a video. It will also automatically catch content used in a critique or parody. YouTube's Content ID system cannot tell the difference between someone who copies a few minutes of, say, a professional sporting event to make fun of it and someone who shares parts of a match in a way that might deprive the distributors of revenue. In these cases, YouTube creators have to go through a process to try to convince the copyright owner that their use is fair. Ultimately, the copyright owner makes the decision; if they reject the user's claim, they are redirected through the DMCA process to lodge a formal takedown request. At this point, unless the YouTube user files a counter-notice, they'll get a "strike" against their account. If a user gets three strikes in ninety days, Google will terminate their account.

It's easy to see why the copyright industry wants to see automated content recognition systems become standard across the web. These industries used to have control of the major physical distribution channels – record stores, video shops, and theaters – and losing control in the digital age is terrifying. The utility of YouTube's Content ID is also that it seems to promise a future that puts the power back in the hands of copyright owners to control how their content is distributed and consumed – and how the advertising revenue is distributed. Finally, technology looks set to provide a solution to the problems it has created. All around the world, copyright owners are working with governments to try to require other companies to invest in using similar technology for controlling copyrighted content wherever it turns up. Automated copyright detection systems have now been built into many other services on the internet. Facebook has developed its own detection systems, and companies like Audible Magic produce software that has been adopted by many platforms.

The worrisome thing about these automated systems is that they have no ability to judge context. This means it is not possible for an automated system to determine whether a particular use of copyrighted material is covered by a license or by fair use. The task of determining whether a use is licensed requires some level of human intervention and judgment. There are many, many examples of Content ID and similar tools making mistakes, and collectively these mistakes add up to a lot of wrongfully silenced speech and lost revenue for ordinary creators trying to reach an audience.

Take, for example, the $1 billion lawsuit that Viacom started in 2007 against Google for copyright infringement by YouTube users. Viacom, a mass media multinational, complained that Google was encouraging users to upload clips of its copyrighted content. Viacom alleged that its clips had been unlawfully streamed billions of times, bringing in substantial advertising revenue for Google. During the trial, it came out that even Viacom's own lawyers couldn't tell whether some of the clips they were complaining about were actually infringing. In many cases, executives within Viacom's group of companies had chosen not to remove clips from popular TV shows, recognizing that they provided valuable publicity. YouTube's chief counsel explained that Viacom asked for clips to be removed from YouTube "countless" times, only to come back and ask for them to be reinstated after complaints from another arm of Viacom's conglomerate.[26]

The most telling examples come from Viacom's guerilla marketing tactics, often unknown to other parts of the company. To stoke excitement about upcoming releases, the media giant for years asked marketing firms to rough up videos to look like leaked footage and then post the clips to YouTube under fake accounts. These efforts to disguise the videos worked so well that not even the lawyers for Viacom could tell that the clips were actually on YouTube with Viacom's permission. A robot is not likely to do better.

These types of mistakes come out when there is effective scrutiny through the legal system. When automated systems are making decisions at a massive scale, the mistakes are hard to track. This is the real danger of creating a parallel system of policing content that does not involve real legal oversight. Given the nontrivial error rate in infringement notices, automated takedown systems pose substantial risks to the legitimate expression of ordinary individuals and the legitimate businesses of new media creators. When these types of automated systems are deployed to stop people from uploading clips of their baby dancing or parodists making fun of politicians, the negative effect on legitimate speech can be massive. Unfortunately, while much money has been spent on improving detection systems, the mechanisms of appeal that platforms put into place are still woefully underdeveloped.

INFRASTRUCTURE COMPANIES AS JUDGE, JURY, AND EXECUTIONER

The problems of due process become even more difficult to deal with when we look at the efforts of copyright industries to enlist internet infrastructure companies in the fight against piracy. The strategy to use automated systems only works when dealing with legitimate companies. It doesn't work at all to combat piracy that is facilitated by peer-to-peer networks whose operators have moved to foreign jurisdictions.

Having essentially run out of people to sue who are directly involved in file sharing, the copyright industry has worked to convince internet access providers to help combat infringement. These companies, like Comcast, AT&T, or Verizon, are known as internet service providers or ISPs. The market for infrastructure companies is very concentrated, and large cable companies provide internet access to tens of millions of subscribers. This makes them prime targets for people who want to cheaply exercise control over users.

For several years, three-strikes schemes were the primary focus of global copyright industries. Also known as graduated response schemes, the goal is to get ISPs to take action directly against subscribers who are suspected of infringing copyright. The idea was attractively simple. Users would be given two warnings, but after three strikes (or notices of infringement) they would be out – that is, cut off from the internet. The exact nature of the schemes differs from place to place, and the obligations of ISPs range from issuing warnings, collating allegations made against subscribers and reporting to copyright owners, to suspending and eventually terminating service.

Copyright owners hoped that three-strike schemes would fix two of the major problems they faced. First, this method makes it cheaper to take action directly against users. Instead of suing users in court, copyright owners could employ people to use automated tools to try to detect infringement and send out allegations of infringement to ISPs by the thousands. Second, it solves some of the public relations nightmare of suing users by tasking either ISPs or public administrative tribunals with the unenviable job of enforcing copyright and disconnecting users who receive too many strikes.

The argument behind three-strikes regimes is both economic and moral. The economic argument is that ISPs are uniquely placed to enforce copyright in a way that could be both effective and cheap. ISPs are the gateway to the internet. By threatening to disconnect users completely, suddenly copyright owners could see a way to introduce a real deterrent without all the legal costs of going to court. When file sharing sites were shutdown, users could easily turn to use other sites; by cutting off the internet connections of users completely, copyright owners finally hoped to solve the problem of dealing with continuously reappearing sites. The moral argument was that ISPs should be required to police the internet because they were the ones responsible for the damage it caused (at least in part). Without the internet, there would be no peer-to-peer file sharing. ISPs made money from giving people access to the internet, rights holders reasoned, and therefore should take some responsibility when their customers use their connections to infringe the rights of others.

The moral argument is one that we see in many different debates about what technology companies should do to regulate the internet. The general rule in liberal democracies is that individuals are responsible for their own actions. It is rare for the law to require a technology company to monitor whether its customers are using its tools to break the law. The standard answer is that, if copyright owners were upset, they should take it up with the people responsible themselves. Nobody seriously suggested that ISPs were encouraging copyright infringement, and ISPs aren't legally obliged to help copyright owners. The argument that ISPs should take some responsibility for their users was based most directly in desperation: if ISPs couldn't help, who could?

ISPs were being pressed into becoming the judge, jury, and executioner of copyright infringement around the world, but the introduction of three-strikes regimes was deeply unpopular. One of the major problems is that the punishment did not seem to fit the crime. The internet has become so vital to everyday life that the threat of disconnection was grossly disproportionate to the cost of downloading a few albums or films. The "always-on" nature of broadband has fundamentally changed the way people access information. Access to online information resources is now critical for research and education. Everyday activities such as paying bills, traveling, banking, and socializing are now all routinely done online. The growth of the internet has spurred business both in the online delivery of goods and services and the creation of innovative new markets. Political parties rely on the internet to reach and mobilize voters, and activists rely on the internet to organize campaigns and social movements. With a home internet connection, it is simple to access the web at any time to quickly look up information, check email and conveniently respond in a timely manner, and to communicate with friends and family long after internet cafés or libraries have closed. Disconnecting users from the internet at home means that information is no longer available on demand, that students need to take their reading books and materials and set up at a café to study, that contractors who work from home need to relocate their office, that families need to take their years of receipts and financial documentation to the library or an accountant to complete their tax returns, and that individuals are required to look up and communicate sensitive health information on public terminals. These problems are magnified because three-strikes rules apply to all members of a household, not just the individual who actually illicitly downloaded the film or album. If one person receives three allegations of infringement, or if three people each receive one allegation, all members of the household risk losing their internet access.

The major problem with graduated response schemes is that they always deal with *allegations* of infringement. Copyright owners employ agents to monitor torrents and other file sharing networks, and log the IP (internet protocol) address of people who appear to be downloading files illicitly. An IP address is a number given to identify a computer on the internet, but these numbers can change frequently and sometimes a single IP address might be used by many different computers on a network. An IP address is not a perfect method of identifying individual users, and infringement notices will often incorrectly target innocent people. A group of researchers at the Computer Science Department at the University of Washington proved how inaccurate the system could be when they set up some experiments to trick rights holders. With a little technical wizardry, they were able to convince copyright owners that one of the university's laser printers was responsible for downloading popular films.[27] Because notices of this kind are always just allegations about what a copyright owner believes a subscriber did in the past, there is no practical way for ISPs to verify their accuracy, and it is very difficult for ordinary users to find evidence to refute the allegations. After all, how do you prove you *didn't* download a movie?

Because being disconnected from the internet is such a serious punishment, three-strikes rules raise very difficult legal problems about due process. Due process requires a fair hearing and a fair process to appeal decisions to an impartial judge. In some of the three-strikes regimes introduced around the world, there is little judicial oversight. ISPs are expected to evaluate notices sent in by copyright owners and make a decision about whether to terminate the account of the relevant subscriber. The subscriber might be able to contest an allegation, but usually the burden was placed on them to prove that they were not responsible – a reversal of the legal principle that people are innocent until they are proven guilty.

These problems of due process proved fatal to the first few three-strikes schemes around the world. France was one of the first countries to introduce a scheme that would see people suspended from the internet, but the legislation was deemed unconstitutional by the French Constitutional Council. The council found that the potential negative consequences to freedom of expression and access to infor-mation were so high that suspension of internet access could be ordered by a court only after a full criminal proceeding.[28] This, of course, does not suit copyright owners, who are looking for a way to avoid costly court processes altogether.

Later schemes tried to deal with the issue of due process by doing away with disconnection as a penalty. Instead of suspending people from the internet, the Copyright Alert System developed in the United States only includes warning notices designed to educate consumers and let them know that their infringement has not gone undetected. It was an almost complete failure. The scheme may have had some educational value, but it was not really effective at changing the behavior of the dedicated infringers that the industry was primarily worried about.[29]

Ultimately, three-strikes schemes have largely been abandoned around the world. They are still deeply unpopular, and the costs of sending and processing notices is still high enough that it largely isn't worth the effort. Announcing the abandonment of negotiations to implement a warning system in Australia that would have cost copyright owners up to $20 per notice, Roadshow co-CEO Graham Burke said, "You might as well give people a DVD."[30]

Instead of continuing to pursue three-strikes schemes, copyright owners have pivoted to get other companies to block access or services to foreign file sharing sites. This was the goal of the Stop Online Piracy Act, called SOPA, and its sister the PROTECT IP Act (PIPA), which spawned a massive opposition campaign in early 2012. The logic is simple: instead of trying to shutdown massive sites like The Pirate Bay, copyright owners would instead try to starve them of traffic and revenue. The draft bills would have allowed copyright owners to require search engines to stop linking to sites dedicated to copyright infringement; ban advertising networks from running ads on those sites; prohibit payment processors like Visa, MasterCard, and PayPal from allowing payments to their operators; and ask ISPs to block their customers from accessing the sites. The language of the SOPA/PIPA bills was drafted in very broad terms, and the tech industry feared that it would require them to do much more to police copyright than they currently were. The definition of a "foreign infringing site" was particularly problematic; it wasn't clear that the bills would actually be limited just to stopping major international pirate sites.[31]

In a way that no copyright legislation ever had before, SOPA and PIPA ignited the tech-savvy internet in the United States.[32] Google and Wikipedia turned their websites black in protest, alerting millions of visitors to what they saw as an extreme threat to the way that the internet worked. The major internet players were worried that SOPA/PIPA would overturn the understanding that they didn't have to monitor internet content as it was posted. Wikipedia's magic relies on anyone being able to edit the free encyclopedia, and Google's search engine runs by crawling and indexing as much of the web as possible. These companies were worried that they would have to manually check links in advance – an obligation that would be so expensive as to essentially cripple them.

The campaign was massively successful. SOPA/PIPA turned out to be the first major loss that the industry suffered in the legislative arena during the copyright wars. Ordinary users were motivated by the threats posed to sites like Google and Wikipedia to contact their representatives in record numbers.[33] After several million phone calls, letters, and emails were received by federal representatives, the SOPA/PIPA legislation was scrapped.

SOPA/PIPA turned out to be only the beginning of efforts to get other internet intermediaries to do more to combat copyright infringement. Website blocking schemes have now been introduced in the United Kingdom, some European countries, Australia, and several other countries. These are similar to the ones proposed by SOPA/PIPA but more carefully drafted – and their political introduction managed much more skillfully. ISPs can now be ordered by courts in these jurisdictions to block access to foreign websites dedicated to copyright infringement.

Other efforts to extend the control of copyright owners over internet infrastructure are ongoing. The World Wide Web Consortium is the standards body that sets the protocols that websites and browsers follow to make the web work. Its standards are hugely influential; they are relied upon to ensure that the hundreds of millions of websites around the world all communicate with browsers in a common, interoperable language. In a controversial move, the consortium has introduced DRM standards that provide enhanced control over the web to copyright owners, without safeguards for accessibility, competition, security testing, or other legitimate acts.[34] Meanwhile, the Motion Picture Association of America has managed to secure agreements with companies that administer domain names that allow it to ask for the cancellation of domain names of sites that appear to be facilitating copyright infringement – effectively shutting down websites without any judicial oversight.[35]

BAKING ENFORCEMENT INTO THE NETWORK

The efforts of the copyright industries to get internet companies to protect their rights have been extremely influential in shaping how the internet has developed. The copyright industries are some of the most well-resourced players in internet governance today, and their experiences show just how difficult it is to work out who should be responsible for enforcing the law online. The real, lasting lesson of the copyright wars is that wars are far less effective than partnerships. The copyright industry spent decades fighting against software companies and users that the industry thought of as pirates. The industry was moderately successful at using the law to stop rogue developers from expanding into strong, legitimate commercial businesses. The industry continues to work against dedicated pirates, but the goal is not to try to stamp them out, but to make piracy just a little more difficult than paying for legitimate access to content. The biggest successes of the copyright industries, however, have come from enlisting the help of ordinary technology companies to build protection for copyright into the very fabric of the internet.

The reason these schemes are worrisome is the same reason that they're effective: they provide real powers to control what people do online without the expense of legitimate legal processes. By entering into agreements with technology companies, copyright owners have tamed some of the lawlessness of the early internet. But the wild west of the early internet was not replaced by democratic, accountable, and fair legal systems. The agreements reached between copyright owners and technology companies strike a bargain between each of their particular sets of commercial interests but have little in the way of protection for the interests of the billions of people who rely on the internet every day. Other interest groups undoubtedly could learn a lot from how the copyright industries have worked to secure a system that works in their favor, but the biggest lesson should be a warning for people who care about the public interest and rights of individuals. Unless we all work hard to create better systems, we risk allowing technology companies and their partners to shape our interactions and our information environments without real accountability or oversight.

6

Censorship

So far, we have heard a lot about how private actors are trying to regulate the internet. Governments across the world have also been very active in trying to get internet companies to regulate what information their citizens can access and share online. The decentralized, resilient design of the internet makes government censorship much more difficult than in the mass media era, where it was much simpler to embed controls within the operations of a small number of major newspaper publishers and television and radio networks. Governments are adapting, though, and quickly becoming much more sophisticated in how they monitor and control the flow of information online.

When we think about censorship online, the great firewall of China generally springs to mind. China learned the lesson about how to control the internet very early on. True, it can only exercise power over any provider within its borders. But it does this very well, by imposing strict requirements on providers to develop their systems in a way that empowers its massive bureaucratic army of censors to block content it finds objectionable. Any service provider wishing to do business within China must agree to these conditions, and the Chinese government has become adept at dealing with speech it deems problematic online.

As for service providers outside of China, the Chinese government has pulled off a feat that other authoritarian states can only dream of. By paying special attention to the handful of points on the network at which China is connected with the rest of the world – the backbone cables that head west to Europe and undersea south and east through Asia and across the Pacific ocean – the Chinese government is able to exercise a massive degree of control over what information its citizens can access and who they can communicate with.[1] The internet was designed to be resilient; "The internet treats censorship as damage," John Gilmore's famous adage goes, "and routes around it."[2] But this is only true if there are uncensored points available – not if all traffic must pass through network infrastructure that is owned or controlled by the Chinese government.

China's censorship regime is not perfect, of course, but it does not need to be. It is possible to use a virtual private network (VPN) to encrypt and "tunnel" connections from within China through servers outside China and then on to sites that would otherwise be monitored or censored. VPN technology is cheap and readily available, and specialist privacy-enhancing software like Tor has become much more popular and reliable in recent years. Importantly, VPNs and many other forms of encrypted communications are vital to foreigners doing business within China. So, while the government can block access to major consumer VPN services, it certainly can't afford to completely block encrypted connections. For most purposes, though, China's censorship regime is highly effective without being perfect. The main concern of the Chinese government is that people might organize to resist and perhaps overthrow the authoritarian regime. To clamp down on efforts to organize collective action, the government doesn't have to control all access to external sources of information. It is sufficient if it is able to monitor communications when it has to, block particular sites and search terms, and restrict access to major encrypted services that it cannot effectively control.[3] Much more important is restricting the ability of the Chinese people to collectively organize through the mainstream media or social media sites. Addressing the mainstream media is easy; the government has long been able to maintain control of the largest publishers. This leaves social media, which is where the massive army of censors comes in.

Thanks to some really smart research by scholars in Hong Kong and Brisbane, we can see just how sophisticated China's social media censorship regime is. Jing Zeng and her colleagues developed a system to track microblog posts on Weibo, one of China's most popular social networks. By collecting posts as soon as possible after they are posted, and then checking again several weeks later to see which of these have been censored, they are able to identify what, exactly, the censors are trying to block. It turns out China is not primarily focused on stopping people from criticizing the government, as many have previously assumed. The posts that are most consistently censored are those that try to organize any form of physical meeting or protest; organized collective action is what concerns the Chinese government the most. As long as people are blowing off steam by complaining about the government on social media and not actually organizing to do anything about it, the censors are happy to stand by. The government then also engages in a sophisticated campaign to correct what it sees as misinformation, both by blocking some rumors and by highly targeted counter-speech.[4]

China's example shows what is possible for states to achieve with enough control over physical internet infrastructure and the organizations that operate internet services. It is unique in the scale of its efforts, but not in its ambition. Many other governments try to exercise control over telecommunications networks – if you're an authoritarian government trying to hold on to power, the last thing you want is to allow free access to the unlimited possibilities and information of the internet.

In recent years, many websites and other internet services have moved to encrypt their services by default. End-to-end encryption means that when you visit a page on Wikipedia or send a WhatsApp message the contents are securely encrypted in a way that is difficult to break and generally not possible to decrypt in real time. Previously, governments – indeed, anyone with access to a router through which your internet communications flow – could intercept and monitor the content of communications and selectively choose to block certain pages or keywords. So, for example, the government of Iran was known to have blocked nearly 1,000 Persian-language Wikipedia articles about politics, sex, religion, human rights, academia, media, drugs, and alcohol in 2013.[5] Now, because those communications are encrypted by default, the government is left with only the choice to block all access to Wikipedia or to leave it all accessible. A recent report by scholars at Harvard's Berkman Klein Center for Internet & Society highlights how authoritarian regimes are shifting strategies to adapt to these technological changes. Filtering internet content is still a key strategy, but governments are also increasing surveillance, engaging more directly in conversations on platforms used by activists, and harassing journalists and activists with targeted criminal investigations to better control the dialogue.[6]

Some governments choose to block all access to major sites, even though this comes at some cost of criticism by their people. In times of emergency, authoritarian states have been known to block internet access completely – like the time in 2011 when the Egyptian military seized control of the major internet access providers and completely shut down internet communications with the outside world in a desperate (and failed) attempt to stop the revolution that forced out President Hosni Mubarak.[7] These types of efforts often backfire; the Egyptian government ended up drawing more attention to the protests from both local and international audiences and came off looking thuggish and out of control to both.[8] Nevertheless, other countries have tried similar tactics in recent years, leading the United Nations (UN) Special Rapporteur on the Promotion and Protection of the Right to Freedom of Opinion and Expression and other leading international free speech experts to issue a joint statement condemning internet "kill switches" and the seizure of broadcast stations as "measures which can never be justified under human rights law."[9]

Shutting down an entire country's internet access is a drastic move, and fortunately one that is quite rare. But it is much more common for governments to require internet ISPs in their country to block access to certain websites associated with particular political causes or groups. Turkey has blocked the entirety of Wikipedia in the past and, even after the revolution, Egypt has blocked Twitter, Skype, and the blogging platform Medium, among hundreds of other sites. New research by scholars at the Berkman Klein Center for Internet & Society shows that at least twenty-three countries actively block political websites and sites that report on armed conflicts.[10] Iran, for example, blocks websites affiliated with Kurdish separatists; Russia blocks websites that are critical of the government;

and Malaysia blocks pornography, gambling sites, and "blogs that report on the Malaysian Prime Minister's alleged involvement in a billion-dollar misappropriation scandal in 2015."[11]

Governments are getting much more sophisticated at pressuring foreign platforms to block specific posts that are illegal within their jurisdictions. The Turkish government is the largest state censor of content on Twitter: in the eighteen months from July 2015 to December 2016, it asked for the removal of tweets approximately 7,800 times and asked for the suspension of more than 31,000 accounts. Twitter complied with only a portion of these; it censored just over 5,000 tweets (preventing them from being viewed from Turkish IP addresses) and blocked or suspended just under 2,000 accounts.

Notably, Twitter is one of the platforms with the strongest public commitment to freedom of speech and is presumably one of the most willing to push back on requests to censor information. It regularly files objections in the courts of foreign countries contesting orders; in the second half of 2016, it filed 314 objections in response to the 844 court orders it received, focusing particularly on the requests to stifle critical political speech (all of the objections were denied). Twitter also regularly refuses requests from law enforcement agencies that it considers to be unjustified, but it does generally comply with the laws of foreign countries.

Other platforms receive similar numbers of requests. Facebook's latest data shows that it received around 16,660 requests to block content from courts and law enforcement agencies in 2016, mostly on privacy, national security, and defamation grounds.[12] Google received more than 22,000 individual notices, together asking for the removal of more than 160,000 individual URLs in total.[13] Different firms have different levels of commitment to contesting requests to censor user content; not all of them will expend the substantial resources involved in evaluating the merits of claims and deciding whether to comply with, contest, or ignore incoming requests. In its extensive report on the practices of major telecommunications and internet companies, Ranking Digital Rights (RDR) was highly critical of the lack of detailed information about how intermediaries deal with requests to block or remove content. Google scored better than other companies, and some internet firms – particularly Yahoo, Facebook, Microsoft, and Twitter – provide some details about the requests they process, but, overall, the RDR team found that "Companies don't tell us enough about how they respond when governments and other parties ask them to block, delete, or otherwise restrict content or restrict users' accounts."[14]

The numbers of requests from law enforcement agencies and from courts to remove or block content are much lower than the numbers of requests sent by copyright owners under the DMCA. But to put these figures into a better perspective we have to remember that they are much more likely to target critical speech. Requests from courts and law enforcement agencies cover a wide range of material, from court orders to remove hate speech, defamatory, or prohibited adult content to government agencies requesting to censor political speech that they think is problematic. The major platforms publish regular "transparency reports" that give examples of the kinds of takedown requests they receive from governments around the world. There are many examples of requests to remove political speech that are questionable, at best, including requests that platform companies remove posts that are critical of the government. Particularly where the requests come direct from law enforcement organizations, not courts, there will at least be a threshold question about whether they are legitimate requests or not. These take time to investigate, and in each case platforms have to make a decision about whether to comply by removing the post or blocking it for users within that country, or to reject the request and deal with the threat of legal action or potentially being blocked altogether.

CONTENT FILTERING AND JURISDICTIONAL OVERREACH

It's not just authoritarian states that are pressuring internet companies to block content on their networks. Many Western democracies are now seeking, with renewed vigor, to assert control over what their citizens can access online. These debates are as old as the commercial internet itself, and there's a certain logic to the claims of the various governments involved. Governments have always been heavily involved in the censorship of immoral and indecent content – or what is often referred to as "content regulation." In the mass media age, this was achieved by imposing obligations on publishers, retailers, and broadcasters. Many countries have classification schemes and standards about what content is acceptable to distribute, in what forms, at what times, and to which audiences. These vary from country to country, of course; Europeans are famously much more tolerant of sex and nudity, while Americans much more permissive about violence and hate. But for elected officials subject to the constant demands from their constituents that they do more to clean up the filth that is available online, it is hard to see why the internet should be treated differently.

The internet is different, of course, but only to an extent. One major difference is practical: classification systems are expensive, and they're only worthwhile for large-scale productions. You can classify a film destined for theatrical release, but you can't efficiently classify every video uploaded to YouTube. Different approaches are required – for example, a system that enables uploaders to self-classify their films and allows viewers to flag content for review after it is posted. But this is just a difference in how regulation is imposed. It's always possible to develop different systems or throw more resources at the problem if a state really wants to be able to regulate content at scale. The bigger difference is the more fundamental question of why we impose content regulation.

This is where there is the most disagreement. There is a deep conflict in society about the harm that speech can cause. The basic liberal argument is generally accepted: the state should only interfere with what people can see and say in cases where their speech causes real harm to other people. But people disagree vehemently about when speech is actually harmful. Those who believe most strongly in unrestricted speech argue that only content that directly causes harm can legitimately be restricted: serious invasions of privacy, traffic in child abuse imagery, copyright infringement, unfounded defamatory accusations, direct incitement to specific acts of violence, and so on. This is a problem made much more difficult in the internet era. People can make a valid claim to be personally harmed (or at least offended) when they or their children are unwittingly exposed to content they believe is indecent that is broadcast on TV or radio or plastered on public billboards. We might expect a similar level of regulation around advertising content – there's a good argument that people should not be exposed to ads they find offensive while innocently browsing the web. Perhaps that might also extend to content on major social media sites; we can imagine people may be genuinely upset if gruesome videos unexpectedly started showing up in their Facebook feeds. The argument is much harder to make about content that consenting adults voluntarily seek out. This is the major difference between broadcasting content and material on the internet that people have to search for explicitly. No one is directly harmed by the consensual consumption of hardcore pornography or violent content. Free speech advocates believe strongly, therefore, that only *illegal* content should be restricted, and that the definitions of what is illegal should be carefully and tightly drawn.

Others believe in a democratic right to create cultural rules that reflect our collective moral values, rules that signal that their society does not tolerate hate speech, pornography, sacrilege, or violence, for example. These moral claims are not generally based on harm to any individual, but in a sense that certain types of content are harmful to a society's collective moral well-being. It is, of course, rare that any given society is unified behind a particular standard about what is acceptable and what is not. Drawing these lines is a politically charged exercise; Justice Potter Stewart, trying to decide whether a film was art or pornography, famously explained that it was probably impossible to define hardcore pornography, "But I know it when I see it."[15] But democratic systems are perfectly used to drawing these lines and redrawing them as standards change. There is nothing inherently wrongful with setting out content standards that reflect the moral standards of a community at a particular time, as long as the rights of minority groups are not trampled. Certainly, there will always be disagreement about what the rules should be and how they should be enforced, but these are not theoretically fatal to a system of national content regulation.

The major problem happens when content regulation is applied antidemocratically. Systems of censorship are theoretically justifiable if they reflect the democratic will, and there are both democratic and constitutional safeguards designed to prevent their abuse. The major fear at the dawn of the commercial internet was that nations with wildly different standards about what content was acceptable would each try to impose those standards on the entire world.

Ever since the French courts sought to prevent Yahoo from displaying auctions for Nazi memorabilia (discussed in more detail in Chapter 4), there has been a major concern about jurisdiction and the collapse of a borderless internet. It is fairly clear that courts are entitled to enforce local laws that prohibit certain types of content, but it has always been less clear whether foreign intermediaries should be obliged to respond. Some intermediaries do not – if a US-based internet or telecommunications firm has no business dealings and no assets in the requesting country, and it is confident that US courts will refuse to enforce any judgment handed down in that country, then it can choose to ignore foreign demands. But the major intermediaries do frequently comply with requests from foreign governments. Typically, they are more likely to comply with requests from courts than from law enforcement agencies, but the firms that are building transnational businesses generally feel the need to abide by the law of the countries in which they operate. There are exceptions, of course – Google, for example, preferred to pull its business interests out of mainland China rather than continue to comply with the restrictions that the Chinese government wanted to impose on it. On the whole, though, the major companies obey valid legal directions from foreign governments and sometimes obey informal requests from law enforcement agencies.

Global blocks are concerning because a request that is valid within one country can affect the rights of people in other countries. This was part of Yahoo's concern – why should the free speech rights of Americans and others be curtailed just because the French had more restrictive standards? The answer has typically been to use geolocation technology to block content only within the requesting country. Ever since the Yahoo case, governments have mostly been okay with blocking access to objectionable content to people within their borders or on the localized country domains of major sites.

In recent years, however, some governments have not been satisfied with blocking access only within their borders. Some governments are starting to ask intermediaries to block or remove content globally – not just for their citizens, but for everyone – on the basis either that geoblocks are relatively easy to get around for people within their country or that information available to others may still cause harm to its constituents.[16] The Canadian Supreme Court, for example, has recently ordered that Google remove search results to a particular website, not just for Canadian users, but worldwide. Daphne Keller is an academic and expert in intermediary liability law (now at Stanford University's Center for Internet and Society, Keller was previously a senior lawyer at Google). She worries about this decision: "If Canada can enforce its laws to limit speech and information access in other countries, does it accept that other countries may do the same? Can Russia use its anti-gay laws to make search results unavailable to Canadians?"[17] Google has challenged the order – not in Canada, but it has applied to the US courts for protection.

All of these problems are magnified when the legal rules of one country seem to be in conflict with international freedom of speech norms. The UN Special

Rapporteur on the Promotion and Protection of the Right to Freedom of Opinion and Expression condemned countries that try to restrict content that is critical of the government,[18] but what should an intermediary who is faced with a valid foreign court order do in these circumstances? They can easily be caught in a difficult decision between disobeying the law or contributing to antidemocratic censorship. Pragmatically, too, intermediaries need to weigh the consequences of refusal; if Twitter refused to obey directions to remove tweets that are critical of Turkey's President Recep Tayyip Erdoğan, Turkey may go back to blocking the entire network. There is often a moral dispute here too, about whether it is better to comply in order to provide some access to information in a censored form, rather than none at all.[19] So far, these global orders are still rare, and platforms have been resisting global obligations because they raise a difficult conflict between different standards of the right to freedom of speech in different countries.[20]

These difficult questions are becoming more common as other countries develop laws that are designed to apply to foreign internet companies based in the United States and elsewhere. The European Union's new General Data Protection Regulation (GDPR), for example, has already had widespread effects on how US companies deal with the personal information of European users, and it has been able to drive enhanced protection for privacy for many users worldwide as a result. But the GDPR also builds on and extends the controversial RTBF ruling in way that might require tech companies to remove content globally, even though standards for what is acceptable vary from country to country.[21] When the European Court of Justice handed down its RTBF ruling, Google was originally only going to censor links for users on its country domains in the European Union, like Google.es and Google.fr.[22] Users within Europe could easily circumvent the restrictions by using the Google.com domain. Google was eventually pressured by the French data protection authority to apply its blocking regime for all users who appeared to be accessing any of its domains from a European IP address. Under the GDPR, it is still unclear how far the obligation extends. This creates clear conflicts between the standards of freedom of expression and protection for privacy between different countries. For example, in the United States it might be considered important to ensure that news articles reflect an accurate factual record, including reports about someone's previous criminal convictions, whereas under European law a person might legitimately apply to have that information scrubbed from the internet after they have served their time.

These issues are becoming increasingly important as requests from governments to restrict speech are growing at an alarming rate. Clearly, some of the requests that intermediaries receive are overly broad or contravene global standards freedom of expression, particularly where they are designed to reduce criticism of the government or its officials. Other requests will be more legitimate, particularly where there is a court order in place that addresses prohibited material like hate speech or defamatory material or evaluating material that is deemed to be obscene or offensive according to the moral standards of the jurisdiction, like pornography, links to gambling sites, or graphically violent content. The increasing visibility of extremist groups on social media has also led to governments around the world becoming much more active in asking intermediaries to remove content and to make counter-speech much more visible.[23] The nonprofit research initiative RDR tries to hold intermediaries to account for how they deal with these various requests and expects intermediaries "to comply with requests that affect users' speech, communication, and access to information only when there is a legal reason for doing so, and to investigate and push back on requests that are unlawful or overbroad."[24] Its 2018 report criticized tech companies for not providing enough data about the requests they receive from governments and how they handle those requests. While some companies – notably Google and Twitter – commit to publicly archiving copies of the government requests they receive, RDR found that most companies still "failed to disclose sufficient information about how they handle government and private requests to censor content and restrict user access."[25] The lack of information available makes it very difficult to evaluate what type of material is being censored online and by whom – something that is very worrisome to advocates of freedom of expression.

The core problem with government takedowns is that standards about what is acceptable differ from place to place, but the internet is global. In these circumstances, internet intermediaries are often caught between conflicting legal systems with no easy way out. Some people worry about the increasing fragmentation of the global internet: as different countries continue to impose different standards, we may see major fault lines in the services available in different regions. The "splinternet," some scholars warn, would put at risk the benefits of a seamless global internet, replacing it with a system where "the Internet is experienced differently by users across national jurisdictions, and the big global Internet players face an ever more complex array of diverse, conflicting and possibly contradictory laws and regulations across territorial boundaries."[26] But the alternatives are also bad; intermediaries simultaneously obeying the law of multiple jurisdictions may impose a lowest-common-denominator standard of acceptable speech, to the great detriment of many. Perhaps more likely, we'll see the standards of major jurisdictions, like Europe and the United States, continue to set the standards for what is acceptable. Intermediaries still have a strong incentive to base their operations from within the United States, where they are protected by CDA 230 and the First Amendment. For supporters of the First Amendment's particular vision of free speech, of course, this is a pretty good outcome; but, for people in countries that expect greater protection for privacy or enhanced restrictions on hate speech, this "American legal hegemony" is less than ideal.[27]

7

Lawless

Two decades ago, the late John Perry Barlow, one of the founders of the digital rights group EFF, proclaimed the independence of the internet from the authorities of nation-states:

> Governments of the Industrial World, you weary giants of flesh and steel, I come from Cyberspace, the new home of Mind. On behalf of the future, I ask you of the past to leave us alone. You are not welcome among us. You have no sovereignty where we gather. [...] I declare the global social space we are building to be naturally independent of the tyrannies you seek to impose on us. You have no moral right to rule us nor do you possess any methods of enforcement we have true reason to fear.[1]

Barlow's declaration of independence was a cry for the preservation of the libertarian wild west of the early internet, an ideal of a space of limitless opportunity that its denizens could shape to their liking. He makes two claims here: first, that governments have no real power over the internet, which is a fundamentally unregulable, separate space, both outside of legal jurisdiction and practical reach of governments. The second – a moral claim – is that the rules of online social spaces would evolve to be better – more democratic, more free – than the rules of territorially bound nation-states.

Barlow had hoped we would "create a civilization of the Mind in Cyberspace," governed by rules and ethics that would be "more humane and fair than the world your governments have made before." This is part of the dream of what the internet could help our societies become – the dream of unlimited access to information and the fundamentally democratic ability for all members of society to speak and be heard. It represents a dream that depends on us, as users, to codevelop the diverse communities that can liberate and empower us. This is a dream of a better future that has not yet been fully realized over the past two decades – while it is true that a great many diverse communities have flourished, the internet is now much more centrally controlled by a handful of major corporations than it was when Barlow wrote his declaration. And, unfortunately, we have few safeguards in place to ensure that the power these corporations wield – and of those who seek to influence them – will be exercised in a way that is more legitimate, more humane, or more fair.

The early cyber libertarians, like Barlow, thought that the best way to ensure that the rules that governed the internet were legitimate was to allow online communities to create and enforce their own rules, without interference from the laws of nation-states. They argued that cyberspace was a new, different space. The internet seemed to offer an alternative to the tricky problems of democracy, where laws have to apply generally to an entire diverse group of constituents – a tyranny of the majority, where minority groups are often subject to rules they don't agree with. On the limitless internet, those who disagreed with the rules of any given community could easily leave to join or create new communities that aligned better with their own individual values. In this utopian vision, because the rules of each community are freely agreed upon by its participants, it seemed that each set of rules had to be a better fit than any set of general laws that could be imposed from outside.[2] From this perspective, the most important task of internet governance is to ensure that internet architecture remains neutral and accessible. The cyber libertarians worried that national governments posed the most important threats to the internet – particularly governments that would impose censorship or surveillance on internet infrastructure and interfere with the neutrality of the 'net.

This utopian vision of a libertarian internet rests on two faulty assumptions. First, it only works if online communities really are frictionless to enter and exit. In the early days of the internet, before it was dominated by major platforms and search engines, this assumption seemed more reasonable. Small groups of relatively like-minded people could cluster around bulletin boards, chat rooms, and blog sites, and they could leave easily to create new ones. The modern internet, in contrast, is much more centralized – it is dominated by a small number of major platforms and search providers. Network effects mean that the value of a connected system grows exponentially with the addition of new connections. Massive social networks like Facebook, Twitter, and YouTube, which connect billions of users, are built on this principle. People go to these sites because they make it easy to connect with their friends and with strangers they want to interact with. It's technically *possible* to leave and create a completely new network, but, unless you can convince all of your contacts to leave with you, the economies of scale involved make it much more difficult to stay in touch. These networks create ways for users with shared interests to create smaller groups and connect together, but they are all subject to the general rules of each platform, which means we should not expect those rules to be better adapted to their needs than any democratically created laws imposed from outside.

The second major problem is that small groups of people can agree to rules that work for their members but cause harm to others. So, for example, subscribers of

Reddit's *TheFappening* sub-Reddit came to an agreement among themselves that it was okay to share leaked nude images of celebrities and ordinary people without their consent,[3] and self-hosted forums like The Daily Stormer created their own norms that encouraged the vilification of people of color. The assumption of the cyber libertarians is that these acts are mere *speech* – people who do not want to participate can simply not listen to what these groups are sharing, or perhaps they can create their own sites with more positive speech in response. Because virtual communication can have real harmful consequences for others in society, there will always be pressure to impose external limits on what groups of users can agree among themselves.

INTERNET INTERMEDIARIES GOVERN THE INTERNET

On a day-to-day basis, the rules that apply most directly to people on the internet are the rules set and enforced by intermediaries. These companies – content hosts, search engines, and infrastructure providers – play a major role in governing the material that users can share and view online.[4] They are the most efficient, and sometimes only, means of effectively enforcing laws and social norms on a global network with billions of users. The choices that intermediaries make have a real effect on what their users are able to say, what information they can search for, what news they see, and with whom they can communicate. We have seen, in the previous chapters of this book, many examples of the power that digital intermediaries exercise over their networks – that is, what it is possible and permissible to do online. They rule, not with law, but with the architecture of their networks, the power to influence social norms, and the power to enforce their rules by removing content and restricting access to their networks. They are not all-powerful, by any means, but they are a key actor in governing our lives. Because of their centrality, they are also subject to the influence of many others, both governments and private entities, that want to see intermediaries regulate our behavior for their own ends. This is the tangled web of governance of the digital age.

Some of these rules are baked into the technical infrastructure of the internet. The standards-setting organizations that create the technical protocols that allow people to communicate across a massive, globally distributed interconnected network of networks, and the infrastructure companies that implement these protocols make decisions that have real effects on how we communicate.[5] These rules are not neutral; the software that allows us to communicate encodes rules that affect who can speak, what sort of content can be transmitted, and which communications are most visible to others. Other intermediaries have a much more direct influence on our online lives. The content hosts, search engines, and social media platforms that we rely on every day to reach other people all have rules about how their networks can be used. These rules are written into the contractual terms of service that businesses and individuals enter into every day, and they are enforced through complex and opaque combinations of automated detection and human intervention.

In one of the foundational books about internet governance, Lawrence Lessig, professor of law at Harvard University, explained how law is not the only, or even the most powerful, tool of regulation. Lessig discusses four types of regulatory forces: law, the market, social norms, and architecture – or, when talking about the internet, the term "code." His book popularized the idea that "code is law": the design choices engineers make in creating the infrastructure of the internet work to constrain what it is possible to *do* online, and those who have power over the software and protocols we use on a day-to-day basis have power to shape how we behave.[6] Lessig gives examples of how this works in the physical world: the placement of walls and ramps in public spaces changes how people can use the space, who can get in and out, and who can exercise control. In the digital world, software code can often be taken for granted, but it is never neutral. The choices embedded in the technical standards upon which the internet is built have political implications. Search engines use algorithms that include value judgments about what pages to index and how we should measure relevance, which directly affects the visibility of different types of content online.[7] Social media platforms make design choices that affect how easily people can upload and share content, and they create different tools that allow different actors different levels of control over how that content is distributed. YouTube's Content ID system is a technical tool that provides a great deal of power to copyright owners; Facebook's flagging mechanism operates differently when it is used by particular trusted government departments than when it is used by ordinary individuals. Lessig's point is that these decisions, in a world dominated by software, are no less political in their effects than the public laws created by the democratic legislatures of nation-states around the world. In a way, they're often more powerful because we tend to take infrastructure for granted; the choices about whose voice can be heard are hidden and enforced in ways that are almost invisible, and they are all the more powerful as a result.

Internet intermediaries also govern in a more direct way through their rules and internal processes. By *govern*, I mean that technology companies seek to influence how people behave in shared social spaces. The tools they use to govern are not laws created by a democratically elected parliament, but rather rules set out in the contractual terms of service documents and the more specific guidelines or community standards documents that accompany them. They govern through the design of the platform – that is, the technical features that they implement that constrain how people can interact on the platform and make certain types of behavior easier or harder. And they govern through the social norms they encourage, through direct statements about what the platform is *for*, and by intervening to enforce rules in particular ways that deter behavior they want to suppress and reinforce values they want to encourage.

INTERMEDIARIES ARE AT THE CENTER OF MANY DIFFERENT
STRUGGLES FOR CONTROL

It is tempting to think that online intermediaries are very powerful, particularly given the outsized influence of the giants of the industry. But they are also vulnerable to a great deal of pressure from a great many actors. At the dawn of the commercial internet, the challenges of regulating billions of users connected through a resilient, transnational network of networks seemed overwhelming. It is clear now, though, that intermediaries are the key to regulating the internet.[8] Control over the technical infrastructure of the internet is crucial to shaping the behavior of users. Intermediaries are the focal points of control, where pressure can be most effectively deployed to influence user behavior.[9] This is a point that has not been missed by nation-states and lobby groups, which have worked hard in recent years to influence the way that intermediaries design and operate their networks.

Digital intermediaries are at the heart of current struggles to control the internet because of the power they have over how users communicate. Intermediaries play a critical role in governing the internet by developing and managing its infrastructure. Intermediaries of all types – the owners of physical pipes, the providers of core routing services, the search engines that make content visible, the content hosts, and the social media platforms – shape how people communicate in important but different ways. All these organizations make decisions that have a real effect on public culture and the social and political lives of their users.[10]

Cyberspace doesn't exist as a separate place; it is actually made up of a lot of physical stuff: cables and data centers; and libraries, universities, businesses, and homes; all connected together through internet access providers of all sizes.[11] All of this physical material is controlled by people and corporations that are subject to the ultimate control of territorial governments.[12] Both the people of the internet and its network of pipes are well within the reach of police and courts. Of course, the level of control that nations exert over the internet is not perfect. But, by and large, states have been able to enforce the law against users directly when necessary, and influence the way that intermediaries do business to achieve their regulatory goals indirectly. There are, of course, particular challenges to internet regulation, but, generally speaking, and with some important exceptions, governments have worked out how to enforce laws online and much more routinely than looked possible in the mid-1990s.

Intermediaries today are subject to pressure from law enforcement agencies and private actors around the world to moderate content in different, and sometimes conflicting, ways. They are increasingly subject to the demands of various groups of governments, users, private interests, and civil society. Tarleton Gillespie, a media and communications scholar working at Microsoft Research, makes the point that the major platforms can be viewed as both extremely powerful and just barely managing to run a network that surfs on a massive tide of user content in a violent storm of public opinion and conflicting demands of governments, businesses, and civil society groups from around the world.[13]

Intermediaries now find themselves at the center of many different struggles to control the internet. The World Intermediary Liability Map, hosted by Stanford University, tries to catalog all the disparate attempts of governments around the world to impose responsibilities for enforcing laws against users on internet intermediaries.[14] The powerful law enforcement and security apparatuses of nation-states want telecommunications providers and platforms to do more to combat terrorism – which means building tools into their services to break encryption between users, logging extensive data about what people do online, helping to identify extremist content, and working to promote counter-speech aimed at reducing radicalization. New laws are being created and enforced around the world to require intermediaries to do more to combat hate speech and fake news, like Germany's NetzDG, which threatens fines of up to €50 million if platforms do not remove obviously illegal hate speech within twenty-four hours of it being reported. Many different jurisdictions are steadily expanding existing laws that govern privacy, defamation, consumer protection, and many other topics to apply to intermediaries of all types, from content hosts to search engines to infrastructure companies like ISPs and even online payment processors.

National governments are not the only ones trying to influence how the internet is regulated. Copyright owners want technology firms to proactively monitor communications and enforce copyright law; privacy advocates and people who have been defamed want search engines to make decisions about what information should be indexed and accessible on the basis of whether it is true and relevant. Civil society groups representing survivors of domestic abuse and celebrities whose accounts have been hacked are lobbying hard for both content hosts and search engines to rapidly remove intimate images and videos posted without permission. A very broad range of people advocating for rights on behalf of disadvantaged people and minority groups are behind many different grassroots campaigns to get platforms to more routinely, more rapidly, and more equally enforce their rules against abuse and harassment.

Importantly, while intermediaries are certainly subject to laws created by nation-states, they can be influenced through other means. Lessig's other two modalities of regulation, the market and social norms, can play an important, but much less visible, role in shaping the actions of both individual users and intermediaries. So, for example, YouTube was never required by law to build Content ID. The law only required YouTube to implement a takedown regime. YouTube could have avoided liability from lawsuits from copyright owners by doing the bare minimum: receiving complaints, removing videos where the notice appeared to be valid, and reinstating them if uploader files a counter-notice. But, once Google bought YouTube, it had to find a way to make the massively popular video-sharing platform profitable. There were two major prongs to Google's strategy: it had to better integrate YouTube into its massive advertising platform and it had to get more legal, high-profile content on the platform. This means it had to develop working relationships with copyright owners – particularly the recorded music industry. Here, we see the market incentives at play: as a condition to dealing with Google, the recording industry required the company to do more than just obey the law – Google had to find a way to proactively search and deal with infringing content as it was uploaded, rather than waiting until a complaint was filed. Content ID is a technical system that regulates what users can upload, and it exists because of the market pressures that acted on Google.

Take another example: none of the major search engines or social media platforms were required by law to create a takedown system for revenge porn. At least for the US companies, CDA 230 gives them immunity. After the high-profile media attention that followed the "celebgate" iCloud leaks, however, tech companies were under massive pressure to do something to help make the leaked content less visible. Reddit had to shutdown a popular sub-Reddit that was being used to share links to the images; in fact, its legitimacy as a mainstream social media platform depended on it. Google, Yahoo, and Microsoft all were forced to provide some way for victims to stop links to their nude images from showing up in search results for their names.

The new rules about revenge porn are an extremely pointed example of how social pressure can shape the design and practices of major intermediaries, but the truth is that these companies are responsive to social pressure on a day-to-day basis. As awareness grows about the problems that Twitter and Facebook, and its subsidiary Instagram, have faced dealing with abusive content and enforcing rules consistently, all of these companies are working to build systems and procedures that will help them avoid social condemnation. Smaller intermediaries too are susceptible to social pressure. Content hosts and operators of discussion boards often express a desire to "do the right thing" when setting and enforcing rules for their users. Of course, there are exceptions to this rule: sites that thrive on controversy and operators, like Hunter Moore, who ran the revenge porn site Is Anyone Up?, who bask in collective social outrage. But, overall, very few people want to run a site that angers large parts of society. Not only is it usually bad for business, but the people running these services, like most of us, are social creatures who are sensitive to the moral judgments of others. The law sets minimum standards, but large commercial intermediaries will often do much more than they are technically required to by the law; they often want to be seen as good actors.

THE INTERNET HAS PROBLEMS, AND REGULATION IS COMING

We are at a moment of great change in how the internet is governed. The attempts of foreign governments to influence the 2016 US presidential election might be one of the last straws that marks a fundamental shift in how the United States thinks about the responsibilities of the major technology companies that operate there. Many of the issues discussed in this book have been brewing for more than a decade now, and they occasionally flare up into major controversies that dominate news cycles for a little while, and then fade away again. Through all of this, the threat that technology companies might actually be held accountable for what their users do has been relatively low. But the revelations that Russia ran an organized campaign of hacking, disinformation, trolling, and harassment involving Facebook, Twitter, Google, and Microsoft in an attempt to influence the election have led to a massive public backlash against technology companies.[15]

When Facebook, Twitter, and Google appeared before the Senate Select Intelligence Committee in late 2017, they sent their lawyers. The most profound criticism came from Senator Dianne Feinstein, who noted that the companies had not sent their CEOs and were not taking the hearings as seriously as they should:

> I must say, I don't think you get it ... what we're talking about is a cataclysmic change. ... You have a huge problem on your hands, and the United States is going to be the first of the countries to bring it your attention, and others are going to follow, I'm sure, because you bear this responsibility. You've created these platforms and now they are being misused, and you have to be the ones to do something about it, or we will.[16]

There's a real sense in Silicon Valley that those in the US Congress do not understand technology businesses and aren't serious about introducing new regulation. Just a few months later, Facebook was again called before Congress, facing the aftermath of revelations that the personal data of millions of users had been used by Cambridge Analytica to target voters based on their personal psychological profiles. This time, Facebook CEO Mark Zuckerberg himself showed up to address the members of Congress who sought to hold him to account for Facebook's collection, use, and disclosure of the personal data of its users. The *New Statesman*'s take on Zuckerberg's performance highlighted how skilled the Facebook CEO was at apologizing while avoiding difficult questions, noting that "the more he talked, the more Facebook stock soared" – the story ran with the headline: "Man Makes $4bn in Two Days Explaining Facebook to Old People."[17] It really looked like Congress wasn't able to keep up and certainly wouldn't be able to develop useful regulation that would help achieve its public policy objectives.

Congress is rapidly becoming much more sophisticated about the options it might have to regulate major platforms. In a policy paper released in July 2018, Senator Mark Warner outlined twenty different ways that the US government might choose to regulate the tech industry. Senator Warner was a founder and investor in several major technology and telecommunications companies, and he understands how complex the regulatory challenge is. The options he presented are well thought out, unlike the knee-jerk reactions we have become used to that are easily made and just as easily ignored. The paper was meant as a provocation – a way to start discussion about realistic options for reform and to signal to technology companies that they had better start taking the threat of regulation seriously:

> The size and reach of these platforms demand that we ensure proper oversight, transparency and effective management of technologies that in large measure undergird our social lives, our economy, and our politics. Numerous opportunities exist to work with these companies, other stakeholders, and policymakers to make sure that we are adopting appropriate safeguards to ensure that this ecosystem no longer exists as the 'Wild West'–unmanaged and not accountable to users or broader society – and instead operates to the broader advantage of society, competition, and broad-based innovation.[18]

The options Warner presented are not perfect, but they certainly send a strong message. One option canvassed is to roll back some of the CDA 230 safe harbor, making technology companies liable under state laws if they don't remove defamatory posts, misinformation, and content that constitutes invasions of privacy. Another is to consider comprehensive privacy legislation, like the European Union's GDPR, that would better safeguard the rights that users have over their own data. Crucially, this would weaken the power of major platforms to lock in users by requiring "data portability," which is a way to allow users to transfer all their data to another service. Warner himself notes that there certainly are flaws in each proposal; there are constitutional challenges from the First Amendment to overcome, and there are always political challenges of enacting regulation that would interfere with America's most successful businesses. But, as a way to "stir the pot and spark a wider discussion … on the appropriate trajectory of technology policy in the coming years," Warner's proposals are serious enough to signal a real change in attitude among members of Congress. The tech industry has so far been treated as an exception – the major firms continue to point out that they're not media companies and therefore shouldn't be regulated like the media is. This won't last forever.[19] Senator Feinstein warned the major United States-based technology companies that regulation was coming: "We are not going to go away, gentlemen, [. . .] and this is a very big deal."[20]

Meanwhile, the rest of the world has moved more quickly.[21] Europe, in particular, is flexing its muscle, and has taken direct aim at US tech companies. In 2018, Google was hit by a $5 billon fine under antitrust law for illegally linking its Chrome browser and search apps to Android devices, just months after receiving a $2.7 billion fine for manipulating search results (Google is appealing both decisions in court battles that may take years to resolve).[22] In 2016, Apple was ordered by the European Commission to pay $14.5 billion in back taxes to Ireland.[23] A series of privacy decisions by the Court of Justice of the European Union have imposed tough new obligations on Google, Facebook, and other companies.[24] The European Union's GDPR came into force in 2018, with major implications for how internet companies around the world deal with personal information, and there is pending copyright legislation that may introduce new responsibilities for technology companies to proactively filter for copyright infringement and to pay newspapers when they link to news articles.[25]

Foreign countries are not limited by the First Amendment, and their politics are much less forgiving of the business interests of United States-based technology industry. They have shown a willingness to regulate, and the major US companies have had to comply. The largest internet companies might have their headquarters in the United States, but most of their users are not. These new laws are effective because major platforms cannot afford to ignore regulation from foreign states where they want to do business. The recent laws and court decisions of Europe in particular have sent shockwaves through the global technology industry, and it seems that governments are likely to continue to legislate new expectations and responsibilities for technology companies in the near future.

RECAP: SOME LESSONS FOR REGULATING THE INTERNET

Barlow's hope that internet communities would govern themselves, in ways more humane and fair than the laws of territorial states, now seems a little overly optimistic. The problems illustrated in the first half of this book are just a sample of the major challenges that have come out of the decision to leave technology companies in charge of setting the rules for participation online. Of course, the same decision has led to great innovation, economic growth, and real increased opportunities for billions of connected people worldwide. Tech companies have used their privileged positions to invest heavily in developing new infrastructure, products, and services, and any new regulation obviously comes at a risk of causing harm to the industry. There is still great value in promoting the autonomy of online communities to create their own rules that reflect their shared values, and we might still see platforms evolve their own governance processes that work well for their participants and don't impose serious harm on others.[26]

Currently, however, we are rapidly approaching a point where new regulation will be inevitable. If we are not careful, badly thought out regulation could be disastrous. But it is possible to regulate the internet and even to regulate it well. The law supports the power of platforms to govern with almost complete autonomy, but, in the words of the late great Greg Lastowka, a law professor from Rutgers University, it could "aspire to find more democratic and participatory structures on this new virtual frontier."[27] The social problems enabled by the internet are so significant that governments will continue try to find ways to intervene. The major challenge we all face is to find ways to improve internet governance without foreclosing the opportunities to create vibrant, autonomous communities that support their participants to flourish.

This is rapidly becoming a pressing problem. Regulating the internet is not impossible, but it does pose specific challenges. The second half of this book turns to consider the future: how do we want to constitute our online social spaces, and how might we get there? Before we move on, however, it's worth reviewing some of the principles we have learned over the past two decades, because it's fundamentally important to understand these when thinking about regulation. Ignoring these lessons often results in laws that are ineffective, costly, and sometimes downright harmful. Regulating the internet is a complex task, and it is important to be aware of the consequences of well-intentioned but misguided laws that do not keep these principles in mind.

The internet presents massive problems of scale. This one probably seems obvious, but it's worth restating. The difference in scale of the internet, compared with regulatory problems in mass media, is not just a difference of degree, but a difference in kind. The tools of regulation that have developed for a mass media environment often do not work for the scale of the internet, and the problem cannot be fixed just by hiring more lawyers, police, or judges. The challenges of scale have to be taken seriously if regulation is to be effective. This means that new techniques have to be developed that rely on automation, architectural design, education, the nourishment of prosocial norms, and the delegation of regulatory work to intermediaries. These new techniques must also allow for selective and targeted enforcement against people or companies where there are real abilities to affect practice.

Sometimes, near enough is good enough. A common mistake when thinking about internet regulation is to focus on the exceptions rather than the routine. Say a website is distributing content that one country deems illegal, but the website is hosted overseas in a country with no extradition treaty, and the person responsible for it has no assets in any countries whose courts would enforce a foreign judgment. In these circumstances, it is always possible for governments to target the people within its borders who are accessing the prohibited material or to require internet access providers to block traffic to and from the foreign site. When John Gilmore said that "the net interprets censorship as damage and routes around it,"[28] and when Barlow said that territorial governments had no methods of enforcement that actually worked, they were in a sense correct. The internet is fantastically hard to regulate. If your goal is to permanently remove all access to a piece of information or to prevent communications between committed, but unknown, participants, you're likely out of luck. The Pirate Bay is a well-known example: despite the best efforts of film, music, and television studio executives and law enforcement around the world, the site is still available. It is kept alive via a complicated network of distributed servers and proxy sites around the world that have proved to be resilient to repeated efforts to shut it down – even if one site comes down, another soon pops up.

Perfect regulation is impossible, but this is just as true with every other law, online and off. The goal of law enforcement is never to stamp out all breaches of the law, but just to make it more difficult to violate – often, just to provide a deterrent to casual offenders. There will always be bad actors who try to skirt the law, and the internet's resilient architecture makes it impossible to block access to these sites and tools completely. But the copyright industries have apparently learned that the most useful use of their time and resources is to focus on making illicit content just a bit more difficult to find – difficult enough that ordinary users may choose an available legal alternative instead. This helps to prioritize takedown efforts, allowing copyright owners to focus, for example, on scrubbing links from the first few pages of Google search results, removing content from major commercial platforms, and introducing blocks on major file-sharing websites (even if these are easy to circumvent). This is often a better strategy than wasting resources trying to enforce the law against highly determined users who are willing to go to great lengths to share infringing content. Copyright owners have basically learned this lesson and have made their legitimate market offerings cheap enough and convenient enough that many ordinary consumers will choose to pay rather than seek out illicit downloads.[29] It is true that the internet is resilient and cannot be perfectly controlled, but sometimes imperfect control is good enough.

Targeting users directly can be very unpopular and is usually expensive and slow. Our judicial systems have evolved over centuries to help make sure that the law is enforced fairly. Unfortunately, this also means that it can be extremely costly and slow; due process is expensive. When faced with a great many potential legal claims against a great number of potential defendants, these costs become prohibitive. It is not just inefficient and deeply unpopular, but also practically impossible to enforce the law directly against individuals in all but the most important or harmful cases. This means that enforcing the law directly against users through the legal system is not scalable. If the goal is to deter users from breaking the law, using the legal system is not an effective approach for routine wrongdoing. It might work for high-profile crimes, but for the law to be a useful deterrent for everyday problems, it would have to be applied much more regularly at a massive scale, and this is not something that the legal system can easily achieve.

Cheaper, more regular enforcement usually means more errors. Relying on intermediaries to do the day-to-day work of governing the internet is the only way to effectively regulate at scale, but it comes at a serious cost. Any system that is effective at scale will always involve trade-offs for accuracy and due process. Broadly speaking, we can divide techniques for screening content online into three main categories: preemptive filtering, post-publication review, and automated detection. At the massive scale of major search engines and social media platforms, filtering material before it gets published inevitably means blocking a lot of material that does not get reviewed, or limiting people to a small set of preapproved material, or using very crude filtering techniques that are only partially effective at sorting prohibited content from legitimate material. Reviewing material after it has been published usually means relying on users to flag objectionable content, which means a lot of controversial material will inevitably be published at least for some time and that mistakes will inevitably be made in review. Also, the reporting system and moderation queue can often be exploited or will at least reflect existing biases against the speech of already-vulnerable groups. Relying on automation to detect problematic content is only effective in limited circumstances, where rules are easy to interpret and large sets of training data are available. So far, algorithmic detection works very well to block spam generated by machines and filter content that has already been identified as prohibited. When applied to other, more complex, problems, particularly where context is important or training sets are biased, incomplete, or flawed, automated detection frequently results in dangerous errors that often harm the most vulnerable among us. Whatever combination of these approaches are deployed, the massive scale means that errors will be regular, and dealing with errors requires processes of review and appeal that are comparatively expensive. So far, no real, easily accessible, and cheap systems of appeal exist that work effectively at this scale.

Moderation is hard and inevitably political. It will always be difficult to make rules that suit the needs of a large, diverse population. If we want these systems to be legitimate, we need to find ways for users to participate in the processes of setting the rules. We will need to create space for debate and discussion. This is not to say that we want private tech companies to become full democracies (we don't), but the social acceptability of rules does depend on some form of consent – which requires more than merely checking a box to accept a provider's terms of service.

More transparency is crucial. Improving moderation requires, as a first step, much greater transparency about how the system works. Many of the concerns that people have about the way rules are enforced online by private companies arise because there is so little information available. Before we can have a real debate about what the rules of online platforms should be and how they should be enforced, we need more information about how platforms are currently moderating content and how well they're doing it. This will not be easy – platforms are reluctant to open their processes to public scrutiny – but it is important.

Regulating at scale requires careful attention to costs, incentives, and risks. Effective regulation at this scale needs to be smarter and much more efficient than conventional approaches. Critically, the business models of the modern commercial internet rely on sites and services being able to scale efficiently. The basic promise of the internet as a democratizing tool – the ability of an unprecedented number of people to be able to publish material online and reach new audiences – hinges on the assumption that access is cheap. A vibrant, innovative internet, generally speaking, is one that does not impose heavy costs on the ability to participate. This means that models of regulation that do not scale well – models that require heavy editorial control, for example, like the models that historically have applied to broadcast and print media – impose major risks for the open internet and the ability of ordinary people to participate. At best, expensive regulatory obligations are unlikely to work and might be ignored; at worst, they really can break the internet as we know it and severely limit the important social value it provides.

Internet intermediaries, like other organizations, respond to incentives created by the legal, economic, and social forces that act on them. When they are made responsible for policing the behavior of their users, they will often respond in reasonably predictable ways. Most importantly, when operating at a massive scale, intermediaries have a strong incentive to minimize their costs. When faced with potential liability for what their users do, this creates a powerful incentive to err on the side of caution – usually at some significant cost to freedom of speech, access to information, and openness. Under their current models, intermediaries simply cannot afford to spend a great deal of time reviewing content and complaints. Ultimately, if these costs become high enough, intermediaries shutdown their services or move their operations out of the jurisdiction.

One of the key challenges of delegating obligations to regulate the internet to tech companies is ensuring that they are not subject to potentially crippling fines or liability for the actions of users over whom they have little control. A great deal of the value of the modern internet comes from major investments from tech companies in new technologies that have uncertain outcomes. Some of these experiments blossom into amazing new services that were previously unthinkable but become extremely important. This is why the various protections of "safe harbors" are seen to be so important – they have been crucial to provide the space for innovation and experimentation with new technologies. By limiting risk and uncertainty, they enable investment in innovation that is particularly important to a vibrant and evolving internet. The general principle that people are responsible for their own actions, and not that of third parties, is an important one with which we should be extremely hesitant to interfere. Safe harbor schemes do not have to provide complete immunities, but they should be well designed to articulate the obligations of intermediaries in as certain terms as possible.

Jurisdiction creates limits on government power. Governments around the world have generally learned how to regulate the internet by targeting technology providers and users within their individual jurisdictions. There are, however, still limits to the power that governments have in trying to effectively regulate a massive global network. Many internet providers have a choice about how they structure their business and whose laws they need to follow. When faced with a legal threat from a particular jurisdiction, the first question facing a provider is a risk assessment: do they have people on the ground, or assets in the country? Are they likely to be blocked in the country if they don't comply? If the answers to these questions are all *no*, providers have a lot more power to choose how to deal with legal threats. This makes it very difficult to effectively target providers that are willing to move around and operate primarily from countries with favorable laws. Of course, many global providers have serious business interests in operating lawfully in many countries, but there are always choices available to them. At the extreme end, providers can always choose not to operate in a particular market that they see as too restrictive or dangerous. More generally, this creates a real incentive for providers to base their operations in jurisdictions with more favorable laws. This is really important where there are real conflicts between the laws of different countries that could cause serious harm to users – like when some countries create laws that require search engines and platforms to censor political speech that threatens the government or hand over data about dissidents. In these circumstances, internet companies face a real challenge to decide where they will base their operations, which countries they will work in, and when they will comply with, challenge, or ignore a legal threat.[30]

Well-organized lobby groups get results. It's no surprise that the most important notice and takedown regime for internet content is designed to address copyright infringement. The copyright industries were well aware of the threat the internet would pose to their distribution models, and they worked hard in the 1990s to ensure that legislation was passed that would protect their interests. In the two decades since the DMCA was introduced, they have been actively campaigning for stronger copyright laws and new enforcement mechanisms. What this means, though, is that the law usually evolves in a very piecemeal way, and the concerns of the most vulnerable and marginalized are often not taken into account. Like with all law-making, serious concerted efforts are required to develop principled governance that works in the public interest, not just in the interests of powerful groups.

PART II

A New Social Contract – Constitutionalizing Internet Governance

8

Constitutionalizing Internet Governance

In 1215, on a floodplain on the bank of the River Thames, King John of England met with a group of rebel barons to negotiate a peace treaty. The meeting at Runnymede, about halfway between the fortress of Windsor Castle and the camp of the rebels, became one of the most significant events of Western political history. After raising heavy taxes to fund an expensive and disastrous war in France, King John was deeply unpopular at home. He ruled with might and divine right; the king was above the law. He regularly used the justice system to suppress and imprison his political opponents and to extort more funds from his feudal lords. The peace charter promised an end to the arbitrary rule of the king, guaranteeing the liberties of feudal lords. The document became known as Magna Carta (the "great charter"), described by Lord Denning as "the greatest constitutional document of all times – the foundation of the freedom of the individual against the arbitrary authority of the despot."[1]

The Magna Carta marks the start of a long process of *constitutionalizing* governance. Constitutionalism means that the government's power to rule over us is limited by law. One of the core complaints that the rebel barons had about King John's rule was that he abused the judicial system to further his own personal agenda. He bestowed great favors on those in his inner circle and dealt harshly with anyone who he suspected to be a threat. He would threaten his political enemies with huge, punitive fines and imprison them and their families without valid reasons and without trial. One of the most significant clauses of the Magna Carta (and one of only three that still remain in English law) is a guarantee that no person may be imprisoned or deprived of their liberty or property without proper legal due process.

The Magna Carta is viewed as the beginning of the concept of the rule of law. It is remembered most for the principle that the king must obey the law and was not permitted to exercise his power arbitrarily. The peace itself was short-lived, and the treaty provided protection mainly for the feudal lords, not their serfs, but this principle has endured and expanded. The rule of law, as an ideal, is a vision that to live under the rule of law is not to be subject to the unpredictable vagaries of other individuals – whether monarchs, judges, government officials, or fellow citizens. It is to be shielded from the familiar human weaknesses of bias, passion, prejudice, error, ignorance, cupidity, or whim.[2]

The principles of the rule of law, derived from the Magna Carta over the last 800 years, are the foundations of what makes governance *legitimate* in the Western liberal tradition. The rule of law tries to limit broad discretionary powers of public regulators by ensuring that decisions are lawfully made. It is a belief that good, legitimate governance requires that the decisions of those who have power over us are made according to clear rules. Legitimacy, in this sense, is defined in opposition to the arbitrary or capricious exercise of human discretion. As it applies to governments and their regulatory agencies, the rule of law requires that decisions are made fairly, according to a set of defined and public criteria, that the reasons for those decisions are made available for scrutiny, and that those decisions can be challenged in a public and accountable system of due process.

Legitimacy, at its core, depends upon some consensus that the regulator has a right to govern in the way that it does.[3] For a system of governance to be legitimate, there must be some consensus that social rules represent some defensible vision of the common good.[4] At a minimum, the consent of the governed requires that governance power is exercised in a way that is limited by rules – not arbitrarily.[5] This is ultimately the most basic value of the rule of law: that power is wielded in a way that is accountable, that those in positions of power abide by the rules, and that those rules should be changed only through appropriate procedures within appropriate limits. In this limited sense, there is good reason to believe that the rule of law is a universal human good – that all societies benefit from restraints on the arbitrary or malicious exercise of power.[6]

LAWLESS: INTERMEDIARIES GOVERN IN ZONES OF BROAD DISCRETION

Technology companies play a major role in governing our actions, but the power they have over us is wielded in a way that does not at all live up to the standards of legitimacy we have come to expect of governments. The way that we currently regulate internet intermediaries means that they are under no requirement to rule in a way that is accountable.

As we have seen throughout the earlier chapters of this book, intermediaries have broad discretion to create and enforce their rules in almost any way they see fit. They make decisions based on their own vision for how they want users to behave, their business plans, and commercial interests, as well as in response to their exposure to legal risk and potential bad publicity. They provide little in the way of due process, leaving their users to wonder how and why decisions affecting them were made and creating deep suspicions about hidden bias and overt discrimination.

This is what I mean when I say that intermediaries govern in a *lawless* way. The broad discretionary powers they exercise are the antithesis to *legal* means of making decisions. The role of law in democratic societies is to create a set of rules that reflect the public interest and the morals of the populace. Laws are made legitimate through democratic institutions that are supposed to work in the public interest and constitutional limitations that protect the rights of citizens. The hallmark of legitimacy in law is the rule of law: an underpinning principle that the rules of a society should be created and enforced in a way that is predictable and fair. The legislative system is designed to ensure that the rules themselves reflect the public interest and the will of the people, and the judicial system exists as a way to check that laws are validly made and fairly enforced. Legal systems are by no means perfect, but they create the infrastructure that allows for public oversight of the rules that we live by.

The most commonly agreed-upon principles of the rule of law are procedural protections. These essentially require that rules are applied equally and predictably.[7] At a minimum, this means that people should be aware of the rules and know the reasons upon which decisions that affect them are made. It also implies that rules should be equally enforced and should be stable enough to guide behavior.[8] There must also be protection for due process that ensures that rules are enforced in a fair way.[9] In any system of governance, the policies and rules will always be imprecisely interpreted and applied; the very fact that they are expressed in language means that there will always be some degree of uncertainty.[10] The way that legal systems deal with this uncertainty is to develop procedural safeguards that ensure, as far as practicable, that decision-makers are impartial, that the reasons for the decisions they make are transparent, that the discretion they exercise is curtailed within defined bounds, and, if something goes wrong, that there are procedures by which to appeal the decision to an independent body.[11]

Technology companies are not *required* to govern in a way that is accountable. They have to be sensitive to market forces, but the way they make decisions is not regulated by law. Normally, this is exactly what we expect of corporations. Their primary duties are to their shareholders, and we expect them to make decisions that promote their business interests. This is fundamentally important for innovation; the amazing leaps in technology and the new products and services that quickly become indispensable to our lives are very often driven by tech companies investing in their own commercial interests. The difficulty comes when we recognize that, in some circumstances, technology companies are making decisions that have an effect on our fundamental rights. This is core to understanding the difference between a consumer transaction and actually governing the way that we communicate, do business, learn, love, and play. When our fundamental rights are at stake – our ability to seek information and express ourselves, our privacy, our rights not to be discriminated against, our rights to education, to work, and so on – then we are entitled to expect a greater degree of legitimacy. The problem is not that tech companies are motivated by commercial incentives, but that sometimes their interests conflict with our fundamental rights. It is in these cases that we should worry about whether decisions are made in a way that takes our rights into account.

The laws that regulate intermediaries set the boundaries of their obligations, but they don't specify how decisions should be made. The discretionary powers that intermediaries have are supported in many cases by the safe harbors of various countries. These safe harbors protect tech companies from liability for what their users do, which means that when their users are misbehaving, intermediaries are under only very limited obligations to police their behavior. Some safe harbor regimes come with more conditions than others; in the United States, CDA 230 creates a blanket immunity that means that intermediaries are almost never liable for hosting content or for removing it. Other safe harbors are more nuanced – the notice and takedown provisions of the DMCA, for example, set out a formal scheme that allows copyright owners to request that intermediaries remove infringing material on their networks. But the DMCA leaves a lot of discretion to the intermediary – it is a voluntary scheme, and a host needs to follow it only if they think they might get sued. The incentives it provides are strong, but they are lopsided: because hosts are potentially liable if they don't take material down, they almost always accept notices that appear to be valid and remove content as requested. There's a reinstatement process under the DMCA that is supposed to protect the rights of users who file counter-notices asserting that they are not infringing copyright, but, because users would have no right to actually sue, content hosts are not bound to follow the counter-notice part of the takedown regime. This lopsided structure is common to most laws that set out obligations for internet intermediaries. When there is no applicable safe harbor, intermediaries are liable if they fail to remove content, but never if they remove it.

Because the laws that make intermediaries liable are usually lopsided, intermediaries still have a great deal of discretion about the rules they implement. Whether intermediaries are immune or liable for what their users do changes their incentives and influences their rules, but does not dictate how they enforce their rules. Their decisions are driven by their assessment of risk and commercial objectives, public pressure, and, often, the personal ideologies of their executives. The policies they adopt and the decisions they make can be influenced by public pressure and market forces, but there are almost no legal mechanisms to make intermediaries accountable for particular decisions. Within these zones of lawlessness, decisions by intermediaries might be arbitrary, capricious, unpredictable, and inconsistent – but they can never be reviewed by any independent judge who has the power to hold them accountable.

To be clear, internet intermediaries operate within our existing systems of law. They derive the authority to govern us primarily through contract law: in exchange for access to their services, users agree to abide by their rules. For the most part, the laws of democratic nation-states have allowed online intermediaries a broad discretion to develop and enforce their own rules. There are some limitations in contract law, but these are relatively minor. The general principle is that intermediaries are free to set out whatever terms they see fit, and we are each free to accept or refuse them accordingly.

The rules that bind digital platforms are set out in their contractual agreements. In 2009, Facebook CEO Mark Zuckerberg called the terms of service "the governing document that we'll all live by."[12] These documents have a foundational impact on how we all use the internet, but they are a poor way to articulate the rights of users and the responsibilities of platforms.[13] The terms of service of major platforms are almost universally designed to maximize the provider's discretionary power and to minimize their accountability. For all major platforms, these rules are carefully crafted to reserve the right to govern without any real accountability. Most terms of service documents have a clause that gives the platform a right to terminate a user's account or remove their content at any time, for any reason, or even no reason at all, at the service provider's sole discretion.[14] They include no meaningful safeguards against arbitrary or capricious decisions, allow the platform to change the rules at any time, and provide no meaningful rights to appeal against mistakes.

The terms of service of major platforms attempt to keep their governance processes beyond the reach of review of any external legal standards. They represent a claim by platforms that the public values of good governance do not apply to disputes over how their rules are created and enforced. By giving platforms almost complete control over who they allow to access their services, these platforms are able to make access conditional upon accepting their absolute power. These clauses are the legal lynchpin of a governance strategy that participants must submit to the authority of the platform in order to gain access ("take it or leave it").

This framing of relationships between users and platforms firmly positions ongoing debates about platform governance as an issue to be negotiated with the platform operators rather than as a public political question. This is deeply problematic, since users have no practical power to negotiate with platforms about the terms, and there is no meaningful competition between established platforms on these issues. It is very difficult to find alternative platforms that connect a large number of people without similar contractual language.[15] Since these contracts are usually not read and definitely not negotiated, it can hardly be said that the interests of users are well represented.[16]

OLD THEORIES OF REGULATION

Like constitutional documents, terms of service documents grant powers, but, unlike constitutions, they rarely limit those powers or regulate the ways they are exercised. The broad zone of discretion in which intermediaries operate means that their decisions play a major role in governing our social lives, but they are not made in a way that we can regard as *legitimate*. Legitimacy, when we talk about decisions by those who have power over us, means that decisions are made according to a set of rules and that the decision-maker is accountable. Ever since the rebel barons met King John of England on the meadow in 1215, these basic principles of the rule of law have been seen as important to help ward off tyrannical governance.[17]

Under current law, these principles of legitimate governance do not apply to internet intermediaries, which are generally private actors. The rule of law evolved in an era where the nation-state was considered to be the most powerful actor in governing the lives of citizens. John Locke, whose writing animates great parts of the US Declaration of Independence, believed that we should only give our government the limited power to protect us, and no more. The core threat to liberty, for Locke and those that followed, was the tyranny of the government, not the power of private companies. The vision of law that we inherited from early liberal scholars was that of a sovereign ruler issuing commands to a populace, who were obliged to obey both morally and by virtue of the state's monopoly on the use of force (its police and courts, tasked with enforcing the law). This way of thinking about law has been dominant for much of the last 400 years.

These theories view law as a formal, written command issued by the state. When we think about the rights of the citizen, these theories direct us to think about the legitimacy of these formal laws. The rules of society and of the market that these old theories teach are distinctly not to be thought of as "law."[18] Under this old way of thinking, these rules belong to the private sphere, and are therefore outside of the scope of public discussions about what makes rules legitimate. Just as the rules of chess are not a matter of concern for public politics because they are not enforceable by the state, the same theories suggest that the rules that Facebook might apply to what type of content is permissible are merely a matter between the user and Facebook.

These old theories do not adapt well to the realities of industrial societies, where institutions other than the state play a massive role in governing day-to-day life. The steady rise of powerful transnational corporations and the influence of religious and other cultural institutions make it clear that the way people act is shaped not just by laws, but also by social and cultural forces. Over the last fifty years, theories of "regulation," the goal of which is to understand how people behave and how their behavior can be influenced, have had to adapt to take this type of power into account.

Over a period of several decades, the role of the state has come to be seen differently. The state is now acknowledged as just one actor in society, and it competes and cooperates with other institutions to achieve its regulatory goals. Regulatory theorists these days take a broader view of regulation that includes not just law, but other mechanisms to influence behavior.[19] This broader type of regulation is sometimes called *governance,* which can be defined as "organized efforts to manage the course of events in a social system."[20] Perhaps the most useful ways of thinking about the role of intermediaries in managing the behavior of users online is to think about governance as a web of relationships, where many different individuals and organizations seek to influence what others are doing and how they in turn influence the behavior of others. Scholars of governance have set out useful theories that can be used to see how regulation can operate "at a distance"[21] like this, and their work is extremely valuable for thinking about the implications for how we should regulate and how we should ensure that the rules to which we are subject are legitimate and fairly enforced.[22]

Technology companies govern the internet. Many companies have power over some aspects of our lives, but the rules of platforms, content hosts, search engines, and telecommunications providers govern how we interact with each other, and they shape the possibilities and nature of public discourse. They don't govern in the manner that governments do – they don't levy taxes or imprison us – but they do set rules about how we can talk to each other, what information is available for us to see, what gets removed or buried, who we can talk to, and how widely we can be heard. They arbitrate disputes between us and, when they punish us, they cut us off from our friends and families and our audiences. The way they influence us is influenced in turn by market forces, by governments around the world, by each other and by their users, and by social pressure from the media, civil society groups, and the public.

We are at a point now where the old theories about law and legitimacy no longer easily apply. The task of identifying and developing social, technical, and legal approaches that can improve the legitimacy of online governance is becoming an increasingly pressing issue.[23] It is not a new issue; scholars have worried for decades that telecommunications providers have a major effect on the fundamental rights of their users but few responsibilities to protect them.[24] It is, however, becoming more relevant, and political pressure is mounting with an increasing recognition about the important role that platforms play in mediating communication.

Under our old theories, we don't have very useful ways to think about how intermediaries govern or how we should limit their power. There's a real danger ahead, because there is now more pressure than ever before for internet intermediaries to take a more active role in shaping our social lives. Because intermediaries are the focal points of control of the internet, this pressure is only going to increase. Governments are rapidly becoming more sophisticated and learning how to more effectively regulate the internet – for good or for ill – by better targeting to require intermediaries to regulate users on their behalf. Governments will continue to make new demands that platforms take responsibility for censoring speech they deem to be offensive and for rooting out terrorist propaganda and illicit copyright content. Civil society groups, other businesses, and loose coalitions of individual users are also learning how to exert sustained pressure on intermediaries to change their policies or to resist influence from others. There inevitably will be more social pressure and new laws that push platforms to do more to combat abuse and hate speech, deal with fake news and fake reviews, safeguard elections from foreign interference, protect the privacy of individuals, and so on.

As this pressure grows, tech companies will be expected to play a larger and larger role in regulating how we act. The companies will adapt, and they will continue to develop processes to make decisions quickly and cheaply. At the scale they operate at, these processes will involve automated systems we can't easily understand working in tandem with large teams of human moderators who operate in secret. The forces that have tamed the commercial internet have put us all on a trajectory where we, as users, will give up much of our ability to set the rules of participation in social life through democratic processes and lose the ability to hold those responsible for enforcing the rules to account for their decisions. This matters most because we are ceding control of how our social lives are governed (which has a real effect on our rights) to systems that we do not know how to hold accountable. To escape this scenario, we need a new way of thinking about how we limit, regulate, and make legitimate the discretionary exercise of power over us. We need a new constitutionalism.

A NEW CONSTITUTIONALISM: A MAGNA CARTA FOR THE 'NET

In 2014, Sir Tim Berners-Lee, the founder of the World Wide Web, called for a "magna carta for the web." Speaking on the twenty-fifth anniversary of his proposal that launched the modern web, he announced the creation of the "web we want" initiative, designed to crowdsource "a global constitution – a bill of rights" that would secure the freedom of the web for the future.[25] Berners-Lee's call to arms was a particularly visible endorsement of the work of many different people involved in many different attempts to develop a charter of rights for the internet. It marks a shift as these efforts grow in the public consciousness – questions about internet governance, once of particular interest primarily to network engineers, now resonate through ordinary users of the web, who are increasingly concerned with who has access to their data, who regulates their speech, who enforces the rules, and what they and others are permitted to do online.

We are now at a moment of profound potential change in the way the internet is governed. This is a constitutional moment, an opportunity to fundamentally rethink how power over us is constrained, to reshape how our shared social spaces are constituted. The giant technology companies that control the bulk of the commercial internet are under unprecedented scrutiny for the policies they set, the decisions they make, and the choices that go into designing their architecture.[26] Never has there been so much attention on the values embedded in technology and the policies of tech companies. This is a major opportunity for us all to think about how the internet should be governed, how power is held to account, and whose values prevail.

There have been many discussions about developing a bill of rights for the internet over the past twenty years. Collectively, these projects are known as efforts to develop a "digital constitutionalism." In short, digital constitutionalism seeks to develop new guiding principles that can be applied to the unique way the internet is governed in different ways by many different actors. These projects are concerned with how the internet is constituted – how it is structured in a way that many institutions and actors exercise power over different aspects of this massive network of networks. The difficult task of digital constitutionalism is to build consensus about how power over the internet should be shared and limited, how those limits may be imposed, and by whom. Unlike regular constitutions, which just have to articulate how power is shared between different parts of a single government, digital constitutionalism requires us to develop new ways of limiting abuses of power in a complex system that includes many different governments, businesses, and civil society organizations.

Most of the declarations about internet governance so far still focus on the role of national governments.[27] They often emphasize the importance of multi-stakeholder governance, an attempt to ensure that individual countries and firms are not in a position to dominate internet architecture and to encourage diverse democratic participation in internet governance debates and decision-making. They set aspirational targets for government investment in internet infrastructure and educational programs that teach digital literacy skills. They also articulate specific human rights principles – particularly freedom of speech and privacy rights – that attempt to limit government censorship and surveillance.

What these declarations don't usually do is create strong expectations about how private organizations should govern their parts of the internet. Private companies and nonprofit organizations provide a great deal of the value of the internet and play a very large role in governing how their users communicate. Ensuring that the core standards and technical infrastructure of the internet are regulated in a legitimate, democratic, and inclusive way is an extremely important and ongoing task. The chapters that follow, however, focus on the specific role that private organizations play and what we should expect from them. So far, this question not been adequately addressed by the range of constitutional declarations that focus primarily on the obligations of nation-states.

The time has come for a more fundamental rethink of how societies govern the internet. We are at a crucial point where there is major public unease and debate about the power that telecommunications intermediaries and internet platforms exercise over our lives and the extent to which they are being pressured by a wide range of governments, businesses, and civil society actors to wield their power over us for many different ends. The controversies over internet governance have become more frequent and more visible in recent years, and the days where intermediaries have been able to claim that their systems are neutral are drawing to an end. As political pressure grows, however, there are clear dangers. Badly designed laws and mounting social pressure on technology companies to do more to regulate online content could lead us further into a situation where intermediaries are routinely responsible for making and enforcing rules about how users behave without increasing their accountability. We must also be wary of creating new obligations for intermediaries to police content in a way that reduces competition, discourages innovation, or overly limits the freedom of individual users to communicate.

There are opportunities here for companies to avoid regulation being imposed from outside by constitutionalizing their own operations. To overcome the core challenge of mistrust that comes from a broad discretion to act however they like, tech companies would have to implement rules that impose real limits on how they make decisions. Obviously, companies are not likely to voluntarily begin limiting their own power, but it's not unheard of. Facebook tried to introduce a form of democratic voting system in 2009, and platforms have experimented with empowering councils of users to arbitrate disputes about how they enforce their rules. Either way, it seems clear that some form of change is coming. Tech companies might be better served in the long term by introducing their own constitutional systems, on their own terms, that satisfy the needs of their users, shareholders, and business interests, rather than waiting for more aggressive regulation from governments.

The central challenge for internet governance is now to find new ways to ensure that the power of online intermediaries over our lives is exercised in a way that is fair and accountable, without destroying the massive benefits that an open and diverse global internet can bring. The big dream for the potential of the internet is that it can enhance our practical capabilities and increase our ability to act and to live fulfilling lives by helping people to connect and to access and participate in the creation of information, education, media, and public and political discourse. People have long worried about how powerful interests might limit the potential of the internet to enhance freedom or even use it to oppress people. The remainder of this book examines what we should expect from the companies that govern the internet and sets out a plan for how we might collectively be able to make internet governance more legitimate. To do this, we're going to turn to the Universal Declaration of Human Rights, or what Eleanor Roosevelt called the "International Magna Carta."[28]

9

Protecting Fundamental Rights

this was an arbitrary decision. . . . I woke up in a bad mood and decided someone shouldn't be allowed on the Internet. No one should have that power.[1]

Cloudflare CEO Matthew Prince

Because technology companies play such a large role in governing our lives, we should expect them to *constitutionalize* their processes for making decisions that affect our fundamental rights. By constitutionalization, I mean particularly the introduction of limits imposed by companies on their own exercise of power.[2] This process of constitutionalization is the transformation of political limits that have historically only applied to governments to apply to a decentralized environment where many different types of actors can be said to play a governing role in society.[3] This is the translation of the concept of the rule of law to formalize the "lawless" internal processes of powerful corporations in a way that limits and regulates how power is exercised. This translation is a shift away from purely legal conceptions of the rule of law that is essential to pursue if the core goal of the rule of law – limiting the arbitrary exercise of power – is to be achieved in the messy social systems of real life where governments are not the only bodies that regulate our lives.[4]

The constitutionalization of technology companies and internet intermediaries requires two main types of limits on power. The first is a set of procedural limits on how rules are made and enforced. This is the opposite of arbitrariness in decision-making – it means that there are limits and processes in place to ensure that decisions are made legitimately, according to clear rules, with adequate due process to correct mistakes. These procedural requirements help to ensure that rules are fairly enforced. The second type are substantive concerns: the idea that social systems should respect and promote our fundamental rights and freedoms. These substantive concerns require that the rules technology companies develop are "proportionate" (meaning that they do not limit fundamental rights more than is necessary to achieve a legitimate purpose) and that their tools are designed in a way that mitigates the potential for harm and empowers people to exercise their rights.

Cloudflare's decision to refuse to host the Daily Stormer Nazi site is an excellent example of how constitutional limits could have helped the company to navigate a difficult challenge and make a more legitimate decision. At the time of the Charlottesville attack in 2017, Cloudflare had no formal public policy in place for dealing with controversial material on the websites it hosted. It did explain, in a 2013 blog post by its CEO Matthew Prince, that it was committed to taking a neutral stance on the content that its users hosted and refused to act as a censor by refusing services to websites hosting controversial speech, unless directly required to by a valid court order.[5] When Prince decided to refuse hosting to the Daily Stormer, the company had no processes to think through its decision. Instead, Prince says "this was an arbitrary decision."[6]

Prince is right that this type of arbitrary decision-making is dangerous. It's a decision by a leader with broad discretionary power, made without reference to any clear standards, without oversight or mechanisms of appeal. It's the antithesis of the type of legitimate decision-making that is at the heart of what we think about as good governance. Substantively, Cloudflare's rules were not based on any sound, well-thought-through policy that could provide a good justification for why it would not host hate speech. Prince was dealing with a real conflict between rights to freedom of expression and freedom from hate speech that incites discrimination, hostility, or violence – but had no tools to articulate a rule that draws a defensible distinction between the types of speech Cloudflare would tolerate and the types it would refuse to host.

INTERMEDIARIES GOVERN IN A WAY THAT AFFECTS OUR FUNDAMENTAL RIGHTS

The reason we should care so much about how technology companies conduct themselves is because our fundamental rights and freedoms are at stake. Many companies make decisions that affect our lives in some way, but, because tech companies are so important to how we communicate and interact, they have a direct effect on the human rights of their users (and others affected by their users). As Rebecca MacKinnon put it: "Unlike companies that produce sportswear or toothpaste, the value proposition of internet-related companies relates directly to the empowerment of citizens."[7]

Over the past few years, human rights experts have explained that, if our rights are to be protected in any real sense, we will need the help of internet intermediaries. The UN Special Rapporteur on the Promotion and Protection of the Right to Freedom of Opinion and Expression, David Kaye, points out that internet intermediaries are in a special position to affect the human rights of people in the digital age. Because internet intermediaries make decisions that have an effect on rights, and because they are subject to pressure from governments and others, Kaye argues that:

> we as users – beneficiaries of the remarkable advances of the digital age – deserve to understand how those actors interact with one another, how these interactions and their independent actions affect us and what responsibilities providers have to respect fundamental rights.[8]

Human rights are powerful because they articulate a set of global standards for fundamental rights. The Universal Declaration of Human Rights, approved by the UN in 1948 after the atrocities of World War II, sets out thirty articles articulating a set of fundamental rights. The declaration is supported by two binding treaties, the International Covenant on Civil and Political Rights and the International Covenant on Economic, Social, and Cultural Rights, which, after decades of negotiation, were adopted in 1966. Together, these documents form the International Bill of Human Rights. They anchor the international human rights framework, which includes a large network of international institutions, monitoring mechanisms, additional treaties and declarations, guidelines, recommendations and guides to interpretation, and human rights organizations dedicated to encouraging compliance and building capacity across the world.

International human rights are generally expressed in a way that is binding against nation-states, not private actors. The early human rights regime grew out of the atrocities perpetrated by governments, and much of the focus over the past fifty years has been on preventing abuses by nation-states and encouraging countries to invest in programs that improve freedom and real opportunities for their people. This way of thinking about human rights emphasizes the role of governments in creating laws that enable people to realize their rights.

The fact that international human rights law is only really legally binding against governments[9] has made it difficult to understand in any detail what role businesses and other private actors should play in promoting human rights. Legally speaking, what individuals and companies choose to do is limited only by the law, not by human rights. For some people, this means it does not make sense to talk about platforms infringing on freedom of speech because they moderate what users post.

But this view of human rights is changing. The UN Guiding Principles on Business and Human Rights (UNGPs) set out a vision for how companies should promote and respect human rights. They come out of a project, led by John Ruggie, a professor at Harvard University's Kennedy School of Government, to articulate the different responsibilities of different types of actors to protect human rights. The "Guiding Principles" set out the "protect, respect, and remedy" model developed to understand the responsibility of state and non-state actors to respect human rights.[10] These principles are the first articulation of UN expectations for how businesses should respect human rights.[11] They are a nonbinding articulation of expectations that moves away from earlier attempts to impose actual duties on firms under human rights law.[12] Governments have the primary responsibility for protecting human rights by creating and enforcing laws that provide meaningful protections for people and by refraining from dealing with people in a way that causes harm to their rights. Governments are also responsible for ensuring that domestic laws are set up to ensure that businesses do not infringe on human rights. But the key point of the UNGPs is that they expect businesses to "respect" human rights. This means, fundamentally, that they should avoid infringing upon the human rights of the people with whom they deal, and they should work to provide meaningful help and redress for violations of human rights with which they are involved.[13]

The language of responsibility from the guiding principles is now becoming more common in internet governance debates.[14] Over the past decade, the international human rights community has been working to articulate what exactly these principles mean for internet intermediaries. Intergovernmental organizations and independent rapporteurs for human rights have issued influential reports that identify how internet and telecommunications intermediaries are deeply involved in a range of issues with relevance to substantive human rights. The Organisation for Economic Co-operation and Development in 2010 recognized that internet intermediaries, from ISPs to search engines, content hosts, marketplaces, and social media platforms, play a major social role in enabling access to the internet, organizing information, and facilitating communication and market transactions.[15] Once we recognize the magnitude of the sphere of influence of major intermediaries, it becomes easier to think of the responsibilities that should come with the extensive power that they wield over our social lives.[16]

International human rights institutions have started to call on internet intermediaries to do more to protect human rights. The core rights that tech companies are most commonly involved in are rights to freedom of expression, privacy, equality, and nondiscrimination. While it is relatively clear how these rights apply to the actions of nation-states, there is a great deal of ongoing work to articulate how they should apply to intermediaries. A UN Educational, Scientific, and Cultural Organization report from 2014 notes that internet intermediaries provide unprecedented access to information and abilities to communicate, but also face substantial challenges in responding to controversial speech in legitimate ways.[17] David Kaye recently issued a major report calling on intermediaries to minimize the impact of laws that require them to censor information and to do better in the enforcement of their own rules for acceptable content.[18] The special rapporteur on violence against women, Dubravka Šimonović, made similar calls in her report to the UN General Assembly, criticizing the "inadequate and substandard responses from intermediaries concerning online gender-based violence."[19] Šimonović noted that intermediaries have responsibilities under human rights law to protect women, but that they were not doing enough either to shield them from abuse or to avoid illegitimately censoring their legitimate speech. Through these reports and the work of civil society groups, it has become clear that advancing human rights online requires the active participation of the businesses that provide a large proportion of internet infrastructure and services.

PROTECTING RIGHTS THROUGH CONSTITUTIONALIZATION

Constitutionalism imposes limits on governance power to safeguard fundamental rights. The central task ahead, for those who care about human rights in the digital age, is to work out how to embed human rights into the internal processes of technology companies. Despite the difficulty of relying on voluntary compliance, really protecting human rights in a digital age will require technology and telecommunications companies to voluntarily commit to protecting rights. We have seen already that the law generally does not do a very good job of imposing enforceable obligations on tech companies. Internet intermediaries are generally free, in a legal sense, to manage their networks in whatever ways they see fit. Improving the legal accountability of tech companies will be a necessary component of protecting human rights, but will not be sufficient.

The challenge of legitimate internet governance is the challenge of finding a way to promote the autonomy of many diverse social systems while also limiting autonomy according to external values. The discretion that technology companies and internet intermediaries have to set their own rules, for their own particular goals and for the benefit of their users, is something that should be encouraged. Too much legal oversight would cripple the operations of these companies and would limit diversity and innovation far more than we would want. Finding a way to make internet governance more legitimate without destroying autonomy implies that we need a way to hold those who wield this discretionary power to account through social – as opposed to legal – means.

Law sets the outer limits of what intermediaries can and must do, but the bulk of day-to-day internet governance happens in the lawless zone of discretionary power. Binding law can promote and support good governance values and accountability among technology companies, but real change must also come from within. Law does not play a primary role in limiting power through constitutions; "[t]he primary aspect of constitutionalization is always to self-constitute a social system."[20] Because technology companies govern with a substantial degree of autonomy, protecting fundamental rights in the digital age requires constitutionalism to deal with decentralized governance power. The top-down, external imposition of law by governments will not be enough to change the way that technology companies think about their governing roles. And changing the way that technology companies conceive of their power is the critical component of constitutionalization, which requires the self-reflexive internalization of limits on an autonomous body's own power. Constitutionalism ultimately involves a paradox that governance power is made legitimate because those who exercise power believe themselves to be bound by their own rules.[21] When we talk about the constitutionalization of technology companies, they are not fully autonomous or independent systems; their internal limits on power are not self-sufficient, but are reinforced and supported by external laws. But, because these systems do have a substantial degree of autonomy, for limits to be effective they must also be supported reflexively from within.[22]

Within the broad discretion that internet companies have at law, human rights principles provide a way to organize social pressure on companies to do better than the minimum legal requirements they are subject to. We'll see in Chapter 11 where new laws might be required to raise the minimum standard and shrink the lawless zone, but binding law can only ever be one part of the solution. In practice, legal enforcement through the courts is rare and very slow, even where strong laws exist. Most corporate regulation happens more informally – through the development of industry standards, reporting mechanisms, and social pressure on companies. The aspirational language of human rights can play a useful role in setting ethical standards above the minimum legal requirements, as well as work to fill in the gaps in the law where it needs to adapt to the needs of particular industries.[23] Often, effectively addressing human rights issues requires active cooperation between different stakeholders, including civil society, governments, and businesses. Even where binding legal obligations are introduced, industry-specific initiatives are likely necessary to monitor compliance and set out best practice guidelines that are not always possible or efficient to do through a government regulatory process.[24]

COORDINATING SOCIAL PRESSURE

Real, effective protections for fundamental rights in the digital age will require technology companies to internalize respect for human rights as limits on their governance power. The challenge of making the decision-making processes of platforms more legitimate is an incredibly difficult one. Constitutionalization requires real commitments from technology companies to impose limits on their own power, and no company is likely to voluntarily adopt limits on its discretion without clear reasons and incentives to do so. But if the problems I've outlined in this book are serious enough to try to address, then real change is what we should collectively be demanding from technology companies and internet platforms – even if this seems impossibly radical at first.

Individual controversies – small shocks that make platform governance look less legitimate – can be weathered by technology companies without real lasting change. Controversies over the involvement of technology companies in human rights abuses are becoming increasingly common, but the way they are reported by the media, dealt with by pundits, and acted on by companies makes it difficult to learn generalizable lessons or develop real, lasting change. There's a certain righteous-ness, and sometimes even glee, among commentators when a major internet company makes a mistake. "Hot takes" abound as pundits line up to give their opinions about each new breach. Few of these have any lasting impact. Platforms have often been able to weather public relations storms by apologizing, making some vague commitments to improve, and waiting out the news cycle. Mark Zuckerberg has made countless public apologies on Facebook's behalf over the last fifteen years, but the company's critics complain that little has actually changed in the way it is run.[25] Twitter has promised to deal with abuse on its platform for years now, but, even when its financial future seemed to be on the line, it has been unable to back up its words with decisive action. While scandals about the governance of tech companies are becoming more common, tech companies are learning to manage the news cycle and weather the storms of negative press and defuse the tensions without real impact on their day-to-day business.[26]

The type of self-limitation that is at the heart of constitutionalization requires a more fundamental change in ideas about how our online social spaces should be governed. A paradigm shift like this occurs at the brink of catastrophes, where the collective weight of previously ignored or dismissed warnings suddenly make change almost unavoidable.[27] Gunther Teubner, a German legal scholar and sociologist who has written extensively about the need to develop constitutional limitations that apply to transnational corporations, explains that constitutional-izing processes are self-corrections that are often brought about by crises; the "constitutional moment," where radical change is possible, emerges through experiences that present potentially destructive consequences "that can be over-come only by a process of self-critical reflection and a decision to engage in self-restraint."[28] Teubner warns that historically, the "paradoxical undertaking" at the heart of constitutionalization processes, where a social system creates its own limits on its power, requires extraordinary change: "It cannot be overemphasized that these self-limitations did not arise automatically by reason of functional impera-tives, but rather only under immense external pressure, as the result of fierce constitutional battles."[29]

Human rights principles do not enforce themselves. Without clear legal obliga-tions, internet intermediaries have been slow to respond to criticisms of their negative effects on human rights. Committing to good human rights practices does not come naturally to technology companies – or most businesses for that matter. This is not just inertia; businesses face real financial incentives that often conflict with their ability or willingness to respect human rights.[30] Firms adopt human rights standards to mitigate their risks and reduce their exposure to negative press that can affect their bottom line. Many technology companies have a culture that is deeply committed to trying to do good in the world through technology, and their employ-ees are often receptive to reforming the parts of their culture that are demonstrably harming that positive social mission. Organized social pressure, then, is the key to improving practice. Understanding how social pressure can be brought to bear on digital intermediaries is the most important challenge for ensuring that tech com-panies implement changes and commit to governing their networks in more legitimate ways.

A recent report by Article 19, a free speech advocacy group, examined the drivers for adoption of human rights standards at internet and telecommunications companies. The report found that real changes in corporate policy generally requires a public scandal that companies cannot afford to ignore, but that scandals are only effective at driving change where there is enough focused external pressure from the media and civil society groups and there are internal champions within the firm who are willing to push for change.[31] Change can be slow at the start, but it does build in momentum. Once some companies introduce processes that promote greater accountability, other companies in the same industry have an incentive to adopt similar standards, either because they learn about the public relations risks that could happen to them if they don't or because it slowly becomes expected of them.

The impetus to change typically comes after a serious incident that is widely reported as a public failure on the part of tech companies. One of the earliest major incidents that triggered a widespread industry shift came in the aftermath of China's imprisonment of Shi Tao for disclosure of state secrets in 2005. Shi had used an anonymous Yahoo email account to release details about a document from the Communist Party instructing journalists not to report on the upcoming fifteenth anniversary of the Tiananmen Square massacre. The Chinese government asked Yahoo to identify the poster and Shi was sentenced to ten years in prison and forced labor.[32] The incident sparked a major controversy and Yahoo executives were brought before the US Congress to explain why they had chosen to release Shi's information to the Chinese government – holding Yahoo responsible for his imprisonment. For the most part, while Yahoo executives expressed regret about Shi's case, they maintained that the company had done nothing wrong by following the local law. Cofounder Jerry Yang explained "We have no way of preventing that beforehand. … If you want to do business there you have to comply."[33] It took several years of public pressure for Yahoo executives to admit moral responsibility, agree to a settlement for Shi's family, and implement procedures to prevent similar problems in the future.

Shi Tao's incarceration (and Yahoo's role in the conviction of at least three other Chinese dissidents) sparked a serious change in the industry. Yahoo's failure was not so much that it acquiesced to a demand from a government that had power over its local operations, but that it had put itself in a position where it would inevitably be forced to comply with government demands that breach human rights standards. In later decisions to expand to other markets, the company would end up undertaking due diligence under what are known as "human rights impact assessments." Before deciding to enter the Vietnamese market, for example, Yahoo had dedicated human rights lawyers evaluate the risks of legal demands from the Vietnamese authorities to hand over data in a way that could threaten freedom of speech.[34] In response, the tech company decided to base its operations in Singapore, where it could more effectively resist requests it deemed to be illegitimate under human rights standards.

Other tech companies took note of the criticism and bad press Yahoo received (and the nearly 8 percent loss in stock value it suffered). Looking for a way to mitigate their risks, and avoid new government regulation, major tech companies ended up helping to launch the Global Network Initiative (GNI), a collaboration between tech industry, human rights groups, academics, and investors, designed to share information and promote industry standards that effectively protect human rights. The extent to which the GNI has been successful is a matter of some debate. Founded with the participation of Google, Microsoft, and Yahoo, the organization has struggled to expand its membership, with only LinkedIn and Facebook joining as additional members from the tech industry. Key civil society groups have refused to participate in the organization. Amnesty International in 2008 chose not to join because the consensus-based principles that underpinned the organization did not go far enough to meaningfully protect human rights.[35] The EFF quit in protest in 2013 when it became clear that the tech companies were prohibited from sharing information about their participation in the US government's extensive surveillance scheme.[36] On the other hand, the GNI has been successful in ensuring that the five major tech companies adopt (or at least begin to adopt) human rights impact assessments as a core part of their businesses.[37] Optimistically, the GNI is a promising forum for a diverse group of stakeholders to work together to develop best practices and work through tough challenges much more effectively than any one company can hope to achieve on its own. It has at least been able to bring representatives from technology companies together with human rights experts, which is a good development in an industry that has been slow to understand the social impact of its work.[38]

The example of the GNI shows some of the promise of industry-led self-regulation, but it also highlights some of the major ongoing challenges. In the immediate aftermath of the scandal concerning Yahoo's involvement in China and the incarceration of Shi Tao, some companies, like Google, managed to structure their operations in a way that avoided obligations to hand over information about dissidents.[39]

Voluntary human rights responsibilities provide a tool that can be used to drive positive change in the business practices of internet intermediaries. They are not the entire answer, but they can be a very useful way to set out the ethical standards that companies should follow, and these standards can then be used by a broad range of civil society groups and monitoring organizations to improve compliance. The strength of the guiding principles is that they are designed to be acceptable to companies, but this is also perceived as their biggest weakness.[40] For the principles to be effective, however, companies have to be encouraged to program respect for human rights into their internal processes.[41] This will require a lot of work from a wide range of groups that are able to exert pressure on tech companies and to hold them accountable. Ultimately, better coordination of external pressure will be required to convince intermediaries to make real changes. The challenge for those who care about the effect of platforms on human rights is to learn to better leverage isolated controversies into long-term change. Doing this effectively will require more extensive ongoing monitoring and sustained social pressure for more targeted, more particular demands – the type of demands that can drive useful change in the internal processes of technology companies. One of the major challenges is that there is little consensus about what we collectively expect from technology companies. There are many different interest groups with different priorities and agendas, and intermediaries often find themselves subject to conflicting demands from a range of different stakeholders.

Human rights law is not directly binding on technology companies, but social pressure, and bad public relations, can be a very strong motivating force – particularly when other companies can also be mobilized to exert pressure in a way that threatens their business relationships and revenue. The example we saw in Chapter 3, when WAM! was able to convince advertisers to threaten to withdraw their campaigns from Facebook unless it addressed misogynistic pages on its platform, shows that these strategies can be successful. The more organized that commentators, regulators, and nongovernmental organizations (NGOs) can become when responding to crises in internet governance, the more likely we are to see real change from platforms. Human rights norms provide a universal set of values that different groups can ask to be protected in very different situations. By focusing on the *processes* for making decisions that have an impact on our rights, there is an opportunity for a broad range of stakeholders to articulate a clear set of expectations for what platforms should do.

The extent to which we are likely to see platforms improve their governance processes really depends on how well civil society can present a clear and relatively unified set of targeted demands to platforms and marshal pressure from government regulators, the media, and the public in support of those demands. The key strength of human rights standards is that they provide a way to coordinate demands across a broad range of different civil society organizations. International human rights provides a baseline upon which most civil society groups can agree, even if their goals and priorities differ, across a broad range of issues. We'll cover some of the most important specifics in the next chapter, but the general ask is that platforms should monitor their impact on rights, work with civil society to identify problems, report on their performance, and implement systems that improve their processes. There's a lot of room for intermediaries to make different decisions about how they design their systems, what rules they choose, and how they choose to enforce them, but the important requirement is that they are somehow held accountable for those choices and can justify them accordingly.

Despite their shortcomings, the voluntary responsibilities of businesses to respect human rights can play a useful role in defining best practices and helping to hold companies accountable in the absence of legal obligations. Human rights are powerful without being legally binding because they provide tools that can be used to focus pressure on technology companies. They are powerful precisely because we do not have binding law: even in the absence of legal liability, companies do not want to be seen to be on the wrong side of human rights.

The next step to holding tech companies accountable is to develop strong civil society institutions and public agencies that are able to monitor performance against standards of good governance and exert pressure on platforms. Human rights are useful here because they have the support of a large global network of monitoring organizations and advocacy groups that are able to exert coordinated social pressure. This global human rights system provides an established framework through which pressure can be applied on the range of actors involved in internet governance to push forward progress toward fulfilling established human rights standards.

International civil society networks are starting to exert more coordinated pressure on technology companies, and this process is gathering momentum. The guiding principles have been adopted by civil society groups in a series of declarations and charters calling on intermediaries to do more to protect freedom of speech, rights of individual privacy, rights to be free from discrimination, harassment and abuse, and obligations to resist pressure to unduly limit freedom of speech, among others.[42] International NGOs concerned with human rights have used these principles to call for greater responsibility from tech companies and have worked to hold intermediaries accountable against human rights principles. Established human rights organizations, like Amnesty International and Human Rights Watch, have begun to pay serious attention to the role of digital platforms, and new organizations have been established to focus specifically on improving the human rights practices of telecommunications providers and internet intermediaries.

THE FUTURE ROLE FOR HUMAN RIGHTS

Working out the responsibilities that intermediaries have is not an easy task. Even understanding what impact internet infrastructure, telecommunications companies, and digital platforms have on human rights is difficult. Indeed, it has taken a long time for internet intermediaries to acknowledge that their actions have implications for the human rights of their users at all. Even when it is clear that some intermediaries have a real effect on rights, it is still very difficult to come to any sort of consensus about what responsibilities different types of intermediaries owe to promote human rights and to whom, or to come to agreement on what exactly this means that they should do. Importantly, though, international human rights law does provide some ways to work through these tricky problems. The basic principles of human rights, agreed on over many years, provide useful tools to identify the impact of internet intermediaries on our lives.

There are also incentives for platforms themselves to align with human rights values. Given that they will always moderate content, and any decision they make is likely to be controversial for someone, they need a way to assure stakeholders that their decisions are somehow legitimate. If platforms aren't able to do this, they will end up losing advertisers and risk regulatory intervention that limits their power or discretion. Implementing human rights safeguards within their business practices provides a way for platforms to justify decisions by assuring those concerned that the decisions have been made in a proper way, according to a rigorous process that can identify risks. Of course, implementing human rights safeguards will impose limits on how platforms can act, but at least human rights principles are flexible enough to allow platforms quite a lot of choice in how they develop. It might be in their long-term interests to adopt human rights processes that make their decision-making process more legitimate, rather than risk losing the trust of their users and being subjected to stricter laws that reduce their power to make their own decisions.

The difficulties that Cloudflare experienced in banning the Daily Stormer are exactly the types of problems that can be prevented by embedding human rights considerations within the day-to-day procedures of a company. The decision troubled Prince, the CEO, and he has since moved to develop better relationships with civil society groups to help make better decisions in the future. In an interview with the Open Technology Institute's Kevin Bankston, Prince explains that he wanted future decisions to go through a more legitimate process, with a clear policy that has been informed by a broader social discussion, in consultation with a wide range of civil society groups that can work through the core conflict between freedom of expression and freedom from hate speech.[43] This is exactly the type of broad consultation that is expected of companies making decisions that have an impact on human rights under the guiding principles. Procedurally, if it were tailored to promote human rights, Cloudflare's policy would limit Prince's ability to make a unilateral decision and instead create an accountable system to apply the rules in a fair way, with adequate due process to handle mistakes.

Developing a human rights approach to internet governance is the best way to promote a free and open internet that empowers people to flourish. Particularly in an environment where companies have few *legal* responsibilities, human rights infrastructure provides a way to organize and influence social pressure. Relying on internet intermediaries to make voluntary improvements to their systems is not a perfect solution to the problems this book describes, but it is part of the answer.

By better connecting the work of digital constitutionalism with the substantial progress the international community has already made in promoting human rights, those who care about internet governance have an opportunity to ground specific internet concerns within established human rights norms, standards, and principles. This is a project that fundamentally requires setting limits on how governments, companies, and other interest groups wield power over the internet. These are powerful, established interests, and this is not likely to be an easy task. Building on established human rights infrastructure provides a very useful tool for advocacy, awareness raising, and political pressure for those of us who believe in the potential of the internet to advance freedom. The rest of this book sets out the opportunities to progress this work. In the next chapter, I examine the practical implications of human rights standards for internet intermediaries and set out an immediate list of the biggest priorities for improvement. Later, in Chapter 11, I examine the areas where voluntary human rights responsibilities are not likely to be sufficient and turn to consider what legal changes will be necessary to improve the legitimacy of platform governance.

10

What Should We Expect of Intermediaries?

The government-sanctioned murder of thousands of Rohingya people in Myanmar's Rakhine state is one of the worst human rights atrocities in recent years. There were approximately 1.2–1.4 million Rohingya people living in Myanmar before 2016, and nearly 725,000 had fled persecution from military forces and Buddhist extremists to neighboring Bangladesh by late 2018.[1] The persecution of Rohingya was fueled by anti-Islamic nationalists, whose voices were amplified through physical leaflets, journals, and DVDs, as well as through social media.[2] Facebook's role in helping to circulate hate speech has been strongly criticized for contributing to the crisis. Facebook is an incredibly important source of news in Myanmar, where it is a major entry point for information and dominates over other search and news services.[3] Hate speech against Rohingya Muslims – often described as the "most persecuted minority in the world"[4] – is rife on Facebook in Myanmar,[5] spreading particularly strongly through influential pages run by organized hate groups posting false news and vilification.[6] Marzuki Darusman, chairman of the UN Independent International Fact-Finding Mission on Myanmar, explained social media had played a "determining role" in the violence in Myanmar:

> It has ... substantively contributed to the level of acrimony and dissension and conflict, if you will, within the public. Hate speech is certainly of course a part of that. As far as the Myanmar situation is concerned, social media is Facebook, and Facebook is social media.[7]

Facebook has come under sustained criticism from human rights groups for its role in helping to spread hate speech that fueled the crisis. The platform's policies prohibit incitement to violence and hate speech, as well as hate organizations and content that expresses support or praise for those groups or their members. These policies, however, were not well enforced during the crisis.[8] The Burma Human Rights Network reported that official government Facebook pages used dehumanizing language in a campaign to "demonize" the Rohingya population, and

"Facebook posts by nationalists have directed abuse towards journalists, NGO workers and Rohingya activists."[9] The military in Myanmar executed an extensive, systematic campaign involving hundreds of military personnel who used fake Facebook accounts to spread anti-Rohingya propaganda, flooding news and celebrity pages with incendiary comments and disinformation.[10]

During the same period, Rohingya activists complained that their content, including news about military atrocities, was being repeatedly censored by Facebook.[11] Facebook's rules don't directly discriminate against the Rohingya, but, in practice, the moderation system reflects and reinforces established patterns of discrimination. In an environment where minority voices are already marginalized, and are likely being flagged for review at a greater rate than hate speech against them, Facebook should have expected that counter-speech might be disproportionately silenced and that extremist content might flourish. The problem could well be exacerbated by problems of localization – Facebook has to rely on moderators who speak Burmese to understand the content of posts, and there is presumably a potential implicit or explicit bias if those moderators are drawn primarily from members of the majority religious and ethnic groups or if moderators are not trained to be sensitive to violence and persecution.

Facebook has promised to do more to combat hate speech in Myanmar. In July 2018, after months of criticism, it moved to take stronger action to ban prominent members of hate groups and to more effectively take action against people who repeatedly post hate speech and incitements to violence.[12] The overarching problem, though, is a systemic one that persists on many platforms. While most major digital media platforms have made public commitments to reducing hate speech and harassment on their platforms, actual progress has been limited. Too often, platforms make rules that they assume will apply neutrally, without taking into account that their systems amplify existing social inequalities. This cannot be addressed without careful attention to the design of a platform's architecture, policies, and procedures.

It's a mistake to look at particular controversies and mistakes in isolation. The real problem is systemic; it's about how platforms are designed, how their rules are set out and enforced, and how they choose to do business. The open question is what we should expect from platforms: what are their obligations? There are no easy answers to many of these questions, many of which involve difficult trade-offs. We can say that Facebook should have done better with identifying and moderating hate speech in Myanmar but disagree about where exactly it should draw the line between valid political expression and speech that promotes genocide. Some think the line should be drawn at incitement – that Facebook should only prohibit posts that directly encourage violence. Others think posts that dehumanize an ethnic or religious minority are a precursor to violence and should be prohibited – like how the common characterization in the media at the time of the Tutsi people as "cockroaches" who should be "exterminated" preceded the genocide in Rwanda that saw more than 800,000 people killed within three months in 1994.[13] Facebook's current rule against hate speech prohibits dehumanization of ethnic, religious, and other protected groups, but some worry that this rule is not enforced regularly enough or that a broader category of disparaging speech should be prohibited. The story is the same with other lines drawn in the sand; we can argue about whether it's better for Google to provide censored search results to Chinese citizens than not provide search services at all or whether Cloudflare was right to pull the plug on Nazis. There's no law that dictates a right answer in these circumstances – so what exactly should the companies have done?

International human rights law provides a set of tools that can help to answer these questions. It doesn't always dictate a specific conclusion in any particular case, but it does provide a way of approaching these problems. Human rights law is particularly useful because it sets out a group of values that have grown out of long periods of negotiation and consensus building. It provides the tools that are necessary to fight for basic rights and freedoms that belong to all people and which should be protected both online and off. These are important tools that can be used to work through some of the most complex challenges of governing the internet to build consensus about how our societies can best promote freedom and equality. Most importantly, for our purposes, they set out guidelines for how businesses can ensure that their internal processes work to treat people with fairness, equality, respect, dignity, and autonomy.

Human rights are rhetorically powerful precisely because they are expressed in ways that are universal; they provide global values that many different stakeholders can get behind, in a way that can bridge the individual controversies over governance that have become so common. These fundamental rights provide a plausible basis for developing new constitutional limitations on the decentralized power of private corporations – but this will require freeing human rights from their historical context to recognize that they do not only apply to the state, but rather to the exercise of political power more generally, including by corporations.[14] Importantly, this does not mean that human rights law should be applied directly to corporations without modification; the challenge of constitutionalization will be to articulate how the universal principles of human rights can be promoted across a wide variety of different social contexts.

In relation to technology companies and telecommunications providers, this means that protections for fundamental rights need to be carefully tailored to the independent norms of different networks and platforms and the various needs and values of the communities of users they support. Well-functioning platforms need to introduce rules that will inevitably affect human rights in some way, and it is important that all platforms have the ability to set different rules that reflect their context, their commercial objectives, and the platform's distinct culture and feel. Platforms curate content and set and enforce rules that suit the needs of their users – this is a core part of the value that platforms provide.[15] Protecting human rights does not mean that platforms should not set rules or that they should all set the same rules, but rather that the rules they set and enforce must be defensible. So, while freedom of expression is a human right, this does not mean that tech companies should always allow users to post whatever they like. Companies can legitimately set policies that restrict freedom of expression for valid ends. Rights will sometimes come into conflict too; creating space for users to communicate meaningfully will often require platforms to limit rights in some way. Tackling abuse, for example, requires platforms to limit the freedom of users to speak in ways that silence marginal voices. The rules of a platform and its design choices create the environment that gives each platform a distinct flavor and makes it useful to its users. Human rights responsibilities mean only that a platform must consider the consequences of its choices on the rights of its users and be able to justify those choices when they are scrutinized.

Human rights are a flexible system that can help ensure that rules are created and enforced in a way that protects fundamental freedoms of individuals and improves their abilities to fully participate in society. The rights are universal, but they are not absolute. The core rights – guarantees of freedom of expression, privacy, equality, and so on – are values that express a common international agreement about the protections all people are entitled to. Because the needs of different societies are different, however, human rights law recognizes that different social systems might introduce different rules that limit rights in different ways. Because human rights are always contextually dependent and contingent, they don't try to dictate a right answer as to which rules can be set. Instead, human rights provide a conceptual tool to ensure that rules that impact on rights are well designed in the particular context in which they are applied.

Human rights principles provide a guide to what we should all expect of the technology companies that exercise power over how we interact with each other. Most importantly, human rights provide a tool to move from high-level aspirations – platforms should do better in how they exercise their power – to a concrete set of requirements. These concrete requirements are the minimum standards to which we should all collectively hold tech companies. The responsibility to respect human rights requires businesses to prevent and address their involvement in human rights violations. This requires companies to exercise due diligence, in "a comprehensive, proactive attempt to uncover human rights risks, actual and potential, over the entire life cycle of a project or business activity, with the aim of avoiding and mitigating those risks."[16] The UNGPs require companies to employ due diligence to ensure that their operational policies and procedures not only refrain from creating or facilitating any human rights violations, but also to ensure that they are not complicit in any violations that occur elsewhere in their supply chains, and that human rights-based approaches and considerations are enmeshed in their policies.[17] Companies need to undertake impact assessment, performance tracking, and consultation with a variety of stakeholders to meet the due diligence standard expected of them.[18] The core improvement we should be asking for is that tech companies embed human rights due diligence within their decision-making processes. This means undertaking human rights impact assessments before planned business decisions and major feature changes, *as well as* after specific incidents. It also requires intermediaries to make a genuine commitment to improving policies, procedures, and the technical design of their systems to limit the risks of human rights violations, and developing adequate responses when violations occur. In this chapter, I'll work through a set of concrete changes that we should be demanding from technology companies to constitutionalize their processes and impose real limits to make their exercise of power more legitimate.

MONITORING IMPACT

For technology companies, the first core challenge in implementing human rights standards is to introduce continuous monitoring systems that assess the effects that their practices, services, and products have on the human rights of their users and others. Telecommunications providers and internet intermediaries have only recently begun developing systems to track their impact on human rights, and these are generally not yet sufficiently comprehensive or transparent. Some of this work is being carried out within major internet companies, although the way that these firms understand human rights is generally skewed toward interference by states rather than a detailed understanding of the effects of their own systems and processes.[19] This can particularly be seen in the transparency reports that major telecommunications and internet intermediaries produce. Among all of these reports, providers are primarily reporting on external demands. Few platforms release clear data about the effects of their own content moderation systems; the focus of these reports is overwhelmingly on state interference with speech and privacy rights.[20]

The enduring lesson from Yahoo's experience in China is that, when making decisions to enter new markets, technology companies should carefully weigh the merits of providing services in these markets against the risks of becoming complicit in human rights abuses. Transnational tech companies should know by now that these are weighty decisions and should have internal systems in place to better evaluate the risks of any business decision that might have an adverse effect on human rights. Facebook's experience in Myanmar shows that it did not adequately learn this lesson. Like many other global technology companies, Facebook has been bullish in its expansion to new markets,[21] and it did not undertake adequate risk assessments before entering Myanmar in earnest.

If Facebook had performed a human rights impact assessment earlier, it could have anticipated that it might face problems expanding into Myanmar. Facebook is no stranger to extremist content – it has been dealing with hate speech for a very long time. If the platform's leaders had adequately consulted with human rights groups, Facebook may have discovered that there was a particularly pronounced and sensitive problem with hate speech in Myanmar. When thinking through the clear implication that it would have to deal with hate speech in Burmese concerning issues about which it had little existing knowledge, its leadership might have recognized that there was a real gap in its staffing to be able to handle the problems that would inevitably arise. It might even have realized that its automated tools would have trouble dealing with posts in Burmese, because the Burmese language is not supported by the common Unicode standard, and the Burmese people often use a custom font to communicate with which their existing text processing software couldn't cope.[22] A thorough human rights assessment when making the decision to invest in entering into the Burmese market could have saved Facebook a lot of trouble by enabling it to take the steps it was eventually forced to take – hiring more local moderators, committing more resources to identifying and removing pages and accounts dedicated to spreading hate speech, and working with local NGOs to understand the issues – before it contributed to the genocide of the Rohingya people.

Google, too, has apparently not yet learned this lesson. Eight years after pulling out of China, it has been unable to resist the lure of access to a booming emerging internet market and has started to secretly develop a censored version of its search engine that would be acceptable to the Chinese government. When the news broke, it sparked outrage from human rights groups and from Google engineers who felt that the decision betrayed the company's values.[23]

To undertake human rights due diligence, digital intermediaries will need to spend considerable time with their stakeholders to understand the range of their impact on rights and develop mechanisms to monitor this impact over time. Michael Samway was a vice president and deputy general counsel at Yahoo when it introduced an extensive commitment to building respect for human rights into its internal procedures in the fallout from the scandal that saw it play a role in the incarceration of Shi Tao and other Chinese dissidents.[24] Samway now runs a consultancy company that advises businesses on integrating human rights protections within their operations. He outlines a practical guide for companies that sets out the basic steps that are likely to be common in any program to successfully implement respect for human rights within a technology or communications company. These basic steps include a genuine commitment to human rights from the company's board of directors and senior executives; a dedicated, internally independent, respected, and powerful human rights team that is well integrated across the range of the company's operations; a well-articulated set of principles that the company has publicly committed to follow with respect to human rights; and an accountable process for continuous monitoring of potential human rights issues that is tightly connected to the ongoing operations of the company.[25]

The development of real commitments to monitoring and respecting human rights is only just starting in major telecommunications and internet firms. RDR is the independent organization that evaluates telecommunications and internet companies against a range of human rights indicators. Its yearly index measures "whether companies demonstrate that they have processes and mechanisms in place to ensure that commitments to respect human rights, specifically freedom of expression and privacy, are made and implemented across their global business operations."[26] The governance indicators that RDR uses look specifically at "board and corporate-level oversight, internal accountability mechanisms, risk assessment, and grievance mechanisms."[27] Its 2018 report shows that telecommunications and internet companies are improving at anticipating and mitigating harms to human rights, but performance is still very uneven across the companies that it monitors. RDR notes that, even though governance practices are improving, "few conduct truly comprehensive due diligence on how all of their products, services, and business operations affect users' freedom of expression and privacy."[28]

INFORMING POLICIES AND RULES

Human rights due diligence should also inform the development of internal rules and policies of internet intermediaries. Because the rules of platforms are often created in an ad hoc manner over time, in response to specific controversies, they could benefit from periodic and systematic review to identify potential problems. So, for example, when Facebook's hate speech policy works to protect "white men" but not "black children" (see Chapter 2), this should raise questions about whether the rule is appropriately tailored. The distinction came about because of how Facebook decided to define the groups it protects, but once the rule was operationalized, its effect was to protect the powerful at the expense of marginalized groups. Similarly, the rule that prohibits female nudity on Instagram and Facebook when it is applied to images of indigenous cultural ceremonies works to silence an already-marginalized group.

The key benefit that human rights principles provide to platforms in these circumstances is a theory of power. The rules of platforms have mostly grown out of a liberal mind-set that prioritizes a formal type of equality (where the rules themselves are not discriminatory) over substantive equality (where unequal rules account for existing social inequality). Platforms make this problem worse when they try to disregard social context in operationalizing these rules to work at a massive scale. There is a real difference between, for example, the poet DiDi Delgado's post that says, "All white people are racist"[29] and white supremacists making disparaging generalizations about people of color. So far, most platforms have been unable to articulate a policy that recognizes that systemic social inequality has an effect on whose voices are heard and that speech on social media feeds and reinforces those underlying inequalities. The result is that platforms continue to struggle with rules that look equal on their face but have the effect of further marginalizing already-marginalized groups.

Human rights principles provide a path away from these problems for platforms. International human rights law has developed specific instruments that address specific vulnerable or disenfranchised groups, including specific declarations and treaties dealing with the rights of women; racial, ethnic, and cultural minorities; indigenous people; people with disabilities; children; migrants; and refugees; among others. But, more generally, human rights principles are based on the overarching need to protect vulnerable groups.[30] A serious commitment to human rights would recognize that rules need to account for structural differences and could provide cover for platforms to articulate and justify policies designed to decrease the risk that they continue to reflect and amplify existing social inequality.

This is not to say that human rights provides a single correct answer, but rather that paying attention to rights can provide a useful process for platforms to arrive at an answer that works for them and their communities. So, for example, Cloudflare's decision to ban the Daily Stormer was an issue that implicates the right to freedom of speech, but human rights law also requires the prohibition of hate speech that is an "incitement to discrimination, hostility or violence."[31] The International Convention on the Elimination of All Forms of Racial Discrimination goes further and requires states to prohibit propaganda and organizations that "attempt to justify or promote racial hatred and discrimination in any form."[32] To be clear, the material on the Daily Stormer website was not illegal under US law, which only prohibits direct incitement to violence (although much of the website's content might be illegal under the broader hate speech laws of other countries). Cloudflare has a very broad discretion about what it can do under US law. CDA 230 ensures that Cloudflare cannot be held legally liable even if some of the content on the Daily Stormer website was unlawful under US law, and the First Amendment would provide strong protection to Cloudflare from any laws that tried to limit its discretion to make choices about what types of websites it will provide services. The issue here is not whether Cloudflare was legally obliged to refuse to host the Daily Stormer (it wasn't) or whether it has the legal right to refuse hosting (it clearly does), but whether it should refuse to host it under its own policies.

For a rule to remove speech to be legitimate, human rights principles require that it be a proportionate means of achieving a legitimate end. Cloudflare, like any other platform, can certainly choose to pursue a policy to prohibit hate speech – that's a legitimate purpose that is accepted, and may even be expected, under human rights law. The point where opinions differ the most is whether Cloudflare's restriction is a proportionate way to achieve that goal. Independent organizations like the Southern Poverty Law Center, which work tirelessly to identify and stamp out racist speech, believe that providers should more aggressively enforce policies against hosting hate.[33] In contrast, groups like the EFF raise important concerns about censoring content at the level of internet infrastructure – like the domain name system, network pipes, or, in this case, content distribution networks. Blocking at this level is a very blunt instrument, and some legitimate speech will inevitably be blocked in the process. When infrastructure providers block speech, the EFF warns, "The risk of powerful voices squelching the less powerful is greater, as are the risks of collateral damage."[34] Because of these risks, some advocates suggest that blocking should never happen at the infrastructure level.

This fundamental tension is not something intermediaries can avoid. Because doing nothing means tolerating hateful speech that will inevitably silence and further marginalize already-marginalized voices, doing nothing is not a neutral policy. Intermediaries have to be able to articulate a rule that draws a line between what they will tolerate and what they will not, and they have to be able to justify that choice. To resolve this tension, intermediaries need to assess, within their own contexts and in collaboration with external experts, what the impact on rights will be. They need to make a reasonable determination that their policy is likely to be effective and will not be overly restrictive on legitimate speech. Their policies should be clear and well known to their users. This means doing much more than current practice, which is to add a catch-all discretion to their contracts that allows them to terminate service for any or no reason.[35] Their decisions should be consultative and transparent with a broad range of stakeholders (including particularly their users, independent experts, and civil society groups) in a way that fosters a useful social debate among those affected.

GREATER TRANSPARENCY

One of the most significant problems of governance by platforms and other intermediaries is that so much of it is done in secret. It turns out that we have no real way to measure how digital intermediaries govern their networks, what external pressures they face, and how they respond. There is little information publicly available about how digital media firms make decisions about content that they prohibit or permit. Almost everything we know about these processes is either obtained through leaked documents and partial information, subject to nondisclosure agreements, or reverse engineered. We know even less about how their governance practices have changed over time, and we have few effective tools to compare performance across different intermediaries.

Technology companies have been under pressure to be more transparent for years,[36] and they have made some major improvements. A key outcome of the Global Network Initiative has been to encourage its members to release regular "transparency reports." Google was the first internet company to publish a transparency report, designed to disclose requests it received from governments to censor content or disclose identifying information about its users. Transparency reporting is a good example of where voluntary standards can work to improve practices across an entire industry. Organizations like the EFF started to rank companies on the information they disclosed – its annual "Who has your back" report awards stars to rank tech companies on their transparency and willingness to resist government demands.[37] A few companies started to compete to improve their ratings, and transparency reports became more common. Many more companies started to produce transparency reports after Edward Snowden's revelations, when global concern rapidly grew about the tech sector's participation in the National Security Agency's surveillance regime.[38]

Several dozen telecommunications and internet firms now provide regular transparency reports, detailing some of their impact on human rights. This is a welcome move, but the data revealed are always selective and partial.[39] Transparency reports typically include quantitative information on legal requests received by intermediaries, breaking down this data on a country-by-country basis and often providing information on what proportion of requests have been complied with. This information sheds light on various issues regarding third-party interference, such as government requests for data and copyright takedown requests. Increasingly, standardization of reporting procedures enables comparison among intermediaries, although there is still a long way to go.[40]

Unfortunately, transparency efforts offer only a partial picture of the legitimacy of companies' practices.[41] Transparency reports do not generally report on decisions to enforce the firm's terms of service in response to private complaints about content, and they predominantly provide summary statistics that cannot be used to evaluate the accuracy or consistency of decisions. Transparency reports also often fail to capture the context within which decisions are made – they provide little detail about the procedures intermediaries go through to make decisions. Moreover, legal requests make up only part of the broader landscape of decisions that implicate legitimacy: policies set by intermediaries and design-level choices also have an effect on the legitimacy of intermediary practices but are not reflected in transparency reports.

This type of information is crucial to understanding the massive systems of content moderation, but it is not sufficient. In calls for greater transparency, there is often an explicit or implicit assumption that transparency – greater information disclosure – leads to greater accountability and trust. By itself, though, transparency does not lead to greater accountability.[42] Indeed, when companies use transparency strategically as theater to ward off claims for greater accountability, it can undermine and obscure real understanding.[43] The lack of detail in transparency reports can allow platforms to respond to demands for more information while avoiding real accountability.[44] For transparency to be useful, it has to be targeted – not just increasing information, but communicating in a way that can be used to help hold decision-makers accountable.[45]

One of the most promising new organizations that tries to make intermediaries more accountable is RDR, which is a new organization that monitors how well tech companies and telcos are implementing human rights standards. It hopes to be able to foster greater accountability by regularly rating their performances on key human rights indicators.[46] It has a rigorous research methodology that it applies to twenty-two prominent telecommunications and tech companies (regardless of whether the companies are willing to participate). The index that RDR produces ranks companies on how well they have integrated human rights standards within their daily business. This includes monitoring the extent to which companies undertake human rights impact assessments before introducing new services or entering new markets, as well as how transparent the companies are about their impacts and processes. By articulating clear, concrete steps that RDR expects companies to implement, it seeks to encourage competition between companies, reward high performers with positive media attention, and single out the worst performers for targeted criticism designed to induce them to improve for the next year's report.[47]

Projects like the EFF's "Who Has Your Back?" reports and RDR's index provide a simple rating system that can be used to drive improvements across the industry. When the EFF started to rate companies on how well they protect user privacy and freedom of expression, it found that many companies were responsive and worked to improve their ratings in future years, even as it made the criteria for each category stricter every year. The EFF is well connected in the US tech industry, and can use its annual reports to identify best practices in a way that pressures other companies to improve. RDR likewise has seen marked improvements in the time it has been releasing its reports – in its most recent report, seventeen of the twenty-two companies studied improved their performance in at least one category.[48] These indexes have been particularly useful to get companies to report more information about external influences from governments – requests to disclose information about their users or to censor content. Unfortunately, progress is still slow in improving the internal processes of companies – most are still reluctant to disclose information about how they make decisions.

Increased transparency is and should continue to be one of the core immediate demands of civil society groups and concerned users. A meaningful commitment to human rights requires not just that intermediaries consider human rights issues in their business practices, but that they foster an open dialogue with external stakeholders about their practices. The Santa Clara Principles is a recent declaration from civil society groups and academics (myself included) that outlines the types of aggregate statistics that present a useful starting point for analysis of content moderation at a systems level.[49] At a minimum, the principles urge platforms to release regular information about the total numbers of posts and accounts flagged or reported and the proportion of content removed or accounts suspended. The declaration requests that this information be broken down along several important dimensions, including type of content, category of rule violated, source and number of complaints (including government actors, other users, and different types of automated detection systems), and locations of flaggers and affected users. In the face of increasing criticism in the mass media and demands from civil society advocates, companies like Facebook and Google have continued to improve their reporting practices, making more information about how they regulate internet content available for public scrutiny.

Greater transparency is a fundamental precondition to improving trust in how technology companies regulate the internet. A major part of the problem at the moment is that users are rarely given good reasons about why their content is removed or why their complaints are rejected. Most platforms have been reluctant to disclose good information about how they make decisions, but it is increasingly clear that this strategy is breeding distrust. In the history of common law legal systems, the provision of public reasons to explain decisions has long been seen to be fundamental to avoiding arbitrariness and promoting good decision-making.[50] The analogy from legal decision-making is "that justice should not only be done, but should manifestly and undoubtedly be seen to be done."[51] The lack of good information about what platforms are doing is not insulating them from criticism – indeed, it seems to be having the opposite effect: because we cannot see how well their systems are working overall, we are left to imagine major systemic biases. Because of the massive scale at which major platforms operate, this means there will always be mistakes. The lack of good information turns each of these mistakes into potential conspiracies, as users develop their own folk theories to explain decisions.[52] The fact that their internal decisions have become so controversial in recent years, leading to a constant churn of scandals and news articles, puts platforms at risk of losing legitimacy in the eyes of the public. There are signs that this is changing, as platforms slowly move to improve their enforcement processes to give better explanations directly to their users.

The bigger challenge will be to develop new ways to understand the operations of platforms at a systems level. This is incredibly difficult, because the operations of platforms are complex and interrelated systems that operate at a massive scale.[53] It is also incredibly important across the entire range of ongoing debates about the role of technology companies in regulating our lives. There are now many emerging debates over, for example, whether and how intermediaries should identify and filter fake news, respond to systemic harassment and digital manifestations of domestic abuse, remove content that infringes on personal privacy rights, target extremist content, and proactively monitor for copyright infringement. Online intermediaries face pressure from many different sectors to regulate their networks in different ways for different ends, and there are deep competing interests at stake. Demands for intermediaries to take on a more active role in moderating content need to be balanced against freedom of speech and access to information rights of individuals, as well as concerns about economic costs and potential impacts on both innovation and competition.

As a key priority, if we care about how intermediaries govern their networks, we need to be able to measure their impact on human rights and work out how we can use this information to help protect them from external pressures that would limit our freedom and how we can hold them accountable for decisions they make on their own initiatives.

Our ability to hold digital intermediaries accountable depends on our ability to understand, at a systems level, what effects they have on our lives. Intermediaries play a large role in promoting human rights – if the internet has the capacity to enhance freedom, it is because of the commercial and nonprofit organizations that provide its infrastructure, the services we use, and the platforms through which we communicate. Intermediaries can also have major negative effects on our rights. We should try to understand how they contribute to our capabilities and real opportunities to act, as well as how their architecture, policies, and procedures can operate to limit our freedoms. Then we should also try to understand the pressures they face to govern their networks in different ways. They are usually positioned to most directly influence the behavior of users, but they are continuously being pushed and pulled in different directions by a range of other actors. These relationships are also continuously evolving, as technology changes and intermediaries adapt to changes in markets, in public opinion and in response to the shifting demands of their changing user base, and in their regulatory environments.[54]

Seriously improving understanding in the complex governance systems of technology companies will require a much greater degree of openness on the part of the companies. Understanding the effects that technology companies have on our lives and identifying potential biases and other problems requires careful attention to the inputs and outputs of these systems and how they actually work in different social contexts.[55] Analysis of this type will require large-scale access to data on individual decisions as well as deep qualitative analyses of the automated and human processes that platforms deploy internally. It will require new methods to investigate how well these systems are working in a way that allows comparison between platforms and over time as rules, architectures, processes, and social norms change.[56]

This research will require the cooperation of research institutions and granting agencies that can provide resources to support them, as well as platforms to provide access to more granular data on moderation processes and outcomes. Specifically, this means at least that platforms should work to find ways to provide access to fine-grained data on their decisions and the operation of different components of their systems in a way that enables independent public-interest research that "can diagnose emergent problems and suggest possible remedies."[57]

Really understanding governance will also require new and ongoing collaborations with journalists[58] and civil society organizations that are able to make content moderation systems understandable to wide audiences in a way that can be used to hold platforms accountable in the context of a set of shared public values.[59] Given the complexity of moderation systems and the contested values at stake, this work is likely to be difficult and require a large and diverse set of collaborations to help monitor and communicate concerns to platforms, users, and regulators in a way that can improve understanding and move forward political debates about accountability. Finding ways to improve transparency and participation in a way that is meaningful is an immense challenge, but it is a crucial component of all efforts to improve the governance of our shared social spaces.

MITIGATING HARM THROUGH DESIGN

Apart from identifying their effects on rights, the guiding principles expect platforms to work to mitigate harms with which they are involved. This is also a major unsolved challenge. All too often, the policies, procedures, and technical features of platforms are designed without a comprehensive understanding about how they will be used and what effects they will have on the human rights of users and external stakeholders. An ongoing commitment to human rights requires companies to continually work through the likely effects of the choices they make to identify and implement opportunities that reduce the risk of harm that could result.

One of the major problems facing platforms today is that policies and technology that look neutral are used in ways that have unintended consequences for already-marginalized groups. Take Reddit's voting mechanism, for example. Reddit tries to let its users sort the massive amount of content on its site using upvotes and down-votes to help the best and most relevant content percolate to the top of its feeds. Reddit is a grouping of many distinct sub-Reddits, each with their own themes and moderation teams (mostly made up of volunteer users). Sub-Reddits develop their own cultural norms about what type of content (posts and comments) is acceptable and relevant, and these are reinforced through the voting mechanism (popular content is more visible; less popular content gets buried), comments between users, and decisions of moderators to remove certain posts.

When it's working well, the system can help communities manage themselves, according to the particular needs and interests of their participants. Unfortunately, the system can also create a fertile breeding ground for abuse and hate. Reddit's voting system rewards people who post popular content and make popular comments. By default, popular comments float to the top of posts and popular posts float to the top of their sub-Reddits and potentially onto the front page of the site. Users are explicitly rewarded individually through a karma score that quantifies their contribution to the site. While Reddit can be a good place for complex discussion, popular content is promoted and rewarded in a way that can hide unpopular or marginal perspectives.[60]

Reddit's user base skews toward a culture of white geek masculinity, and the content that is rewarded and encouraged reflects the particular biases of its participants. The best of geek culture celebrates niche and unpopular interests, but the worst parts of geek culture includes really toxic perspectives on gender and racial issues.[61] Reddit's design choices to use voting to determine the visibility of content, to use karma to reward users, and to rely on volunteer moderators to create and enforce the rules of each sub-Reddit have a strong combined effect on the cultures of the platform and the content circulating on it. Reddit is generally reluctant to step into debates about content, preferring to play the role of an impartial or neutral platform and to leave the task of moderating the site to the moderators of individual sub-Reddits.[62] This choice allows hateful and abusive content to thrive in niche sub-Reddits where the moderators allow or support it and flow from there to other sub-Reddits and the front page as it gains popularity.[63] It is no coincidence that some extremely controversial groups have found a home on Reddit – including people who circulate stolen nude photos, the misogynistic gamergate controversy, and the incels (a portmanteau of "involuntary celibates") who blame their social isolation on women, as well as a host of sub-Reddits dedicated to racism and white supremacy. Eventually some of these issues cause enough controversy that Reddit has to step in and ban the sub-Reddit,[64] but the platform's design and culture tend to provide space for hateful content to thrive.

Reddit's mechanisms for incentivizing and rewarding popular content means that the site can serve, in Adrienne Massanari's terminology, as "a nexus for various toxic technocultures to thrive."[65] When abusive and hateful content circulates in a highly visible way on the platform, and people are explicitly rewarded for posting it, social norms can emerge that make harmful content seem acceptable and encouraged. These norms might start on a particular sub-Reddit, but, once established, can spread to other parts of Reddit. When abuse becomes normalized, and posters of abusive content are rewarded with upvotes, social esteem, and greater visibility, other users quickly learn the social rules or are marginalized, silenced, or forced out.

A key example that forced Reddit's operators to take a more active role in what sub-Reddits were doing came in the celebrity iCloud leak scandal in 2014. Attackers broke into the Apple iCloud accounts of hundreds of people, including several dozen celebrities, and released hundreds of intimate images to the public at large (known as "the Fappening"). Shortly after the iCloud celebrity attacks, another cloud-based leak saw attackers release more than 100,000 private images sent through the Snapchat app. Large discussion board sites like Reddit were the primary places for people to post and seek links to the images. The sub-Reddits hosting the links to images were self-selectively made up of people who believed it was morally permissible to share them, and these sub-Reddits flourished in the face of criticism from other Redditors and the media. Reddit eventually had to step in, banning the sub-Reddits involved and subsequently committing to removing links to any non-consensually posted intimate content reported to it.[66]

Of course, good social norms can also become established in the same way. A promising example, in response to concerns about nonconsensually posted images, comes from the "Gonewild" sub-Reddit.[67] Gonewild exists specifically for the purpose of sharing intimate imagery for enjoyment in an environment that facilitates anonymity.[68] Reddit Gonewild's rules require that all content that is uploaded be done with the consent of the subject. To ensure this, the moderators of the site require users to undergo a process of verification. Before being permitted to post content, users must demonstrate their consent by posting images that clearly identify the poster's body, along with a handwritten sign. Once a user has been verified, that user is identified by a distinctive icon on the user profile. Moderators may require verification if they are not convinced that the person posting the images is in fact the subject. Users who post images without consent are banned, and moderators may delete content posted if verification is not completed sufficiently quickly. The Gonewild story is interesting and insightful as a direct, community-driven response to the problems faced by women who lose control over their images. By prioritizing control and consent, Gonewild squarely places the responsibility for preventing abuse on the posters and moderators of content. Rather than require victims to go through the difficult process of seeking to have content removed, Gonewild is able to flip the burden of proof. In this way, Gonewild seeks to create an empowering space that enables women to maintain a greater degree of control over the way their images are viewed, without creating a stigma that delegitimizes their sexuality and agency in choosing to share intimate images.[69] In the face of frequent victim blaming, where women are admonished for taking or sharing intimate images in the first place, Gonewild's efforts to help women regain control stands out as a singularly empowering move.[70]

The challenge for many platforms is to find ways to encourage different communities to develop and adopt social norms that work for them, while preventing the spread of toxic norms that have a negative impact on others. There are many other examples where the culture of a platform, or parts of a platform, have worked to silence minorities and further entrench discrimination against disadvantaged groups. Stefanie Duguay has studied the way that content moderation systems on Tinder, Instagram, and Vine worked to reinforce prejudice against queer women.[71] The rules of each of the platforms purport to prohibit abuse and harassment, but they are not enforced in a consistent and systematic way. Because these platforms rely primarily on users to detect and flag content that breaches their rules, the content that gets flagged inevitably reflects dominant biases like homophobia, racism, and misogyny. The system for evaluating complaints may well be operating in a way that doesn't discriminate, but, because the inputs to the system are biased, the platforms can end up censoring a greater proportion of content from marginal groups and never reviewing large swathes of content that is abusive or harassing. This quickly creates a cycle that reinforces a culture that perpetuates racism, sexism, and homophobia, and eventually drives minority users off the platform.

The guiding principles provide some insight into the responsibility of platforms to address underlying social inequalities that are enabled and exacerbated by their systems, but there is no easy solution to understanding how this can be done. Ultimately, platforms can avoid infringing on the human rights of others by considering human rights throughout the design and operation of their systems and by working in closer collaboration with experts on human rights. Local knowledge is particularly important here. Ariadna Matamoros-Fernández studies the spread of racism on social media. One of the major problems she points to is that it is difficult for major platforms, the rules and policies of which are often designed in Silicon Valley, to become aware of the complicated ways that hatred can manifest in different regions and cultures. The interpretation of particular content may differ significantly based on local and context-specific knowledge – for example, the use of racist imagery may seem more innocuous to moderators who do not have experience with the cultural dynamics of racism within specific national contexts.[72] When platforms don't invest in understanding the local context, they are inevitably likely to misunderstand how hate speech is interpreted and, therefore, likely to continue to overcensor counter-speech and underblock hate.

One of the most dangerous engineering practices in this regard is to treat the technology being developed as neutral and, as a consequence, avoid making considered choices about how potential harmful uses of the tools can be mitigated. Because online abuse reflects deep social inequalities, telecommunications tools that do not actively take inequality into account will almost inevitably contribute to the amplification of inequality. There have been important advances in recent years to more actively understand how design and engineering choices can exacerbate underlying inequality, and these moves should be encouraged. A great deal more work remains to be done, however, to ensure that contemporary communications tools work to empower marginalized people and amplify their voices, rather than continue to exacerbate well-established patterns of inequality and abuse.

SCALABLE DUE PROCESS

No matter how good a platform's policies are, mistakes are inevitable. When companies deal with millions of complaints every week, and perhaps even more automated decisions, even very low error rates translate to hundreds of thousands of mistakes every week. Ensuring that there are adequate mechanisms of due process to appeal and to seek redress is a critical, but underdeveloped, component of platform governance.

The only way to mitigate the risks of either overblocking legitimate speech or underblocking prohibited speech is to develop an enforcement system that includes adequate due process safeguards. Civil society groups have been working for several years now on guidelines for how these types of decisions should be made. The Manila Principles on Intermediary Liability, a joint declaration between a group of civil society organizations, provide some minimal guidelines for what a legitimate decision-making process should include.[73] Most relevantly, the Manila Principles require that users be given an opportunity to appeal decisions to restrict content, and these processes should be as transparent as possible without harming the privacy rights of individuals.

These procedural safeguards are the hallmark of legitimate decision-making. Under the standards of the rule of law, rules must be clear, well known, and fairly applied, and they must represent some defensible vision of the common good. When Cloudflare CEO Matthew Prince made the decision to stop hosting of the Daily Stormer's site, he hoped that it would be a one-off decision that would spark a broader social conversation about the policies not just of Cloudflare, but of other intermediaries as well. This is the work that needs to be done next, and it is becoming more pressing as pressure on intermediaries to take a more active role in policing the internet continues to build.

This is exactly the work that the UNGPs expect companies faced with these decisions to do to embed a commitment to respecting human rights in their systems. As part of their responsibility to respect human rights, telecommunications providers and digital media platforms will need to develop better complaints systems and mechanisms for due process that are able to effectively mitigate harm perpetrated through their networks. The UNGPs emphasize the importance of developing effective remedies when businesses are involved in human rights violations. The enforcement of rules about acceptable content triggers concerns at least about freedom of speech and access to information, as well as having implications for rights to equal treatment, nondiscrimination, rights against hate speech, and many other interrelated rights. Both of these problems – underblocking and overblocking – raise concerns that tech companies are expected to try to address under the UNGPs. Both of these problems raise the need for better enforcement processes, but, so far, no major platforms have been able to develop truly legitimate systems that work at a massive scale.

These are extremely difficult problems to solve at the massive scale of major intermediaries. The simple, cheap, and scalable mechanisms that platforms have developed to date to enforce their rules are not well suited to dealing with these challenges. Modern digital media platforms rely primarily on relatively simple systems to moderate content – flagging systems that allow users to identify content for review,[74] and a limited set of blocking and filtering tools that help users manage the material to which they are exposed. These systems have so far proved to be deeply inadequate to the task of addressing online abuse at any serious scale.[75] Relying on flagging means that there will often be a problem of systematic under-enforcement because not all content that is technically prohibited will be brought to the attention of the platform or make it through the moderation queue with a correct decision. Most major platforms have rules that prohibit harmful speech, but these are inconsistently applied and enforced. These systems place responsibility for reporting content on the target of abuse, and they have been effective at stemming the tide of widespread abuse. Instead, abuse has become normalized on many platforms.

At the same time, these systems are routinely abused to silence legitimate speech. Marginalized groups who are often the targets of coordinated attacks complain about regular overenforcement of rules in ways that hinder their legitimate communication and participation. In Chapter 2, we saw a common complaint from targets of abuse on social media that they were often unable to get useful help from platforms. Groups of malicious harassers have learned how to coordinate campaigns to flag content they disagree with. Women who routinely receive floods of abuse have complained that not only do platforms not enforce the rules against their abusers, but that they themselves are often silenced, suspended, or banned when they point out abuse or try to take matters into their own hands out of frustration with the platform. Moderation systems have to operate quickly, and because it can be hard to separate out legitimate speech from prohibited content, there is always a risk of overblocking.

This is not a problem that is unique to abuse, but is common to many different moderation problems. All flagging systems can be gamed and are vulnerable to coordinated attacks motivated by any number of reasons. We see this not only in the censorship of counter-speech by marginalized groups, but also in the enforcement of copyright policies and other rules informed by legal obligations. Businesses regularly use copyright law to try to get search engines and content hosts to remove content that is critical of them. People who take offense at negative comments, reviews, or news reports that paint them in a negative light will often make complaints under defamation or privacy law to protect themselves. Often, a platform faces legal liability if it fails to remove content that infringes on the rights of others, but not if it removes content it is not legally obliged to. CDA 230 reduces this risk in the United States, but not for intellectual property claims. In many other countries, laws designed to prohibit defamation, protect privacy, or target hate speech will often create similarly lopsided incentives for platforms to remove content. The predictable result is that platforms are likely to err on the side of caution in removing content alleged to be unlawful, with significant negative impact on freedom of expression.

For states, the conventional way of making decisions legitimate is to provide court oversight. Real judicial review of content moderation decisions, however, is far too expensive and slow to be a workable option. Working out how to enforce rules in a legitimate way, at a massive scale, without the direct oversight of the courts is a difficult and unsolved problem. The Manila Principles set out a baseline set of requirements: clear rules and processes; a right to be heard for the people affected by a decision, preferably before a decision is made; and a useful and accessible avenue to appeal decisions.[76] The Santa Clara Principles also emphasize the need for meaningful and timely appeals, including human review, an opportunity to provide new contextual information, and an explanation that is sufficiently detailed to allow the user to understand the reasons for the decision.[77]

One of the most promising options is an idea to create independent review bodies that would work to enforce the rules and arbitrate disputes once the internal processes of a platform have been exhausted. The Manila Principles envision a future where governments, intermediaries, and civil society groups "work together to develop and maintain independent, transparent, and impartial oversight mechanisms to ensure the accountability of the content restriction policies and practices."[78] In a recent report, David Kaye, the UN Special Rapporteur on the Promotion and Protection of the Right to Freedom of Opinion and Expression, raised the idea of companies working together to create an independent "social media council" that would provide an industry-wide complaints system and allow users to seek remedies for violations of their human rights.[79] This suggestion came from Article 19, the free speech advocacy group, and is based on the press councils that provide industry-wide complaints mechanisms.[80]

While platforms have not yet invested in developing appeals processes that are workable at scale, an industry-led solution could conceivably provide adequate safeguards for due process. Recent developments in low-cost arbitration and dispute resolution suggest that it might be possible to build a cheap but independent review system. We can envisage a fully web-based workflow that allows all parties to easily provide the relevant information to a commercial arbitrator who can make a determination relatively quickly. For the most common types of disputes, the entire process could conceivably be handled cheaply enough that the cost could even be borne by the aggrieved user at first, unless they are successful. Most major platforms keep their dispute resolutions in-house and are reluctant to cede power to external arbitrators. However, a well-designed system could work to the advantage of platforms – allowing them to remain more neutral in disputes by placing the responsibility for resolving contentious decisions on independent arbitrators, while leaving the platform free to set the general rules. Ultimately, if even independent commercial arbitration fails, it is possible to imagine a system that allows parties to escalate disputes into a judicial system. This might be a harder practical step – platforms would have to change their policies and give up some protection from binding legal rulings that might entail substantial legal fees and real compensation payments. Platforms are unlikely to take this step voluntarily; a truly legitimate system will probably require intervention by government regulators. The specter of regulation on many of these issues is a real possibility. We'll see in the next chapter some steps that some governments have already taken and that they could take to encourage the industry to adopt better schemes and, ultimately, to impose scalable dispute resolution through new laws. In the meantime, as pressure increases, platforms will likely have a good incentive to develop better systems to provide meaningful remedies to aggrieved users themselves in order to improve trust in the system and head off the introduction of new laws and binding obligations.

VOLUNTARILY EMBEDDING HUMAN RIGHTS

The standards provided by international human rights law are not perfect. They don't extend to cover every issue that different groups might like to see improvements in; they often don't dictate particular substantive outcomes; and they don't oblige companies to comply under any legal penalties. But they are as close as we have to a universal common denominator of principles that almost everyone can agree on. They have been negotiated at length over many decades by a very broad range of stakeholders, and they have a good claim to represent a global consensus about the values that matter most. As work continues to extend the guiding principles and perhaps even develop a binding treaty for businesses, they also provide a clear statement of what businesses should do to ensure that they limit the harm they cause or are involved with. They are, in short, a useful starting point for the ongoing discussion about what we collectively expect from technology companies to make their decisions more legitimate.

Convincing intermediaries to fully commit to embedding human rights into their operations may well be an impossible task without introducing binding legal requirements. It certainly won't be easy. But there are important opportunities to marshal social pressure in a way that makes more productive use of the massive media attention that accompanies each new controversy about the power of technology companies over our lives, our information environments, and our public discourse. If a great many of us who care about these issues can express our expectations in a common set of targeted demands, we may be able to influence technology companies to constitutionalize their own internal processes. The explicit demands of human rights law that apply to businesses through the guiding principles are a good start. Collectively, our best opportunity here is to seek real commitments to implement routine human rights impact assessments to monitor their impact on rights; provide meaningful transparency to a broad range of external stakeholders; pay particular attention to the impacts of design choices; and work to invent new ways of protecting due process at massive scales.

There are important opportunities for technology companies, too, to benefit from explicitly adopting human rights as a guide for decision-making. While real commitments come at some cost to flexibility, they may just help to improve trust in how platforms govern. One of the hardest issues for platforms to navigate is that there is no universal agreement on what their rules should be. There is no decision they can make – to allow content or to prohibit it – that is not inherently political.[81] Whatever rule they choose will inevitably upset some set of people. And, at the scale they operate, any rule will inevitably be enforced inconsistently – wrong decisions not only are bound to happen, but they are bound to happen often. At the moment, platforms bear all of the responsibility for the decisions they make. They have often tried to hide their responsibility by pretending to be neutral, but this strategy is not working anymore. As both public pressure and the threat of legal regulation increase, there is a clear opportunity to use a set of universal values – like human rights – to ensure that decisions are justifiable to the people that they affect. When Cloudflare and other infrastructure companies refused to provide services to the Daily Stormer, they came off as arbitrary and capricious. If those decisions were instead based on a well-articulated policy that had been vetted by a respected set of human rights organizations and the Daily Stormer had been afforded a level of due process, the decision would have seemed much more legitimate. It probably didn't matter in this particular case – Cloudflare, Google, and others do not seem to have suffered very much commercially as a result of their arbitrary decision-making – but it may well start to matter as the pressure on tech companies continues to grow. Human rights processes could provide a mechanism for platforms to truly transfer some of the responsibility (and the blame) for the decisions they make to others. This might be the only way for tech companies to increase trust and avoid losing their social license to operate. At a time when there is growing pressure for new legal regulation and public demand for market alternatives, adopting human rights safeguards could actually be in the direct interest of technology companies.[82] New laws are almost inevitable. If tech companies do not improve their own governance, any new laws are likely to be much less favorable to their interests.

11

The Role of States and Binding Law

In an article in January 2018 warning of an impending "techlash," *The Economist* painted a bleak picture for the CEOs of Amazon, Facebook, Google, Apple, Netflix, and Microsoft. "Things have been rough in Europe for a while," the article pointed out, and "America is not the haven it was" for the giants of tech that dominate the internet.[1] From the presidential candidates in the next election to a group of concerned state attorneys general, *The Economist* predicted a great deal of anti-tech sentiment was coming from regulators. The year didn't get much better for major tech companies from there. As the investigation into Russian interference in the 2016 presidential elections unfolded, not just Facebook, but all of the major technology companies faced a sudden shift in public opinion on a wave of negative press.

States are under a lot of pressure to regulate the internet. If enough powerful technology companies are able to constitutionalize their own systems and really become more accountable for their decisions, they might avoid real government intervention. If they cannot, as the pressure to regulate continues to mount, internet companies can certainly expect more legal changes to come. Even if regulation in the United States is unlikely in the near future, it's already happening in Europe, and other countries are rapidly learning how to flex their legal muscles.

But as we have seen in previous chapters, regulating the internet is *hard*. So far, most attempts to regulate the internet through intermediaries have been quite blunt – lawmakers around the world have typically not paid sufficient attention to the complex trade-offs that this book highlights. In this chapter, I'm not going to try provide a comprehensive answer to what different governments should do to address the challenges facing the internet. Instead, I want to emphasize four key points to keep in mind when evaluating policy proposals. Hopefully, when lawmakers are faced with the inevitable urgent desire to introduce new laws to govern activity on the internet, they might consider these issues and avoid some of the biggest problems in regulating intermediaries. This is admittedly a pretty optimistic hope (some would say naive). So, I also present these principles for all of us, as concerned citizens who care about the future of the internet, to try to demand better laws from our elected officials. These basic principles can help us evaluate proposed new laws in a great many different circumstances; they highlight what is most important in designing laws that encourage good governance and promote the ideal of a vibrant, flourishing, free, and innovative internet.

AVOIDING BAD LAWS

The first key point is that governments should avoid creating bad laws that cause people harm. This seems straightforward, but so many governments over the past two decades have been unable or unwilling to work through the difficulties of creating good law. There are different types of bad laws that aim to regulate the internet. There are laws that are bad because lawmakers are directly and intentionally trying to use their power in illegitimate ways that infringe on the rights of their own citizens and others, and then there are laws that have a justifiable objective but are bad mainly because they're poorly thought out and risk breaking the internet.

In the first category, governments too frequently create laws that are specifically designed to interfere with human rights. Rulers of oppressive regimes often see the internet's value for freedom of expression and association as a threat to their hold on power. As we saw in Chapter 6, countries like Egypt, Turkey, China, Russia, Saudi Arabia, and Iran – all nation-states that often perform badly on measures of media freedom[2] – have a reputation for creating restrictive rules that require internet companies to censor political speech that is critical of the regime.[3] When the former Egyptian government shut down the entire country's internet access to the outside world, it clearly contravened international human rights law. The Egyptian government tried to prevent people from using services like Facebook to organize protests and tried at the same time to restrict the flow of news about the revolution within the country and outside of it to the concerned international community looking on.[4] The government's goal was clearly not a valid one; trying desperately to hold on to power in the midst of a popular revolution is not a valid goal recognized by international law. The measures imposed by the former Egyptian government directly breach its duty to protect the rights to freedom of expression and freedom of association.[5]

The internet brings great benefits and opportunities to help social movements. It has become so crucial to the way we communicate that it is now vitally important to the functioning of democracy. It can be used to help coordinate, draw attention to, and nourish political action from small protests to large movements to overthrow authoritarian regimes.[6] This makes the internet powerful, but also makes it a key target for the powerful to try to control. Like social movements, the internet is both powerful and fragile.[7] These efforts to limit freedom of expression and association must be resisted, and the international community has a responsibility to try to prevent governments from abusing their power. When governments try to hold on to power by shutting down internet access or implementing political censorship, this should provoke widespread condemnation.

There are many groups working to ensure that the internet remains free, but governments are not doing enough to hold each other accountable for human rights violations. In 2011, the freedom of expression rapporteurs from the UN, the Organization for Security and Co-operation in Europe, the Organization of American States, and the African Commission on Human and Peoples' Rights issued a joint declaration that "Cutting off access to the Internet, or parts of the Internet, for whole populations or segments of the public (shutting down the Internet) can never be justified."[8] Access Now, a global advocacy group, leads the #keepiton campaign to monitor and protest deliberate moves by governments to shut down the internet or block certain mobile apps.[9] A large number of other civil society groups have worked tirelessly to resist internet censorship by governments for as long as the internet has been widely available. Unfortunately, censorship is getting worse, as governments become more sophisticated in their techniques and get access to more sophisticated technology to help them. Article 19, an NGO dedicated to protecting freedom of expression, publishes a metric that rates the state of freedom of expression and information internationally. It reports that "Internet censorship has dramatically increased since 2006," and that new threats have been emerging in recent years.[10] The Berkman Klein Center reports that these trends are increasing: more countries are blocking content, and they are getting more sophisticated about how they block content all the time.[11]

Even in liberal democracies, governments often pressure intermediaries to govern their citizens in illegitimate ways. The massive surveillance regime of the five-eyes countries – the United States, the United Kingdom, Canada, Australia, and New Zealand – works by collecting private information about users directly from telecommunications companies and laundering it through the intelligence agencies of foreign governments in order to avoid laws that prohibit governments from spying on their own citizens.[12] Many countries give power to their executive governments to require internet intermediaries to block websites or remove content, without adequate safeguards for due process.[13] Some of these regimes go much further than is permitted under international standards of freedom of expression. In some cases, governments even avoid their own constitutional protections by leaning on tech companies to remove or block access to extremist material, bullying content, or obscene content, even though the tech companies technically are not legally obliged to. One of the most notorious examples was the US government's informal pressure on technology companies after WikiLeaks published several troves of classified documents in 2010 relating to the conflict in Afghanistan and Iraq. The First Amendment prevents the US government from ordering technology companies to block WikiLeaks. Instead, government officials pressured Amazon, convincing it to drop hosting for WikiLeaks; PayPal, convincing it to stop processing donations to WikiLeaks, a move followed by MasterCard, Visa, Discover, and major banks; Apple, which pulled a WikiLeaks app from its store; WikiLeaks' domain registrar, which de-registered the domain; and even Tableau, a company that produces data-analysis tools, which had been presenting graphical analyses of the leaked documents.[14] By applying pressure informally, rather than through laws, governments are able to bypass constitutional protections that are designed to limit their power and protect the rights of their citizens. Constitutional protections don't apply because they still focus on an old model of governance, where only actual laws by the state are subject to review, not the "voluntary" practices of intermediaries.[15]

The second category of bad laws are laws that are unintentionally bad because they are not well designed. These are laws that address legitimate goals but are not sufficiently attuned to the challenges of regulating the internet. In the United States, the Stop Online Piracy Act/PROTECT IP acts (SOPA/PIPA), which were described in Chapter 5, were examples of laws that tried to achieve a legitimate goal (reducing copyright infringement) but that went about it in a way that would impose unacceptably large burdens on internet companies, to the great detriment of ordinary users. The campaigns against SOPA/PIPA focused on how they would "break the internet" by flipping the assumption that most people on the internet are behaving lawfully most of the time and instead requiring internet intermediaries to do much more to police what people post in advance.[16]

Both types of bad laws are easy to analyze through international human rights law. Most laws that affect the internet will have some impact on human rights – usually at least the right to freedom of expression or the right to privacy. Often, there will be other rights involved too, and some of these might be in conflict at times. Proposals to limit hate speech online, for example, are designed to promote the right to be free from vilification, and depending on how they are implemented might encourage or discourage freedom of speech. The tools developed by international human rights law provide mechanisms to identify and evaluate these effects. Concerns about underblocking hate speech and overblocking counter-speech, for example, can be expressed as a proportionality problem that is very familiar to human rights law. Proportionality requires the assessment of the risks that any given measure will infringe on rights, the likelihood that it will be effective at achieving its intended goals, and the justification that those goals are valid or desirable.[17] Only measures that are carefully tailored are permissible under human rights law. The benefits of this type of analysis is not that it guarantees a particular result, but that it provides a rigorous analytical approach to be able to understand and evaluate the impacts of government proposals on fundamental rights.[18]

In countries with strong human rights protections, courts are able to strike down laws that are not carefully tailored. This happened when France first introduced the HADOPI system, which would have required ISPs to disconnect their subscribers from the internet if they were alleged to have infringed on copyright by downloading films, television, and music. The French Constitutional Council struck down the law, finding that it was a penalty that was disproportionate to the harm that copyright owners would suffer and that it was likely to impermissibly interfere with rights to access information and communicate.[19] Other laws have been struck down on privacy grounds. For example, also in Europe, data retention laws that would require telecommunications providers and ISPs to store details about who their customers communicate with were invalidated because they interfered too much with privacy rights.[20] These processes encourage better legislation because governments can be required to prove to courts that the regulations they impose are both necessary and proportionate.

Other countries do not all have the same strong protection for human rights built into their constitutional systems. International human rights law can help at least to draw attention to some of these problems. The rights established under international law come with processes that can be used to judge whether laws are legitimate and to marshal pressure on governments intent on circumventing their own constitutional limitations. This, unfortunately, is where human rights law has been least effective in the past. Governments intent on introducing bad laws might be criticized in the international community, but many governments have ignored these criticisms in the past. Unless a country's courts are empowered to strike down illegitimate laws or the international community is willing to impose sanctions, the actual legal protections of international human rights law in practice are very weak.

This is not the book that will convince government intent on abusing the rights of their citizens to stop. Human rights law clearly says that Turkey and China should not censor political speech and that the United States, the United Kingdom, Canada, New Zealand, and Australia should not spy on their citizens in a mass surveillance regime. The most we can say here is that technology companies have a responsibility to resist obligations that would require them to infringe on the rights of their users. Apple, for example, should be commended for its efforts to resist requests from law enforcement personnel to weaken the encryption on its iPhones.[21] We should expect technology companies to challenge excessive demands in public and in the courts, even if they end up complying with valid court orders. We should encourage and support intermediaries to resist where they can and sometimes make decisions to ignore valid legal demands from countries that would infringe on human rights. We might also expect companies to refuse to do business in countries where they would be obliged to help restrict human rights. We should criticize Google, for example, for trying to build a censored search engine that would allow it to re-enter the Chinese market.[22] In all of these cases, though, intermediaries bear only part of the responsibility. Human rights are important tools in the ongoing work to pressure countries to do better, but getting countries to abide by human rights continues to be a major challenge in all areas, not just internet regulation.

CREATING LAWS THAT ENCOURAGE GOOD GOVERNANCE

In the rest of this book, let us focus on governments that want to regulate the internet in ways that do not infringe on human rights. The key takeaway message of this book, for governments, is that the challenges of regulating the internet in a legitimate manner are not going to be solved just by making intermediaries liable for what their users do. Obviously, targeting intermediaries is often the most efficient strategy, but good regulation cannot stop there. When we make intermediaries liable, we just exacerbate the problem of lawlessness. For example, a law that requires social media platforms to address hate speech that is posted within twenty-four hours, like NetzDG does in Germany, might reduce the amount of hate circulating on major platforms. Or the so-called Right to Be Forgotten might create an effective obligation on search engines to remove links to content that infringes on the privacy rights of individuals, including old news stories about their past. Reasonable people differ in their opinions about whether these rules strike the right balance between protecting freedom of speech and limiting harm, and the calculus is different in different jurisdictions. But whatever you think about the substance of these rules, the common problem is *procedural*: if a government is going to introduce new internet regulation, how should it operate to ensure that the rules are legitimately enforced? When governments require platforms and search engines to decide what counts as hate speech or which news reports are in the public interest, they sometimes do not pay sufficient attention to *how* these decisions are made. This problem gets much worse when the law creates a lopsided incentive that encourages intermediaries to remove content when they are in doubt. The trap for lawmakers to avoid here is the pitfall of requiring intermediaries to make decisions that affect us all in a way that cannot be described as legitimate. If they are not carefully designed, these types of laws can create systems of censorship that undermine democratic oversight and limit protections for fundamental rights.

Designing good laws that regulate the internet is not easy, and the political conflicts at stake make progress in internet governance debates extremely difficult. Different stakeholders are frequently talking at cross-purposes, and there are real substantive political differences. Pressure to regulate the internet is mounting, and internet intermediaries are subject to an increasing range of demands from all sides. They're under pressure from governments to help enforce laws against their users, from other businesses to regulate in their favor, from groups of vocal users with conflicting demands, and from a very wide range of civil society organizations with diverse priorities that often disagree. Take, for example, the problem of dealing with abuse and hate speech. Some governments, like the previously mentioned example of Germany, have introduced laws requiring platforms to very quickly remove hate speech, but the distinction between lawful political expression and unlawful hate speech, vilification, or incitement to violence differs from country to country. Some governments, like Turkey, use incitement to violence as a pretext for requiring platforms to clamp down on political speech that is critical of the regime. Other countries, like the United States, have much stricter definitions for protected speech and are constitutionally prevented from requiring intermediaries to remove a large range of content that other countries deem unlawful. At the same time, civil society groups are deeply divided about what intermediaries should do. Those groups that focus on freedom of speech want commitments from intermediaries to not stifle legitimate expression and worry about the silencing of minority voices. Other civil society organizations, concerned about the spread of abuse and hate and its consequences, want intermediaries to be much more active in removing content and banning known abusive figures and groups. And then there's the technical groups that would often prefer that these messy social distinctions are dealt with by others, leaving the engineers to get on with the task of keeping a "neutral" internet running.

Creating good rules that impose obligations on technology companies requires governments to pay more attention to the impact the rules will inevitably have on the human rights of individuals. Over the past two decades of laws designed to regulate the internet, very few have been able to do this effectively. Individual users of the internet are the targets of regulation, but when laws focus on the obligations of intermediaries to police their users, the interests of users are often neglected.[23] In large part, this is because many laws end up being developed in a compromise between the technology and telecommunications sector, on the one hand, and the well-organized lobby group pushing for new regulations on the other. One of the core problems in internet policymaking is that it is often so furiously contested that the different stakeholders rarely work together to develop tailored laws – which means when one side finally wins the political battle, the rules are often overly broad and not well suited to the difficult technical and social challenges of regulating the internet. Alternatively, when stakeholders do work together, the laws that emerge are often compromises between the interests of the tech sector and the other side, but the individuals who are the ultimate targets of regulation are not well represented. The DMCA, for example, struck a compromise between copyright owners and tech companies, but it has few effective protections for the rights of individuals.[24] This is a problem that happens often in copyright, where there are powerful established interests but where individuals are not well organized. But it also happens in other areas, where as long as the tech industry's interests are protected, it is willing to agree to rules that might harm users.

The interests of internet users – the public interest – is usually only represented by a handful of digital rights organizations, with comparatively much less influence in the political process. User interests have been able to be protected when they align with the interests of the tech sector. But often, technology companies are most worried about their own legal risks and costs. Time and again, around the world, when these concerns are dealt with, the resulting legislation is a compromise position that marginalizes the rights of individual users.

It's not possible to avoid heated debates about the goals of regulation. This type of debate is a fundamental part of the political process of a functioning democracy. But it should be possible to come to a better agreement about how laws should be designed to best achieve their goals while limiting the negative impact they have on our fundamental rights. Here's where international human rights law can help. Human rights don't remove the political differences, but they do provide a common language for debate.

Focusing on human rights means that the impact of any proposed law on people must be a primary concern. All internet regulation involves human rights interests in some way. The most common concerns revolve around freedom of expression and privacy, but any given proposal might involve other rights as well. The common demand we should all have of lawmakers is that rules designed to govern the internet have a legitimate purpose, are reasonably likely to be effective, and don't go further than necessary to achieve that goal.

The Manila Principles set out the most important human rights considerations when dealing with laws designed to regulate internet content.[25] One of the primary points made by the civil society organizations responsible for designing these principles is that governments should not be liable for what their users say or do online. This is extremely important – when governments are trying to regulate the internet, their first inclination is usually to try to make technology companies do the work. This is understandable, of course; the scale of most internet content problems means that we need to rely on intermediaries to develop effective solutions.

The Manila Principles don't prohibit governments from turning to intermediaries for assistance in enforcing the law. Rather, they focus on *how* internet companies are compelled to regulate. The core threat that the Manila Principles warn about is the danger of lopsided incentives. Often laws designed to address a type of problematic content will simply make internet intermediaries liable for what their users do. Where content hosts, search engines, and social media platforms can't rely on a blanket immunity like CDA 230, or a detailed procedure like the DMCA regime for copyright notice and takedown, they have to make decisions about the likelihood that they will get sued (or be criminally responsible) if they don't remove content. Inevitably, this means that firms will remove content that they're not legally required to remove. Some firms will have a greater appetite for risk and might push back on demands they receive, but, overall, this type of legal uncertainty leads to the chilling of speech. The risks of liability are often too great, and firms are only liable if they fail to remove prohibited content, not if they choose to remove lawful material.

This is why safe harbors are so important. Laws that make intermediaries liable for certain types of content and require them to make decisions about what content to remove or block pose a major threat to freedom of speech. Content hosts in countries without safe harbor protections invariably respond quickly to legal threats demanding that they remove content on their network. Most of them build in quite restrictive rules into their own policies, to minimize the risk that people might complain in the future. Some companies have an admirable commitment to freedom of speech and will develop their own standards for the risk they're willing to bear. But, in general, lopsided liability regimes make companies more likely to refuse to publish something that is lawful when they are in doubt.

But safe harbor regimes that are too strong can also undermine our fundamental rights. Safe harbors like CDA 230, along with contract law that allows intermediaries the broad discretion to set their own rules, combine to create a lawless zone, in which intermediaries are free to regulate their users as they see fit, with minimal responsibilities to govern legitimately. Intermediaries are almost completely immune from liability for what their users say but are also given total discretion to control users' speech. Some scholars are strongly supportive of the broad immunity, on the basis that the market will eventually force platforms to demonstrate that their governance systems are legitimate.[26] Others are not as convinced; in the words of Rebecca Tushnet, a professor at Harvard Law School, CDA 230 "allows Internet intermediaries to have their free speech and everyone else's too."[27]

The strong protection that CDA 230 provides is under a great deal of pressure.[28] The immunity that it provides means that internet companies often have no legal incentive to police content that is clearly unlawful, false, or harmful.[29] Particularly for sites that thrive on hosting harmful content and can ignore social pressure, like Hunter Moore's revenge porn site, this immunity often seems far too strong.[30] Tarleton Gillespie points out that, historically, when the media and communications sector was given a major benefit like this, it came with some matching conditions.[31] These conditions could create responsibilities for the sector to act in the public interest in some way – like a telephone company's obligations to serve everyone in an area or a broadcaster's duty to carry certain types of content. CDA 230 gives internet intermediaries all the power to control content but none of the responsibility that usually entails. Originally, CDA 230 was part of a package that required internet companies to block access to adult content. This was an overly broad restriction on freedom of speech, and the Supreme Court struck down that obligation but left the immunity.

It would be disastrous to remove CDA 230 altogether. The incredible, empowering diversity of the internet as we know it only works because internet companies are not required to screen the content we post in advance against all manners of difficult-to-interpret laws.[32] But this does not mean that CDA 230 could not come with other obligations. Like many others, Tushnet would prefer to see a scheme that imposes obligations on how internet intermediaries censor speech; in order to protect users rights, she argues, it would be better to only grant immunity in exchange for some guarantee of due process, a prohibition on discrimination, or some form of democratic self-governance to ensure that rules are fairly created and enforced.[33] Gillespie suggests a quid pro quo that could require greater transparency, a minimum standard of due process, and better consultation with regulators and external experts.[34] Mark Lemley, a law professor at Stanford University, suggests that an ideal safe harbor would provide people with a legal claim mechanism to identify anonymous posters who had caused them harm, would provide a quick and cheap procedure to remove objectionable material, but would also discourage intermediaries from automatically siding with people who complain at the expense of their users.[35] These types of changes could go a long way toward rebalancing the obligations of internet intermediaries and creating effective and efficient processes to enforce the law, while still protecting the rights of internet users.

There is a lot to be done to fix laws that attempt to regulate users through internet intermediaries. Countries without effective safe harbors should find ways to protect internet intermediaries from liability to better protect the freedom of expression. But at the same time, governments will have to work out what new obligations are appropriate to impose on intermediaries. The Manila Principles can help point the way toward developing internet regulation that enlists the help of intermediaries without unduly restricting freedom of expression. The most important principle is to try to minimize the discretion that intermediaries need to exercise. If intermediaries are to be expected to enforce the law by moderating content that their users create or access, then it should be very clear what they are obliged to do. We should generally try to reduce their discretion by providing clear guidelines that explain what type of evidence a complainant needs to show to support a valid takedown request. Intermediaries should be able to safely operate with the knowledge that, if they follow the procedures set out by the law, they will not be liable for honest mistakes. And the users who are going to be impacted by a takedown or block preferably need to know how they can contest it in advance, or at the very least how they can appeal it afterwards.

The massive scale of the internet is still the most difficult problem. For any rule to be useful at a large scale, it has to be cheap to enforce regularly. But for enforcement to be cheap, decisions need to be automated, distributed out to users, or made quickly by platforms. Due process suffers in each case: automated systems often contain hidden biases; enforcement mechanisms that rely on users to make decisions can be gamed; and moderators making hundreds or even thousands of decisions per day will inevitably make mistakes, miss important context, or disagree on the correct interpretation and application of the rules. At such a massive scale, even a slight error rate still results in a great many mistakes every day.

If intermediaries are to be legally required to remove or block content, developing a scalable system of due process is critically important. So far, there are no good takedown regimes for internet content. The DMCA is the most widely used, as we have seen in Chapter 5, but it is too rigid. Its counter-notice regime has no ability to offer parties with demonstrably good histories the benefit of the doubt, which means that it is subject to abuse by unscrupulous copyright owners and unscrupulous uploaders. The counter-notice system is also lopsided in its voluntariness. A host does not have to follow the takedown procedures at the request of a copyright owner, but it usually faces a real threat of litigation and liability under copyright law if it doesn't. Conversely, because a host can never be liable for wrongfully removing content, it doesn't have to follow the counter-notice scheme – and users have no recourse if their counter-notice is ignored. The biggest problem with the scheme is that there is no cheap intermediate stage to resolve disputes – if the parties disagree, the only way out is a full copyright trial, which is expensive and slow. This means that disputes rarely get resolved properly.

The so-called three-strikes regimes that were introduced several years ago provide another good example of what can go wrong when governments require telecommunications companies to do regulatory work, without developing adequate due process safeguards. The idea, as we saw in Chapter 5, was to get ISPs to enforce copyright rules against their subscribers by forwarding on allegations of infringement and imposing access restrictions and suspensions on subscribers who receive multiple strikes. These were almost all bad schemes from which we can learn a lot. They failed on basic measures of due process: they tried to fix the problem of regulating at scale by doing away with legitimate oversight. Copyright owners had an incentive to send as many notices as they could, as quickly and cheaply as possible, and the quality of these notices was often questionable at best. The ISPs had little incentive to investigate the claims in the thousands of notices they received, and, even if they wanted to, they had no way to evaluate whether the claims were true or not. ISPs are not courts – they don't have the ability to compel evidence, evaluate competing claims, and make a legitimate finding about the facts. This means that there's no legitimate way to impose a penalty on a subscriber based on the mere allegation of a copyright owner.[36]

Graduated response schemes are examples of the types of laws that simply cannot be effective and proportionate at a large scale. The penalties they contemplated were serious – disconnection from the internet for an entire household is a big deal – and the harm they were designed to address, illicitly downloading a film that might cost a few dollars to rent, was trivial by comparison. After the first schemes were rejected, some countries tried to introduce schemes that included due process safeguards, including using administrative tribunals to make decisions and allowing full access to the judicial system in the case of serious disputes. These schemes have been almost complete failures because the costs of enforcing a copyright claim in a legitimate way far exceeds the value to the copyright owner.

All of this, of course, was known to the copyright lobby and the governments that implemented these schemes beforehand, but they were never forced to think through the implications of their proposals. If they had been, they might instead have saved a great deal of effort and focused on developing solutions that were actually likely to work (like investing in cheap and convenient marketplaces and streaming services).[37]

There are long-term lessons to be learned from these schemes that can be applied to other laws. Intermediaries are not well placed to make decisions about whether material or behavior is lawful or not. If they have to make a decision about whether something is lawful, they are not set up with the independent protections that courts have for anyone to trust that their decision is legitimate. If it is difficult to work out whether a claim is valid or not in relation to an issue that affects a person's rights, this is the stage where we should involve the judicial system. This is not to say that every request to remove content on the internet needs to come from a court – that would be far too slow to be effective, in most cases. Instead, it is possible to design takedown schemes that don't rely on intermediaries to evaluate whether a complaint is accurate but that allow any disputes to be resolved by an independent process. Ultimately, we should be able to envisage a system of oversight that includes an escalating series of reviews by arbitrators, tribunals, and courts until disputes are resolved. This is the common structure of legal due process that allows societies to have confidence in decisions without requiring expensive and slow bureaucratic processes at every turn. The tribunals lower down in the hierarchy are cheaper processes that can quickly check that decisions appear to be properly made, and most disputes can be resolved relatively rapidly. For the small proportion of serious disputes that remain, these might be escalated to the normal courts of the land, which have the power and impartiality required to investigate the facts at issue and to rule on the application of the law.

This is an area for experimentation, as the pressure on governments to regulate the internet continues to grow. The current models of regulating intermediaries are not well suited to dealing with these problems, and our legal systems are not well equipped to deal with disputes on a massive scale. These are of course difficult trade-offs: if we require a court order before an intermediary is obliged to remove content, nations will never be able to enforce their democratically created laws. But, without judicial oversight, there will inevitably be mistakes, and there are no guarantees that they will be fixed. The only legitimate approach to enforce laws online at scale must be to experiment in the middle ground – to find ways to move between cheap and routine enforcement by platforms and other internet intermediaries and a series of escalating processes that provide independent review where it is needed. In the coming years, as governments consider new laws to regulate internet content, developing effective schemes of due process that work at scale will become critically important.

ADDRESSING HUMAN RIGHTS VIOLATIONS

In the last two chapters, I suggested that tech companies could usefully develop their own constitutional rules to better deal with many of these issues. The nonbinding UNGPs provide good guidance about how they can start down this path. But these principles are not likely to be sufficient, on their own, to achieve lasting and fundamental social change and adequate protection for human rights. There are serious limits to the extent that tech companies are going to be willing to self-regulate, and they will not be able to address all the many and varied concerns people have about internet content and behavior on their own.

Constitutionalizing internet intermediaries – reducing their discretionary power – is not an easy thing for a government to legitimately do. Legally, there is a world of difference between the duties that governments owe to their citizens and what we expect from online platforms making decisions about their networks. Governments are subject to stricter rules because they have a monopoly on the use of force; that is, the rules are ultimately backed by police forces and the state's military strength. Jack Balkin, a constitutional law professor at Yale University and expert on the First Amendment, made this point in 2004, when thinking about the types of rules that should apply to the internet. As a thought experiment, imagine a game that simulates the rules of a Soviet-era prison camp in Siberia – rules that would, if imposed without consent, clearly breach human rights. We would want to support the rights of developers and players to create and participate in The Gulag Online; both clearly have freedom of expression interests in the experience.[38] Likewise, we would not want courts to interfere when a group of friends set specific rules about acceptable topics of conversation in a forum dedicated to their book club.

But the issue becomes much more problematic when we deal with larger platforms that feel like public spaces. Sarah Jeong, in her book *The Internet of Garbage*, explains that "large-scale platforms are different. Although they are technically private property and not subject to First Amendment speech protections even when their users and servers are based in the US, they are beginning to resemble public squares of discussion and debate, the main staging grounds of the kind of speech that connects people to other people and forms the foundation of democracy."[39] In a recent interview with *Wired*, Twitter CEO Jack Dorsey explained that

> A lot of people come to Twitter and they don't see a service. They see what looks like a public square and they have the same expectation as they have of a public square.[40]

Dorsey is right. These services *feel* like public spaces, even if they're not legally treated the same.

It is clear that private platforms have a substantial impact on our fundamental rights in practice. David Kaye, the UN Special Rapporteur on the Promotion and Protection of the Right to Freedom of Opinion and Expression, argues that these old distinctions between public and private spaces are no longer fully appropriate for the digital age. In a recent report, Kaye explains that "In the digital environment, human rights impacts may arise in internal decisions on how to respond to government requests to restrict content or access customer information, the adoption of terms of service, design and engineering choices that implicate security and privacy, and decisions to provide or terminate services in a particular market."[41] The rules that private companies adopt are often vague or unpredictable, and they are enforced inconsistently. Platforms find themselves caught between demands that they do more to regulate offensive content – like abuse or copyright infringement – and demands that they stand up for their users' rights to speak and to seek information.

There's no easy answer yet about what different societies expect from digital media platforms. We wouldn't want even the largest platforms to be bound by the same rules that regulate state power. A massive part of the attraction of digital platforms is that they curate and moderate content. As Gillespie explains, moderation is the key commodity that platforms offer.[42] Users expect Google to exercise judgment about which links are more relevant to searchers, and many users expect Facebook to try to present updates in a way that prioritizes the content they want to see. These decisions might often be controversial, but the massive flood of information available on the internet means we rely on certain gatekeepers and tastemakers to curate the content we see. If private companies couldn't discriminate between different content and sources, we would lose a lot of the value of the internet.[43]

And yet we do often feel aggrieved when private companies make decisions on grounds we don't approve of. We worry about the rules of platforms in a way that discriminates on the basis of gender, race, or religion. We worry about the algorithms that search engines and other companies use to rank content that embed these biases in a way that invisibly shapes our information environment.[44] We worry about political bias, like when Facebook employees seemed to curate lists of trending news articles in a way that favored the candidate Hillary Clinton over Donald Trump in the presidential election, or later when it failed to deal with Russian interference that favored Trump and, some think, delivered up the presidency. We worry about Instagram blocking innocent images of women with average or larger body sizes, and we worry about it not doing enough to block hateful and abusive images.

There are people working hard within major technology companies to improve the way their systems work. I am optimistic that social pressure from a wide network of activists, civil society groups, journalists, and intergovernmental organizations can help convince intermediaries to constitutionalize on their own, but I'm not naive enough to think this will work in all cases or well enough to fix all of the problems we have seen over the past twenty years or are likely to see in future.

International human rights law requires governments to enact rules that protect the rights of their citizens. When technology companies act in ways that are harmful to human rights, governments have obligations under international law to change the rules that regulate those companies.[45] The challenge of relying on human rights to improve the business practices of internet companies is that they're not law, and, therefore, they don't come with binding legal penalties. The human rights responsibilities of businesses are largely voluntary, which means that, although they have some serious momentum, they are not actually enforceable in any real sense. Global advocacy groups have expressed a great deal of skepticism about the voluntary framework set out by the guiding principles. Human Rights Watch has called the guiding principles a woefully inadequate approach to business and human rights issues. That is because without any mechanism to ensure compliance or to measure implementation, they cannot actually require companies to do anything at all. Companies can reject the principles altogether without consequence – or publicly embrace them while doing absolutely nothing to put them into practice. The principles do not explicitly insist that governments regulate companies with the requisite scope and rigor; they also fail to push governments hard enough to ensure that companies respect human rights.[46]

Groups like Human Rights Watch and Amnesty International believe that binding legal obligations are required to hold corporations responsible for their impact on human rights. Many human rights scholars are also critical of the compromises struck to achieve consensus in the UNGPs, which has resulted in the watering down of duties not to violate rights in favor of a "responsibility to respect."[47] Some scholars warn that voluntary compliance with human rights standards is only likely to work when it is backed up by legally binding obligations.[48] Real, meaningful legal obligations would require governments to introduce new laws that require companies to undertake regular assessments and report on their impact on human rights, as well as the introduction of enforceable legal remedies where a company is found to have breached its duties under international human rights standards of due diligence.[49]

At the very least, where technology companies are not able to adequately protect our rights themselves, we will need smart and well-crafted laws that can make them more accountable. For governments to meet their obligations to protect human rights, they will need to actively monitor the extent to which human rights violations are being adequately dealt with through the voluntary actions of businesses. In some circumstances, we will need specific laws that try to change industry practice. Where technology companies are failing to adequately protect fundamental rights, governments have direct obligations under human rights law to intervene and change their domestic laws to better protect the people they are responsible for. For example, tech companies have not been able to adequately protect vulnerable groups of people from human rights violations perpetrated via digital technologies. Groups against domestic violence warn that telecommunications technologies are routinely used as tools of coercion and control to perpetrate violence against women, and governments may need to step in to oblige technology companies to build better safeguards into their tools or develop better responses when people are at risk.[50] We have also seen that many technical systems work to reinforce and exacerbate discrimination on racial grounds, and these biases are being built into automated systems that influence many aspects of ordinary social life.[51] When the algorithms and policies of tech companies work to discriminate on the basis of race or other protected characteristics, or to help their users to unlawfully discriminate, governments have a role to play in protecting equality and reducing discrimination. These are just a few examples; there will be many more issues that arise where the discretionary power of tech companies needs to be curtailed in the public interest.

DIGITAL CONSTITUTIONALISM: MONITORING AND
IMPROVING GOVERNANCE

There are a few different approaches to regulation that can address some of the problems raised by the unchecked discretion of technology companies over our lives. Only one approach – the self-constitutionalization of technology companies – can maintain the autonomy and diversity that makes the internet so special. Other approaches are necessarily more blunt. They require either breaking up massive technology companies under antitrust rules to reduce their power or embedding heavy bureaucratic oversight that strips them of their discretion and unique flavor. If we care about an open, vibrant, flourishing internet, and we care about how our social spaces are governed, we have to do better than either of those options. We have to imagine new ways to hold technology companies (and those who influence them in turn) accountable.

One of the fundamental challenges of regulating advanced technologies is that technological development often outstrips the pace of innovation in regulatory tools that might be used to govern it.[52] In these situations, regulation often lags behind or doesn't quite fit the technology it seeks to address.[53] The difficulty is exacerbated because public regulatory agencies face major challenges in monitoring and understanding the social effects of technological change. Private companies are investing heavily in research and development, and there are information asymmetries between those companies and public regulators seeking to understand the potential impact of new technologies.[54] From a public regulator's perspective, the design of many new technologies are often opaque, largely incomprehensible, and sometimes even unknowable.[55] Even when regulators are able to obtain better information about technical systems, they are often not well equipped or resourced to predict what effects they may have on individuals, societies, and economies.[56]

The challenge of digital constitutionalism is to find new, hybrid forms of accountability that promote both autonomy and accountability.[57] Digital constitutionalism ultimately has to be driven from within technology companies. The work of governance, for the most part, is ordinary. It happens in routine decisions and day-to-day interactions that shape a social system. Making this everyday work more legitimate – subject to real limits with real accountability – can only be done through internal reflection.[58] External laws can set real obligations, but this just shifts the boundaries of the lawless zone of discretion that intermediaries enjoy. The essence of digital constitutionalism is not so much about these boundaries – the exceptions where governments have to intervene with actual laws and familiar legal tools – but is instead concerned with the everyday, routine exercise of power. Legal compliance at the edges will not drive the cultural change upon which the process of constitutionalization depends. Importantly, though, industry-led constitutionalization does not mean the development of independent systems cutoff from the rest of society. The internet is not a separate place, and technology companies always operate within an existing social system.

The aim of constitutionalizing internet governance is, therefore, not to create new, separate, and independent spaces, but to develop new governance structures that work in a heavily decentralized context. This is a major challenge – existing models of constitutionalism are not at all adapted to decentralized systems. Traditional constitutionalism proceeds on the basis that the state is the most important source of power and, therefore, focuses on holding governments accountable. Digital constitutionalism must instead find a way to regulate power that is distributed among many actors within complex systems with many separate interacting components. For governments, this means radically rethinking how regulation can operate in a decentered environment – where the state is not the only, or even the most powerful, actor seeking to regulate behavior.[59] Effective decentered regulation must be "hybrid (combining governmental and non-governmental actors), multifaceted (using a number of different strategies simultaneously or sequentially), and indirect."[60]

The challenge ahead is to develop hybrid systems of accountability that promote legitimate governance among the many different and interconnected actors that influence our online lives. Governments have an important role to play here: if technology companies are to constitutionalize their internal processes and become more accountable, governments can and must encourage and support them to do so. Actually achieving cultural change among technology companies means that diverse external forces, including governments wielding soft regulatory power and creating hard laws, as well as wide range of civil society – users, NGOs, journalists, academics, trade unions, professional organizations, and so on – must be able to "exert such massive pressure on the ... system so that it will be constrained to build up internal self-limitations that actually work."[61] This pressure then has to be sustained over time, so that the system remains accountable both to its users and to those external stakeholders who are in some way affected by what its users do.

There is no easy answer to guide the process of digital constitutionalism. There is no single model that will work in all circumstances; rather, the goal must be to work toward a diversity of systems that are accountable and legitimate to their users and to the external stakeholders that they affect. Ideally, good digital constitutionalism would promote the autonomy of technology companies to develop their own rules and deliver useful and innovative networks and services. It would encourage diversity in rules and design and allow different networks to adapt governance structures that align with the expectations of users and each platform's unique flavor and context. At the same time, it must also ensure that there are appropriate external limits on the autonomy of these systems that reflect the baseline expectations of democratically created laws. So far, this is not too far off from what we have now – intermediaries are free to govern their networks within the limits established by the law. The core differences, for a constitutionalized system, are that the power of platforms must be limited by clear rules, with working systems of review, in a way that is accountable both to users and external stakeholders (including government regulators, but also groups of people whose rights are somehow affected by what people do through the platform).

Working out how to best progress the project of digital constitutionalism is still an unsolved challenge. What accountability means and looks like will differ greatly according to place, time, culture, and context. The one thing that is clear is that, in order to progress these debates, we will need a lot more knowledge about how we are governed by a complex interrelated network of infrastructure, software, governments, technology companies, and other actors. Identifying the impact of all of these actors will require a great deal of work in order to understand how these networks operate at a systems level. Because information is so fragmented, this can only be done through extensive collaboration. There is a pressing need for strong, multistakeholder networks of industry, civil society, academic researchers, journalists, and public agencies that are empowered to monitor the development and deployment of new technologies against human rights standards.[62]

We are still at an early stage in working out how to hold accountable those who exercise power through networked technologies. The most important issue that governments can focus on in the immediate future is encouraging understanding of these incredibly complex issues. This means prioritizing increased transparency from technology companies, perhaps through legally mandated disclosure requirements. It also means fostering ongoing opportunities for multistakeholder collaboration and sharing of information and expertise. Eventually, it will mean taking targeted legal action to encourage the constitutionalization of technology companies and creating new oversight mechanisms to hold these processes accountable. Before we get there, though, we will need a great deal more participation from other sectors of society – journalists, academics, NGOs representing all manners of social issues, and industry groups, as well as networks of user communities. We may be at a constitutional moment, but that just means that the hard work to develop consensus about a new constitutionalism is just beginning.

12

Conclusion

Digital intermediaries govern the internet. The telecommunications companies that provide the infrastructure, the standards organizations that design the protocols, the software companies that create the tools, the content hosts that store the data, the search engines that index that data, and the social media platforms that connect us all make decisions that impact how we communicate on a broad level. They govern us, not in the way that nation-states do, but through design choices that shape what is possible, through algorithms that sort what is visible, and through policies that control what is permitted. The choices these intermediaries make reflect our preferences, but also those of advertisers, governments, lobby groups, and their own visions of right and wrong.

Technology companies govern, but they are losing popular support. Legitimacy, in governance terms, comes from the consent of the governed – a common acceptance that those that exert power over us have the right to govern us. For years, technology companies have been able to justify their prerogative to govern the same way other companies do – because we choose to use their services in a competitive marketplace. Up until this moment, we might have said that tech companies' right to govern comes from the contracts we enter into. The market provided legitimacy: we, as consumers, each choose to abide by their rules, no matter how poorly they are defined or how arbitrarily they are enforced. If these intermediaries are seen as just providing services to consumers, who are free to vote with their wallets, then their actions are almost certainly legitimate, but as the influence of technology companies on our lives becomes clearer, these companies need to do more to justify themselves and maintain their legitimacy.

Slowly, tech companies have been losing our collective consent. The tide of public opinion is now challenging the assumed right that technology companies have to govern our lives in the way that they do. The pressure on technology companies to be more accountable is growing steadily. This pressure has been building for years because technology companies have been making decisions that affect us all behind closed doors, without any real accountability. It increases with every shock and controversy that casts doubt on whether the industry has our best interests at heart or is doing as much as we would like to fight all manner of bad actors online. This pressure is fed by media industries that delight in attacking technology companies – particularly those parts of the mainstream media that have suffered the most in the shift to digital and blame big tech for their ongoing struggles. It's stoked by governments that want to protect their citizens from the dangers of the internet (or at least look like they are) and by governments that want to better control their citizens through technology companies.

This pressure is not sustainable in the long term. No matter how benevolent and thoughtful tech executives appear to be, the lack of transparency and accountability will continue to breed allegations that they are uncaring, incompetent, biased, or even just downright evil. No matter how much technology companies protest, their central power as focal nodes on the internet makes them irresistible targets for people who want better control over users.

The core argument of this book is that, because online intermediaries play such a crucial role in regulating how users behave, we should find a way to ensure that their decisions are legitimately made. For this, we need what I call digital constitutionalism. Traditional constitutionalism focuses on power exercised by the state and is not well adapted to ensuring that the decisions of private actors are legitimately made. A more modern view of regulation can help us to understand that the type of power that intermediaries exercise over users is a type of governance power and that this power is subject to influence by a wide range of different actors. This recognition requires us to pay attention to the work that intermediaries do to govern the internet, as well as the different methods that state governments, the private sector, the media, and civil society use to influence the practices of inter-mediaries. Once we recognize how the internet is governed in practice, it becomes clearer that traditional ways of thinking about how the exercise of power is made legitimate are no longer adequate to protect people online.

There is no simple, single definition of what it means to govern legitimately. It is impossible to define, because it is a concept that depends fundamentally on context and constantly changes. People who exercise power have legitimacy because we collectively give it to them. So, whether social media platforms, search engines, content hosts, telecommunications companies, and other entities are acting legitim-ately when they shape our actions and our environment depends on how much we expect from them. This is still very much up for grabs; we are still in the early days of the commercial internet, and we do not yet have an easy answer or even common agreement on the exact shape of the limits people want to see imposed on the power of tech companies.

Working out what limits we, as a society, want to impose on the exercise of power in the digital age is the first challenge of digital constitutionalism. Constitutionalism is fundamentally about the limitation of governance power; *digital* constitutionalism requires us to think about not just national governments, but also about how the power that platforms wield ought to be limited. It is important to emphasize that digital constitutionalism does not mean we would want to treat private intermediaries as if they were exactly like nation-states. We hold governments to a higher standard of legitimacy because they control armies and police, can levy taxes and imprison us, and are responsible for maintaining and organizing our core social and physical infrastructures – from education, health care, and social security, to roads and public utilities. The high standard of legitimacy we hold governments to comes at a major bureaucratic cost. It would be disastrous to try to apply these standards directly to private platforms and telecom providers.

Human rights is probably the most powerful tool we have to encourage intermediaries to make their governance processes more legitimate. The language of human rights provides a universally agreed-upon set of values that governments and businesses should work to promote. These values – and the responsibilities that accompany them – provide a useful way of making explicit concerns over the constitution of our shared online social spaces. The voluntary component of human rights compliance is already helping to set standards for what intermediaries should do, and it provides a guide for civil society to work cooperatively to amplify the pressure for more legitimate processes. The frame of human rights can also guide governments to implement better laws, with binding legal obligations. Human rights do not enforce themselves, and they are not sufficient to hold technology companies accountable, but they do provide a common language that we can use to build consensus about what we expect from those who govern us.

The key next steps toward accountability in platform governance are both straightforward and very difficult. Platforms should immediately improve their transparency practices, focusing on how they can help people understand decisions that affect them and their systems as a whole. They should hire human rights lawyers and empower them to review and advise about improving technical features and business practices. Platforms will need to reach out more to others in working through some of the tough decisions they will have to make – they should cultivate stronger relationships with experts, civil society groups, government regulators, and find some new ways to encourage genuine participation from their user communities. The rules that platforms develop should be clearer and better justified, and they must start to experiment with new systems of independent review and appeals processes that adequately deal with inevitable mistakes.

The second challenge of digital constitutionalism is building enough consensus and enough social pressure to force technology companies to create their own constitutional limits. Rulers usually do not give up power voluntarily. We are at a constitutional moment now, where change might be possible but is by no means guaranteed. For all of us who care about how the internet is governed, now is the time to work together to hold power accountable. We need to make visible the influence that technology companies have on our lives and the influence that others have on them in turn. We need to trace how governments and private interests regulate how we behave and communicate; what we can see and share; and how we live, love, and work through the technologies that we use. For those of us who are academic researchers, this means we need to devise new research methods that can help us understand complex regulatory systems, made up of human and technical components, at massive scales, over time, and across national borders and platform boundaries. For this, we will need better data, and we should be working with technology companies and governments to ensure that good data is made available and accessible for ongoing research. We will also need new theory to understand how power can and should be held to account in a decentralized environment.

And then we will need to mobilize. We will need to seize this moment to marshal and coordinate pressure on technology companies to fundamentally change their cultures – to recognize that, as powerful governors of our social lives, they owe us real accountability. At the same time, we need to resist the efforts of governments around the world to introduce new restrictions that unjustifiably limit our freedoms or threaten the conditions for autonomy and innovation that make the internet so great.

All of this means that we need new collaborations. We do not yet have the institutions that are able to regularly and consistently hold power to account at scale. A digital constitutionalism requires not just change from platforms, but new structures that can monitor compliance, continue to exert pressure, and address wrongdoing. There is a role for courts and legislatures here, but there is also a need for new institutions that can more effectively marshal social pressure in day-to-day governance where the legal system is too cumbersome. These new institutions require some imagination – we will have to invent them. Academics, activists, and journalists will have to work together to engage tech companies, governments, and concerned users. As for concerned users, it's easy to feel disempowered, but there is great power in collective action. For all of us, it's time to participate in the emerging debates about how we want our shared social spaces to be governed, to make our concerns heard to governments and technology companies, and to lend our support to the activists and the civil society organizations fighting for our freedoms.

Achieving real change is not going to be easy, but what is at stake is the possibility of constructing an internet that is vibrant, diverse, and accountable. There's a lot of work ahead of us, but never has there been a better opportunity to make serious change than now.

Notes

1 THE HIDDEN RULES OF THE INTERNET

1 Joe Heim, "Recounting a Day of Rage, Hate, Violence and Death," *Washington Post*, August 14, 2017, www.washingtonpost.com/graphics/2017/local/charlottesville-timeline/; see also, Jason Wilson, "Charlottesville Reveals an Emboldened Far Right That Can No Longer Be Ignored," *The Guardian*, August 14, 2017, www.theguardian.com/world/2017/aug/14/charlottesville-far-right-neo-nazis-violence.

2 Andrew Anglin, "Heather Heyer: Woman Killed in Road Rage Incident Was a Fat, Childless 32-Year-Old Slut," *The Daily Stormer*, August 13, 2017, www.dailystormer.com/heather-heyer-woman-killed-in-road-rage-incident-was-a-fat-childless-32-year-old-slut/.

3 Keegan Hankes, "Eye of the Stormer," *Intelligence Report*, February 9, 2017, www.splcenter.org/fighting-hate/intelligence-report/2017/eye-stormer.

4 Ibid.

5 Ken Schwencke, "How One Major Internet Company Helps Serve Up Hate on the Web," *ProPublica*, May 4, 2017, www.propublica.org/article/how-cloudflare-helps-serve-up-hate-on-the-web.

6 Matthew Prince, "Why We Terminated Daily Stormer," Cloudflare (blog), August 16, 2017, http://blog.cloudflare.com/why-we-terminated-daily-stormer/.

7 "Cloudflare Transparency Report for the First Half of 2017," Cloudflare, accessed August 31, 2017, www.cloudflare.com/transparency/.

8 Timothy B. Lee, "Unable to Get a Domain, Racist Daily Stormer Retreats to the Dark Web," *Ars Technica*, August 22, 2017, https://arstechnica.com/tech-policy/2017/08/unable-to-get-a-domain-racist-daily-stormer-retreats-to-the-dark-web/.

9 Jeremy Malcolm, Cindy Cohn, and Danny O'Brien, "Fighting Neo-Nazis and the Future of Free Expression," Electronic Frontier Foundation (blog), August 17, 2017, www.eff.org/deeplinks/2017/08/fighting-neo-nazis-future-free-expression.

10 Matthew Prince, "Why We Terminated Daily Stormer," Cloudflare (blog), August 16, 2017, http://blog.cloudflare.com/why-we-terminated-daily-stormer/.

11 Kate Conger, "Cloudflare CEO on Terminating Service to Neo-Nazi Site: 'The Daily Stormer Are Assholes,'" *Gizmodo Australia*, August 17, 2017, www.gizmodo.com.au/2017/08/cloudflare-ceo-on-terminating-service-to-neo-nazi-site-the-daily-stormer-are-assholes/.

12 Natasha Lomas, "DigitalOcean and Cloudflare Ditch Neo-Nazi Client, The Daily Stormer," TechCrunch (blog), August 16, 2017, http://social.techcrunch.com/2017/08/16/digital-ocean-and-cloudflare-ditch-neo-nazi-client-the-daily-stormer/.

13 Copyright owners already have agreements with some domain registrars, payment processors, and advertising networks to cut off websites accused of hosting or even linking to infringing copyright material, without any oversight by the courts: Annemarie Bridy, "Copyright's Digital Deputies: DMCA-Plus Enforcement by Internet Intermediaries," in *Research Handbook on Electronic Commerce Law*, ed. John A. Rothchild (Edward Elgar, 2016), 185–208, https://doi.org/10.31235/osf.io/grzeu.

2 WHO MAKES THE RULES?

1 Mark Zuckerberg, "Update on Terms," Facebook, February 17, 2009, www.facebook.com/notes/facebook/update-on-terms/54746167130.

2 Ibid.

3 James Grimmelmann, "Virtual World Feudalism," *Yale Law Journal Pocket Part* 118 (2009): 126.

4 Nicolas Suzor, "Digital Constitutionalism: Using the Rule of Law to Evaluate the Legitimacy of Governance by Platforms," *Social Media + Society* 4, no. 3 (July 1, 2018): 2056305118787812, https://doi.org/10.1177/2056305118787812.

5 Ibid.

6 Mike Ananny makes the point that "Publics emerge when technologies create associations by aggregating people." Mike Ananny, "Toward an Ethics of Algorithms: Convening, Observation, Probability, and Timeliness," *Science, Technology, & Human Values* 41, no. 1 (January 1, 2016): 93–117, https://doi.org/10.1177/0162243915606523.

7 Dick Costolo, "The 'Town Square' in the Social Media Era: A Conversation with Twitter CEO Dick Costolo," accessed July 22, 2017, www.brookings.edu/wp-content/uploads/2013/06/20130626_social_media_twitter_costolo_transcript.pdf.

8 Mark Zuckerberg, "Building Global Community," Facebook (blog), February 16, 2017, www.facebook.com/notes/mark-zuckerberg/building-global-community/10154544292806634/.

9 Zeynep Tufekci, *Twitter and Tear Gas: The Power and Fragility of Networked Protest* (Yale University Press, 2017), 145–146.

10 Jean Burgess and Joshua Green, *YouTube: Online Video and Participatory Culture*, second edition, Digital Media and Society Series (Polity Press, 2018).

11 Nancy K. Baym, *Personal Connections in the Digital Age*, second edition, Digital Media and Society Series (Polity Press, 2015).

12 Celeste Liddle, "Looking Past White Australia and White Feminism," *New Matilda* (blog), March 9, 2016, https://newmatilda.com/2016/03/09/looking-past-white-australia-and-white-feminism/.

13 Ibid.

14 Celeste Liddle, "Facebook: Aboriginal Women Practicing Culture Are Not Offensive," *Change.org*, accessed June 28, 2017, www.change.org/p/facebook-aboriginal-women-practicing-culture-are-not-offensive.

15 Chris Graham, "Facebook Re-Re-Suspends Black Feminist, Writer for 'Offensive' Images of Aboriginal Ceremony," *New Matilda* (blog), March 13, 2016, https://newmatilda.com/2016/03/13/prominent-black-feminist-writer-petitions-facebook-as-more-users-suspended-over-offensive-images/.

16 Philip Napoli and Robyn Caplan, "Why Media Companies Insist They're Not Media Companies, Why They're Wrong, and Why It Matters," *First Monday* 22, no. 5 (May 2, 2017), https://doi.org/10.5210/fm.v22i5.7051.

17 Mike Ananny and Tarleton Gillespie, "Public Platforms: Beyond the Cycle of Shocks and Exceptions," The Internet, Policy and Politics Conference, Oxford University, accessed July 9, 2016, http://blogs.oii.ox.ac.uk/ipp-conference/sites/ipp/files/documents/anannyGillespie-publicPlatforms-oii-submittedSept8.pdf.

18 Tarleton Gillespie, "The Politics of 'Platforms,'" *New Media & Society* 12, no. 3 (May 1, 2010): 347–364, https://doi.org/10.1177/1461444809342738.

19 Tarleton Gillespie, *Custodians of the Internet: Platforms, Content Moderation, and the Hidden Decisions That Shape Social Media*, first edition (Yale University Press, 2018), 17.

20 James Grimmelmann, "The Virtues of Moderation," *Yale Journal of Law and Technology* 17 (2015): 42.

21 Mary L. Gray and Siddharth Suri, *Ghost Work: How to Stop Silicon Valley from Building a New Global Underclass* (Eamon Dolan/Houghton Mifflin Harcourt, 2019).

22 Sarah Roberts, "Commercial Content Moderation: Digital Laborers' Dirty Work," in *The Intersectional Internet: Race, Sex, Class and Culture Online*, ed. Safiya Umoja Noble and Brendesha Tynes (Peter Lang Publishing, 2016), http://ir.lib.uwo.ca/commpub/12.

23 Frank Pasquale, *The Black Box Society* (Harvard University Press, 2015).

24 Adrian Chen, "Inside Facebook's Outsourced Anti-Porn and Gore Brigade, Where 'Camel Toes' Are More Offensive Than 'Crushed Heads,'" Gawker, February 16, 2012, http://gawker.com/5885714/inside-facebooks-outsourced-anti-porn-and-gore-brigade-where-camel-toes-are-more-offensive-than-crushed-heads.

25 Nick Hopkins, "Revealed: Facebook's Internal Rulebook on Sex, Terrorism and Violence," *The Guardian*, May 21, 2017, www.theguardian.com/news/2017/may/21/revealed-facebook-internal-rulebook-sex-terrorism-violence.

26 Julia Angwin, "Facebook's Secret Censorship Rules Protect White Men from Hate Speech but Not Black Children," *ProPublica*, June 28, 2017, www.propublica.org/article/facebook-hate-speech-censorship-internal-documents-algorithms.

27 Tarleton Gillespie, *Custodians of the Internet: Platforms, Content Moderation, and the Hidden Decisions That Shape Social Media*, first edition (Yale University Press, 2018), 122.

28 Sarah Myers West, "Censored, Suspended, Shadowbanned: User Interpretations of Content Moderation on Social Media Platforms," *New Media & Society*, May 8, 2018, https://doi.org/10.1177/1461444818773059.

29 Nicolas P. Suzor, Sarah Myers West, Andrew Quodling, and Jillian York, "What Do We Mean When We Talk About Transparency? Towards Meaningful Transparency in Commercial Content Moderation," Forthcoming.

30 "Community Standards," 2016, www.facebook.com/communitystandards.

31 Katharine Schwab, "How ProPublica Became Big Tech's Scariest Watchdog," Fast Company, February 16, 2018, www.fastcompany.com/90160486/how-propublica-became-big-techs-scariest-watchdog.

32 "Captain Clay Higgins – Posts," *archive.is*, June 5, 2017, http://archive.is/95FO1.

33 Julia Angwin, "Facebook's Secret Censorship Rules Protect White Men from Hate Speech but Not Black Children," *ProPublica*, June 28, 2017, www.propublica.org/article/facebook-hate-speech-censorship-internal-documents-algorithms.

34 Julia Angwin, Ariana Tobin, and Madeleine Varner, "Have You Experienced Hate Speech on Facebook? We Want to Hear from You," *ProPublica*, August 29, 2017, www.propublica.org/article/have-you-experienced-hate-speech-on-facebook-we-want-to-hear-from-you.

35 Marvin Ammori, "Freedom of the Press: The 'New' New York Times: Free Speech Lawyering in the Age of Google and Twitter," *Harvard Law Review* 127 (2014): 2259–2593.

36 Kate Klonick, "The New Governors: The People, Rules, and Processes Governing Online Speech," *Harvard Law Review* 131 (March 20, 2017), https://papers.ssrn.com/abstract=2937985.

37 Catherine Buni and Soraya Chemaly, "The Secret Rules of the Internet: The Murky History of Moderation, and How It's Shaping the Future of Free Speech," *The Verge*, 2016, www.theverge.com/2016/4/13/11387934/internet-moderator-history-youtube-facebook-reddit-censorship-free-speech.

38 Jeffrey Rosen, "The Delete Squad," *The New Republic*, April 29, 2013, www.newrepublic.com/article/113045/free-speech-internet-silicon-valley-making-rules.

39 Julia Angwin, "Facebook's Secret Censorship Rules Protect White Men from Hate Speech but Not Black Children," *ProPublica*, June 28, 2017, www.propublica.org/article/facebook-hate-speech-censorship-internal-documents-algorithms.

40 Sarah Myers West, "Censored, Suspended, Shadowbanned: User Interpretations of Content Moderation on Social Media Platforms," *New Media & Society*, May 8, 2018, https://doi.org/10.1177/1461444818773059.

41 Deepa Seetharaman, "Facebook Employees Pushed to Remove Trump's Posts as Hate Speech," *Wall Street Journal*, October 21, 2016, www.wsj.com/articles/facebook-employees-pushed-to-remove-trump-posts-as-hate-speech-1477075392.

42 Michael Nunez, "Former Facebook Workers: We Routinely Suppressed Conservative News," Gizmodo, accessed July 4, 2017, www.gizmodo.com.au/2016/05/former-facebook-workers-we-routinely-suppressed-conservative-news/.

43 Alice E. Marwick and Rebecca Lewis, *Media Manipulation and Disinformation Online* (Data & Society Research Institute, 2017), https://datasociety.net/output/media-manipulation-and-disinfo-online/.

44 Robyn Caplan, Lauren Hanson, and Joan Donovan, *Dead Reckoning: Navigating Content Moderation after 'Fake News'* (Data & Society Research Institute, February 2018), https://datasociety.net/pubs/oh/DataAndSociety_Dead_Reckoning_2018.pdf.

45 Whitney Philips, *The Oxygen of Amplification* (Data & Society Research Institute, 2018), https://datasociety.net/output/oxygen-of-amplification/.

46 Rupi Kaur, Facebook (blog), March 26, 2015, www.facebook.com/rupikaurpoetry/posts/821304554630489:0.

47 Deepa Seetharaman, "Facebook Employees Pushed to Remove Trump's Posts as Hate Speech," *Wall Street Journal*, October 21, 2016, www.wsj.com/articles/facebook-employees-pushed-to-remove-trump-posts-as-hate-speech-1477075392.

48 Kate Klonick, "The New Governors: The People, Rules, and Processes Governing Online Speech," *Harvard Law Review* 131 (March 20, 2017), https://papers.ssrn.com/abstract=2937985.

49 Tarleton Gillespie, *Custodians of the Internet: Platforms, Content Moderation, and the Hidden Decisions That Shape Social Media*, first edition (Yale University Press, 2018), 14–15.

3 THE INTERNET'S ABUSE PROBLEM

1 Catherine Mayer, "I Got a Bomb Threat on Twitter. Was I Right to Report It?," *Time*, August 2, 2013, http://world.time.com/2013/08/02/i-got-a-bomb-threat-on-twitter-was-i-right-to-report-it/.

2 Emma A. Jane, *Misogyny Online: A Short (and Brutish) History*, Sage Swifts (SAGE Publications Ltd, 2017), 89.

3 Amanda Hess, "The Next Civil Rights Issue: Why Women Aren't Welcome on the Internet," *Pacific Standard*, January 6, 2014, https://psmag.com/social-justice/women-arent-welcome-internet-72170.

4 Emma A. Jane, *Misogyny Online: A Short (and Brutish) History*, Sage Swifts (SAGE Publications Ltd, 2017), 88.

5 Amanda George and Bridget Harris, *Landscapes of Violence: Women Surviving Family Violence in Regional and Rural Victoria* (Deakin University, 2014), www.deakin.edu.au/__data/assets/pdf_file/0003/287040/Landscapes-of-Violence-online-pdf-version.pdf; Bridget Harris, "Violent Landscapes: A Spatial Study of Family Violence," in *Locating Crime in Context and Place: Perspectives on Regional, Rural and Remote Australia*, ed. Alistair Harkness, Bridget Harris, and David Baker (The Federation Press, 2016), 70–84.

6 Amnesty International, "Amnesty Reveals Alarming Impact of Online Abuse Against Women," November 20, 2017, www.amnesty.org/en/latest/news/2017/11/amnesty-reveals-alarming-impact-of-online-abuse-against-women/.

7 Maeve Duggan, *Online Harassment 2017* (Pew Research Center, July 11, 2017), http://assets.pewresearch.org/wp-content/uploads/sites/14/2017/07/10151519/PI_2017.07.11_Online-Harassment_FINAL.pdf.

8 Amnesty International, "Toxic Twitter – A Toxic Place for Women," 2018, www.amnesty.org/en/latest/research/2018/03/online-violence-against-women-chapter-1/.

9 Mariana Palumbo and Delfina Schenone Sienra, *EROTICS Global Survey 2017: Sexuality, Rights and Internet Regulations* (Association for Progressive Communications, 2017), www.apc.org/en/pubs/erotics-global-survey-2017-sexuality-rights-and-internet-regulations.

10 Fred Turner, *From Counterculture to Cyberculture: Stewart Brand, the Whole Earth Network, and the Rise of Digital Utopianism* (University of Chicago Press, 2006).

11 Wired Staff, "Dear Internet: It's Time to Fix This Mess You Made," *WIRED*, August 24, 2016, www.wired.com/2016/08/open-letter-to-the-internet/.

12 Ibid.

13 Melvin Kranzberg, "Technology and History: 'Kranzberg's Laws,'" *Technology and Culture* 27, no. 3 (1986): 545, https://doi.org/10.2307/3105385.

14 Adrienne Massanari, "#Gamergate and the Fappening: How Reddit's Algorithm, Governance, and Culture Support Toxic Technocultures," *New Media & Society* 19, no. 3 (2017): 336, https://doi.org/10.1177/1461444815608807.

15 Whitney Phillips, *The Ambivalent Internet: Mischief, Oddity, and Antagonism Online* (Polity Press, 2017), 59.

16 Ryan M. Milner, "FCJ-156 Hacking the Social: Internet Memes, Identity Antagonism, and the Logic of Lulz," *The Fibreculture Journal*, no. 22 (2013): 78.

17 Arab American Institute, Asian Americans Advancing Justice, Center for Media Justice et al., "Open Letter to Facebook," *Politico*, October 30, 2017, www.politico.com/f/?id= 0000015f-72d6-d783-a15f-f7d65c8d0000.

18 Andrew Quodling, "Platforms Are Eating Society: Conflict and Governance in Digital Spaces," in *Negotiating Digital Citizenship Control, Contest and Culture*, ed. Anthony McCosker, Sonja Vivienne, and Amelia Johns (Rowman & Littlefield Publishers, 2016).

19 Angwin, Tobin, and Varner, "Facebook (Still) Letting Housing Advertisers Exclude Users by Race;" Julia Angwin, Noam Scheiber, and Ariana Tobin, "Dozens of Companies Are Using Facebook to Exclude Older Workers from Job Ads," *ProPublica*, December 20, 2017, www .propublica.org/article/facebook-ads-age-discrimination-targeting; Ariana Tobin and Jeremy B. Merrill, "Facebook Is Letting Job Advertisers Target Only Men," *ProPublica*, September 18, 2018, www.propublica.org/article/facebook-is-letting-job-advertisers-target-only-men.

20 Josh Halliday, "Twitter's Tony Wang: 'We Are the Free Speech Wing of the Free Speech Party,'" *The Guardian*, March 22, 2012, www.theguardian.com/media/2012/mar/22/twitter-tony-wang-free-speech.

21 Rich McCormick, "Twitter's Reputation for Abuse Is Turning off Potential Suitors," *The Verge*, October 19, 2016, www.theverge.com/2016/10/19/13328380/twitter-abuse-disney-sales force-bids-pulled.

22 Nitasha Tiku, "Twitter CEO: 'We Suck at Dealing with Abuse,'" *The Verge*, February 5, 2015, www.theverge.com/2015/2/4/7982099/twitter-ceo-sent-memo-taking-personal-responsi bility-for-the.

23 Amnesty International, "Toxic Twitter – A Toxic Place for Women," 2018, www.amnesty .org/en/latest/research/2018/03/online-violence-against-women-chapter-1/.

24 Emma A. Jane, "'Your a Ugly, Whorish, Slut': Understanding E-Bile," *Feminist Media Studies* 14, no. 4 (July 4, 2014): 532, https://doi.org/10.1080/14680777.2012.741073.

25 Jessica Vitak, Kalyani Chadha, Linda Steiner, and Zahra Ashktorab, "Identifying Women's Experiences with and Strategies for Mitigating Negative Effects of Online Harassment," The ACM Conference on Computer Supported Cooperative Work and Social Comput- ing, February 25–March 1, 2017, 1236, https://doi.org/10.1145/2998181.2998337.

26 Nicolas P. Suzor, Molly Dragiewicz, Bridget Harris, Rosalie Gillett, Jean Burgess, and Tess Van Geelen, "Human Rights by Design: The Responsibilities of Social Media Platforms to Address Gender-Based Violence Online," *Policy & Internet*, 2018, https:// doi.org/10.1002/poi3.185.

27 Danielle Keats Citron, *Hate Crimes in Cyberspace* (Harvard University Press, 2014).

28 Michael Salter, *Crime, Justice and Social Media: New Directions in Critical Criminology* (Routledge, 2017), www.routledge.com/Crime-Justice-and-Social-Media/Salter/p/book/ 9781138919679; Cindy Southworth, Shawndell Dawson, Cynthia Fraser, and Sarah Tucker, *A High-Tech Twist on Abuse: Technology, Intimate Partner Stalking, and Advocacy* (Violence Against Women, 2005), http://citeseerx.ist.psu.edu/viewdoc/download?doi= 10.1.1.581.4&rep=rep1&type=pdf.

29 Amanda Lenhart, Michelle Ybarra, Kathryn Zickuhr, and Myeshia Price-Fenney, *Online Harassment, Digital Abuse, and Cyberstalking in America* (Data & Society Research Institute, 2016), www.datasociety.net/pubs/oh/Online_Harassment_2016.pdf.

30 Molly Dragiewicz, Jean Burgess, Ariadna Matamoros-Fernández, et al., "Technology Facilitated Coercive Control: Domestic Violence and the Competing Roles of Digital Media Platforms," *Feminist Media Studies* 18, no. 4 (2018): 609–625, https://doi.org/10.1080/14680777.2018.1447341.

31 Delanie Woodlock, *The Abuse of Technology in Domestic Violence and Stalking* (Violence Against Women, 2017), 19.

32 Michael Salter and Thomas Crofts, "Responding to Revenge Porn: Challenges to Online Legal Impunity," in *New Views on Pornography: Sexuality, Politics, and the Law*, ed. L. Cornella and S. Tarrant (Praeger, 2015), 233–256.

33 Michael Salter, "From Geek Masculinity to Gamergate: The Technological Rationality of Online Abuse," *Crime, Media, Culture* 14, no. 2 (2018): 247–264, https://doi.org/10.1177/1741659017690893.

34 Molly Dragiewicz, Jean Burgess, Ariadna Matamoros-Fernández, et al., "Technology Facilitated Coercive Control: Domestic Violence and the Competing Roles of Digital Media Platforms," *Feminist Media Studies* 18, no. 4 (2018): 609–625, https://doi.org/10.1080/14680777.2018.1447341.

35 Umair Haque, "The Reason Twitter's Losing Active Users," *Harvard Business Review*, February 12, 2016, https://hbr.org/2016/02/the-reason-twitters-losing-active-users.

36 Liz Kelly, *Surviving Sexual Violence* (Polity Press, 1988).

37 F. Vera-Gray, "'Talk about a Cunt with Too Much Idle Time': Trolling Feminist Research," *Feminist Review* 115, no. 1 (March 1, 2017): 61–78, https://doi.org/10.1057/s41305-017-0038-y.

38 Martha Craven Nussbaum, "Objectification and Internet Misogyny," in *The Offensive Internet* (Harvard University Press, 2010), 68–90.

39 Emma A. Jane, *Misogyny Online: A Short (and Brutish) History*, Sage Swifts (SAGE Publications Ltd, 2017), 1.

40 Martha Craven Nussbaum, "Objectification and Internet Misogyny," in *The Offensive Internet* (Harvard University Press, 2010), 73.

41 Martha Craven Nussbaum, "Objectification and Internet Misogyny," in *The Offensive Internet* (Harvard University Press, 2010), 75.

42 Evan Stark, *Coercive Control: The Entrapment of Women in Personal Life* (Oxford University Press, 2007).

43 Anastasia Powell and Nicola Henry, "Policing Technology-Facilitated Sexual Violence against Adult Victims: Police and Service Sector Perspectives," *Policing and Society* 28, no. 3 (2018): 291–307, https://doi.org/10.1080/10439463.2016.1154964.

44 Nicolas P. Suzor, Molly Dragiewicz, Bridget Harris, Rosalie Gillett, Jean Burgess, and Tess Van Geelen, "Human Rights by Design: The Responsibilities of Social Media Platforms to Address Gender-Based Violence Online," *Policy & Internet*, 2018, https://doi.org/10.1002/poi3.185.

45 Frank La Rue, *Report of the Special Rapporteur to the General Assembly on Hate Speech and Incitement to Hatred* (United Nations General Assembly, 2012), http://ap.ohchr.org/documents/dpage_e.aspx?si=A/67/357.

46 Bailey Poland, *Haters: Harassment, Abuse, and Violence Online* (University of Nebraska Press, 2016), 174–175, www.jstor.org/stable/j.ctt1fq9wdp.

47 Amnesty International, "Toxic Twitter – A Toxic Place for Women," 2018, www.amnesty.org/en/latest/research/2018/03/online-violence-against-women-chapter-1/.

48 J. Nathan Matias, Amy Johnson, Whitney Erin Boesel, Brian Keegan, Jaclyn Friedman, and Charlie DeTar, *Reporting, Reviewing, and Responding to Harassment on Twitter* (Women, Action, & the Media!, 2015), https://ssrn.com/abstract=2602018.

49 Ariadna Matamoros-Fernández, "Platformed Racism: The Mediation and Circulation of an Australian Race-Based Controversy on Twitter, Facebook and YouTube," *Information, Communication & Society* 20, no. 6 (2017): 940, https://doi.org/10.1080/1369118X.2017.1293130.

50 Pamela Turton-Turner, "Villainous Avatars: The Visual Semiotics of Misogyny and Free Speech in Cyberspace," *Forum on Public Policy* 2013, no. 1 (2013): 1–18.

51 Ryan M. Milner, "FCJ-156 Hacking the Social: Internet Memes, Identity Antagonism, and the Logic of Lulz," *The Fibreculture Journal*, no. 22 (2013).

52 Amnesty International, "Toxic Twitter – A Toxic Place for Women," 2018, www.amnesty .org/en/latest/research/2018/03/online-violence-against-women-chapter-1/. "Open Letter to Facebook," Women, Action, & the Media, 2013, https://womenactionmedia.org/faceboo kaction/open-letter-to-facebook/; Andre Oboler, *Aboriginal Memes & Online Hate* (Online Hate Prevention Institute, 2012), www.ohpi.org.au/reports/IR12-2-Aboriginal-Memes.pdf; Clementine Ford, "Hey Facebook, Rape Is Not a Punchline," *Daily Life*, 2013, www.dailylife.com.au/news-and-views/dl-opinion/hey-facebook-rape-is-not-a-punch line-20130527-2n6tx.html.

53 Thomas E. Ford and Mark A. Ferguson, "Social Consequences of Disparagement Humor: A Prejudiced Norm Theory," *Personality and Social Psychology Review* 8, no. 1 (February 2004): 79–94, https://doi.org/10.1207/S15327957PSPR0801_4; Thomas E. Ford, Christie F. Boxer, Jacob Armstrong, Jessica R. Edel,"More Than 'Just a Joke': The Prejudice-Releasing Function of Sexist Humor," *Personality and Social Psychology Bulletin* 34, no. 2 (2008): 159–170, https://doi.org/10.1177/0146167207310022; Simon Weaver, "Jokes, Rhetoric and Embodied Racism: A Rhetorical Discourse Analysis of the Logics of Racist Jokes on the Internet," *Ethnicities* 11, no. 4 (2011): 413–435, https://doi.org/10.1177/ 1468796811407755.

54 Open Letter to Facebook," Women, Action, & the Media, 2013, https://womenactionme dia.org/facebookaction/open-letter-to-facebook/.

55 Ibid.

56 Emma A. Jane, *Misogyny Online: A Short (and Brutish) History*, Sage Swifts (SAGE Publications Ltd, 2017), 81.

57 Robin Knowles, "Facebook 'rape' Page to Stay despite Charity Criticism," *BBC Newsbeat*, October 7, 2011, www.bbc.co.uk/newsbeat/article/15130624/facebook-rape-page-to-stay-des pite-charity-criticism.

58 Marne Levine, "Controversial, Harmful and Hateful Speech on Facebook," *Facebook*, 2013, www.facebook.com/notes/facebook-safety/controversial-harmful-and-hateful-speech-on-facebook/574430655911054.

59 Association for Progressive Communications, *Online Gender-Based Violence: A Submission from the Association for Progressive Communications to the United Nations Special Rapporteur on Violence against Women, Its Causes and Consequences* (Association for Progressive Communications, 2017), www.apc.org/sites/default/files/APCSubmission_UNSR_VAW_GBV.pdf.

60 Association for Progressive Communications, Association for Women's Rights in Development, Asociación Trinidad, et al., "Joint Statement on Facebook's Internal Guidelines

for Content Moderation," Association for Women's Rights in Development, August 16, 2017, www.awid.org/news-and-analysis/joint-statement-facebooks-internal-guidelines-content-moderation.

61 Kate Crawford and Tarleton Gillespie, "What Is a Flag for? Social Media Reporting Tools and the Vocabulary of Complaint," *New Media & Society* 18, no. 3 (2014): 410–428, https://doi.org/10.1177/1461444814543163.

62 Julian Dibbell, "A Rape in Cyberspace," *The Village Voice*, December 23, 1993, www.villagevoice.com/2005/10/18/a-rape-in-cyberspace/.

63 Adrienne Massanari, "#Gamergate and the Fappening: How Reddit's Algorithm, Governance, and Culture Support Toxic Technocultures," New Media & Society 19, no. 3 (2017): 329-346, https://doi.org/10.1177/1461444815608807.

64 Eshwar Chandrasekharan, Umashanthi Pavalanathan, Anirudh Srinivasan, Adam Glynn, Jacob Eisenstein, and Eric Gilbert, "You Can't Stay Here: The Efficacy of Reddit's 2015 Ban Examined through Hate Speech," *Proceedings of the ACM Human–Computer Interaction* 1, no. CSCW (2017): article 31, https://doi.org/10.1145/3134666.

65 danah boyd, "The Politics of 'Real Names,'" *Communications of the ACM* 55, no. 8 (2012): 29–31, https://doi.org/10.1145/2240236.2240247.

66 Sarah Myers West, "Ambivalence in the (Private) Public Sphere: How Global Digital Activists Navigate Risk," seventh USENIX Workshop on Free and Open Communications on the Internet, 2017, www.usenix.org/system/files/conference/foci17/foci17-paper-west.pdf.

67 Emily van der Nagel and Jordan Frith, "Anonymity, Pseudonymity, and the Agency of Online Identity: Examining the Social Practices of r/Gonewild," *First Monday* 20, no. 3 (2015), https://doi.org/10.5210/fm.v20i3.5615.

68 Clementine Ford, *Fight like a Girl* (Allen & Unwin, 2016), 176.

69 Clementine Ford, *Fight like a Girl* (Allen & Unwin, 2016), 176.

70 Clementine Ford, *Fight like a Girl* (Allen & Unwin, 2016), 176–177.

71 Jon Ronson, *So You've Been Publicly Shamed* (New York: Riverhead Books, 2015).

72 Kate Klonick, "Re-Shaming the Debate: Social Norms, Shame, and Regulation in an Internet Age," *Maryland Law Review* 75, no. 4 (2016): 1029–1030.

73 danah boyd, "What World Are We Building?" (October 20, 2015), www.danah.org/papers/talks/2015/ParkerLecture.html.

74 A technique that has become popularly known as "sea lioning." The term was coined in 2014 to refer to a tactic of the GamerGate movement. It originates from a cartoon by David Malki: http://wondermark.com/1k62/.

4 LEGAL IMMUNITY

1 Eugene Volokh, "Cheap Speech and What it Will Do," *The Yale Law Journal* 104, no. 7 (May 1, 1995): 1805–1850, https://doi.org/10.2307/797032.

2 Cade Metz, "Paul Baran, the Link between Nuclear War and the Internet," *WIRED*, April 9, 2012, www.wired.co.uk/article/h-bomb-and-the-internet; "Paul Baran and the Origins of the Internet," *RAND Corporation*, accessed September 18, 2017, www.rand.org/about/history/baran.html.

3 Tim Weitzel, Oliver Wendt, and Falk V. Westarp, "Reconsidering Network Effect Theory," Proceedings of the Eighth Conference on Information Systems, ECIS 2000, 91.

4 Axel Bruns, *Gatewatching: Collaborative Online News Production*, Digital Formations (P. Lang, 2005).

5 Osama K. Najjar, Murad Salem, and Samar Samara, "Yahoo vs Google," Birzeit University, Palestine, 2008, http://dx.doi.org/10.2139/ssrn.1375406.

6 "YouTube Company Statistics," *Statistic Brain*, 2016, www.statisticbrain.com/youtube-statistics/.

7 Kate Crawford and Tarleton Gillespie, "What Is a Flag for? Social Media Reporting Tools and the Vocabulary of Complaint," *New Media & Society* 18, no. 3 (2014): 410–428, https://doi.org/10.1177/1461444814543163.

8 Tarleton Gillespie, *Custodians of the Internet: Platforms, Content Moderation, and the Hidden Decisions That Shape Social Media*, first edition (Yale University Press, 2018), 36.

9 Michael Salter and Thomas Crofts, "Responding to Revenge Porn: Challenges to Online Legal Impunity," in *New Views on Pornography: Sexuality, Politics, and the Law*, ed. L. Cornella and S. Tarrant (Praeger, 2015), 234. Alex Morris, "Hunter Moore: The Most Hated Man on the Internet," *Rolling Stone*, November 13, 2012, www.rollingstone.com/culture/news/the-most-hated-man-on-the-internet-20121113; Janice Richardson and Erika Rackley, *Feminist Perspectives on Tort Law* (Routledge, 2012), 145; Kelly Bourdet, "What Revenge Porn Did to Me," *Refinery29* (blog), April 9, 2014, www.refinery29.com/2014/09/57495/revenge-porn; Annmarie Chiarini, "I Was a Victim of Revenge Porn. I Don't Want Anyone Else to Face This," *The Guardian*, November 19, 2013, www.theguardian.com/commentisfree/2013/nov/19/revenge-porn-victim-maryland-law-change.

10 Some of the material in the following paragraphs was originally published in Nicolas P. Suzor, Bryony Seignior, and Jennifer Singleton, "Non-Consensual Porn and the Responsibilities of Online Intermediaries," *Melbourne University Law Review* 40, no. 3 (2017): 1057–1097.

11 Michael Salter and Thomas Crofts, "Responding to Revenge Porn: Challenges to Online Legal Impunity," in New Views on Pornography: Sexuality, Politics, and the Law, ed. L. Cornella and S. Tarrant (Praeger, 2015), 238.

12 Martha Craven Nussbaum, "Objectification and Internet Misogyny," in *The Offensive Internet* (Harvard University Press, 2010), 68–90. Daniel J. Kindlon, Michael Thompson, and Teresa Barker, *Raising Cain: Protecting the Emotional Life of Boys* (Ballantine Books, 2000).

13 Ganaele Langlois and Andrea Slane, "Economies of Reputation: The Case of Revenge Porn," *Communication and Critical/Cultural Studies* 14, no. 2 (2017): 120–138, https://doi.org/10.1080/14791420.2016.1273534.

14 Danielle Keats Citron and Mary Anne Franks, "Criminalizing Revenge Porn," *Wake Forest Law Review* 49 (2014): 347–352.

15 Nicola Henry and Anastasia Powell, "Beyond the 'Sext': Technology-Facilitated Sexual Violence and Harassment against Adult Women," *Australian & New Zealand Journal of Criminology* 48, no. 1 (2015), 113, http://anj.sagepub.com/content/48/1/104.

16 Danielle Keats Citron and Mary Anne Franks, "Criminalizing Revenge Porn," *Wake Forest Law Review* 49 (2014): 353.

17 Derek Bambauer, "Exposed," *Minnesota Law Review* 98 (2014): 2029–2030.

18 Adrian Chen, "Internet's Sleaziest Pornographer Calls It Quits: 'I'm Done with Looking at Little Kids Naked All Day,'" *Gawker*, April 19, 2012, http://gawker.com/5903486/internets-sleaziest-pornographer-calls-it-quits-im-done-with-looking-at-little-kids-naked-all-day.

19 Camille Dodero, "Hunter Moore Makes a Living Screwing You," *Village Voice*, April 5, 2012, www.villagevoice.com/2012/04/04/hunter-moore-makes-a-living-screwing-you/.

20 Sam Kashner, "Both Huntress and Prey," *Vanity Fair*, November 2014, www.vanityfair.com/hollywood/2014/10/jennifer-lawrence-photo-hacking-privacy.

21 Kate Crawford and Tarleton Gillespie, "What Is a Flag for? Social Media Reporting Tools and the Vocabulary of Complaint," *New Media & Society* 18, no. 3 (2014): 410–428, https://doi.org/10.1177/1461444814543163.

22 "Strafgesetzbuch (Criminal Code, Germany)," accessed September 21, 2017, www.gesetze-im-internet.de/englisch_stgb/index.html; "Code Pénal (France)," accessed September 21, 2017, www.legifrance.gouv.fr/affichCode.do?cidTexte=LEGITEXT000006070719&dateTexte=20170922.

23 *Dow Jones & Company Inc* v. *Gutnick*, 210 CLR 575 (High Court of Australia 2002) (Callinan J).

24 *Dow Jones & Company Inc* v. *Gutnick*, 210 CLR 575 (High Court of Australia 2002) (Gleeson CJ, McHugh, Gummow and Hayne JJ).

25 Amy Sawitta Lefevre, "Thai Junta Says Google Removing Content with Royal Insults," *Reuters*, October 22, 2016, www.reuters.com/article/us-thailand-king-google/thai-junta-says-google-removing-content-with-royal-insults-idUSKCN12M073; "Criminal Code (Thailand)," accessed September 18, 2017, http://library.siam-legal.com/thai-law/criminal-code-royal-family-sections-107-112; "Computer Crime Act (Thailand)," BE. 2550 § (2007), www.thailawforum.com/database1/thailand-computer-crime-law.html, art 14.

26 Justin Clark, Rob Farris, Ryan Morrison-Westphal, Helmi Noman, Casey Tilton, and Jonathan Zittrain, *The Shifting Landscape of Global Internet Censorship* (Berkman Klein Center for Internet & Society, Harvard University, June 2017), 20, https://cyber.harvard.edu/publications/2017/06/GlobalInternetCensorship.

27 "A New Approach to China," Official Google Blog (blog), December 1, 2010, https://googleblog.blogspot.com/2010/01/new-approach-to-china.html.

28 "A New Approach to China," Official Google Blog (blog), December 1, 2010, https://googleblog.blogspot.com/2010/01/new-approach-to-china.html.

29 "A New Approach to China: An Update," *Official Google Blog* (blog), March 22, 2010, https://googleblog.blogspot.com/2010/03/new-approach-to-china-update.html.

30 *Google Spain SL* v. *Gonzalez*, No. C-131/12 (Court of Justice of the European Union May 13, 2014).

31 "Transparency Report – European Privacy Requests for Search Removals," September 2014, www.google.com/transparencyreport/removals/europeprivacy/.

32 "Transparency Report – European Privacy Requests for Search Removals," September 2014, www.google.com/transparencyreport/removals/europeprivacy/.

33 Kenneth Adelman and Gabrielle Adelman, "California Coastal Records Project," accessed September 18, 2017, www.californiacoastline.org/cgi-bin/imagerandom.cgi.

34 Mike Masnick, "For 10 Years Everyone's Been Using 'The Streisand Effect' Without Paying; Now I'm Going to Start Issuing Takedowns," Techdirt (blog), August 1, 2015, www.techdirt.com/articles/20150107/13292829624/10-years-everyones-been-using-streisand-effect-without-paying-now-im-going-to-start-issuing-takedowns.shtml.

35 Fred Locklear, "'DVD Jon' Acquitted on All Charges," *Ars Technica*, January 7, 2003, https://arstechnica.com/uncategorized/2003/01/753-2/.

36 Jack Cheng, "Photoshop Rebels Rip Great HD DVD Clampdown," *WIRED*, May 3, 2007, www.wired.com/2007/05/photoshop-rebels-rip-great-hd-dvd-clampdown/; Eric Bangeman, "HD DVD Cracks: There's No Going Back," *Ars Technica*, May 3, 2007, https://arstechnica.com/tech-policy/2007/05/hd-dvd-cracks-theres-no-going-back/; Keith Burgun, "Oh Nine, Eff Nine," *YouTube*, 2007, www.youtube.com/watch?v=L9HaNbsIfp0; R. Stevens, "Kill Me Three Times, Shame on Rasputin," *Diesel Sweeties*, 2007, www.diesel sweeties.com/archive.php?s=1744.

37 *Duffy v. Google Inc* (No 3), No. 1 (SASC 2016). Six separate posts on the website "Ripoff Report" variously accused Dr Duffy of being a stalker, obsessively harassing psychics, spreading malicious lies, and so on. The South Australian Supreme Court found that the reports were defamatory, as were the snippets extracted in google search results. Google was held liable for publishing both the snippets and the links to defamatory material, and it failed to establish defences of innocent dissemination, qualified privilege, justification or contextual truth. Duffy was awarded $100,000 in damages.

38 Unlike many other countries, US defamation law only prohibits false statements that are made maliciously or negligently. See Kyu Ho Youm, "Actual Malice in U.S. Defamation Law: The Minority of One Doctrine in the World," *Journal of International Media and Entertainment Law* 4 (2011): 1–30.

39 'Transparency Report.'

5 HOW COPYRIGHT SHAPED THE INTERNET

1 William Patry, *Moral Panics and the Copyright Wars* (Oxford University Press, 2009).

2 "RIAA v. The People: Five Years Later," Electronic Frontier Foundation, September 30, 2008, www.eff.org/wp/riaa-v-people-five-years-later.

3 James Grimmelmann, "The Ethical Visions of Copyright Law," *Fordham Law Review* 77 (2009): 2005–2038.

4 *Capitol Records, Inc. v. Thomas-Rasset* 692 F.3d 988 (8th Cir. 2012).

5 Paula Dootson and Nicolas Suzor, "Game of Clones and the Australia Tax: Divergent Views about Copyright Business Models and the Willingness of Australian Consumers to Infringe," *The University of New South Wales Law Journal* 38 (2015): 206–329.

6 *A&M Records, Inc. v. Napster, Inc.*, 239 F.3d 1004 (2001) (n.d.).

7 Ernesto, "BitTorrent: The 'One Third of All Internet Traffic' Myth," *TorrentFreak* (blog), September 17, 2006, https://torrentfreak.com/bittorrent-the-one-third-of-all-internet-traffic-myth/.

8 Tara Touloumis, "Buccaneers and Bucks from the Internet: Pirate Bay and the Entertainment Industry Comment," *Seton Hall Journal of Sports and Entertainment Law* 19, no. 1 (2009): 253–282; Joost Poort, Jorna Leenheer, Jeroen van der Ham, and Cosmin Dumitru, "Baywatch: Two Approaches to Measure the Effects of Blocking Access to The Pirate Bay," *Telecommunications Policy* 38, no. 4 (May 1, 2014): 383–392, https://doi.org/10.1016/j.telpol.2013.12.008.

9 Ramon Lobato and Julian Thomas, "The Business of Anti-Piracy: New Zones of Enterprise in the Copyright Wars," *International Journal of Communication* 6 (April 12, 2012): 606–625.

10 Chris Francescani, "The Video Prince Doesn't Want You to See," *ABC News*, October 10, 2009, http://abcnews.go.com/TheLaw/home-video-prince/story?id=3777651.

11 *Lenz* v. *Universal Music Corp*, 815 F.3d 1145 (9th Cir. 2016).

12 Google make their data available at: Google, "Content Removals Due to Copyright," *Google Transparency Report*, accessed October 3, 2018, https://transparencyreport.google .com/copyright/explore?hl=en.

13 Daniel Seng, "'Who Watches the Watchmen?' An Empirical Analysis of Errors in DMCA Takedown Notices," SSRN *Scholarly Paper* (January 23, 2015), 26, http://papers.ssrn.com/ abstract=2563202 (a single notice can include multiple requests; the proportion of invalid requests was 5.8 percent).

14 Jennifer M. Urban, Joe Karaganis, and Brianna L. Schofield, "Notice and Takedown in Everyday Practice," SSRN *Scholarly Paper* (March 29, 2016), 88, http://papers.ssrn.com/ abstract=2755628.

15 Jennifer M. Urban, Joe Karaganis, and Brianna L. Schofield, "Notice and Takedown in Everyday Practice," SSRN *Scholarly Paper* (March 29, 2016), 88, http://papers.ssrn.com/ abstract=2755628.

16 17 US Code §512 (g)(3)(C).

17 Jennifer M. Urban, Joe Karaganis, and Brianna L. Schofield, "Notice and Takedown in Everyday Practice," SSRN *Scholarly Paper* (March 29, 2016), 44-46, http://papers .ssrn.com/abstract=2755628.

18 Tarleton Gillespie, *Wired Shut Copyright and the Shape of Digital Culture* (MIT Press, 2007), 254.

19 Rowland Manthorpe, "Cory Doctorow Dreams of a DRM-Free Utopia – so He's Suing the US Government to Get It," *Wired UK*, April 25, 2017, www.wired.co.uk/article/cory-doctorow-walkaway-science-fiction-drm.

20 Rebecca Tushnet, "I Put You There: User-Generated Content and AntiCircumvention," *Vanderbilt Journal of Entertainment and Technology Law* 12 (2010): 889–946.

21 Paul Harpur and Nicolas Suzor, "Copyright Protections and Disability Rights: Turning the Page to a New International Paradigm," *The University of New South Wales Law Journal* 36, no. 3 (2013): 745.

22 Jean Burgess and Joshua Green, *YouTube: Online Video and Participatory Culture*, second edition, Digital Media and Society Series (Polity Press, 2018).

23 Ibid.

24 *How Google Fights Piracy* (Google, 2016), 4, accessed October 3, 2018, https://drive.google .com/file/d/0BwxyRPFduTN2cl91LXJoYjlYSjA/view?usp=embed_facebook.

25 "YouTube in Numbers," *YouTube*, 2017, www.youtube.com/intl/en-GB/yt/about/press/.

26 Zahavah Levine, "Broadcast Yourself," Official YouTube Blog (blog), March 18, 2010, https://youtube.googleblog.com/2010/03/broadcast-yourself.html.

27 Michael Piatek, Tadayoshi Kohno, and Arvind Krishnamurthy, "Challenges and Directions for Monitoring P2P File Sharing Networks, or, Why My Printer Received a DMCA Takedown Notice," *HotSec*, 2008, http://static.usenix.org/legacy/events/hotsec08/tech/ full_papers/piatek/piatek_html/.

28 See Loi favorisant la diffusion et la protection de la création sur internet (Act Furthering the Diffusion and Protection of Creation on the Internet), Conseil constitutionnel (French Constitutional Court) Décision n° 2009–580 DC du 10 juin 2009 (June 10, 2009) finding that the original HADOPI legislation impermissibly violated the presumption of innocence under French law.

29 David Kravets, "RIP, 'Six Strikes' Copyright Alert System," *Ars Technica*, January 30, 2017, https://arstechnica.com/tech-policy/2017/01/rip-six-strikes-copyright-alert-system/.

30 Claire Reilly, "Three Strikes out: Anti-Piracy Scheme Shelved over 'prohibitive' Costs," *CNet*, February 18, 2016, www.cnet.com/au/news/three-strikes-out-manual-anti-piracy-scheme-shelved-over-prohibitive-costs/.

31 John Blevins, "Uncertainty as Enforcement Mechanism: The New Expansion of Secondary Copyright Liability to Internet Platforms," *Cardozo Law Review* 34 (2013): 1821.

32 Yochai Benkler, Hal Roberts, Robert Faris, Alicia Solow-Niederman, and Bruce Etling, "Social Mobilization and the Networked Public Sphere: Mapping the SOPA-PIPA Debate," *Berkman Center Research Publication* (2013), https://papers.ssrn.com/sol3/papers.cfm?abstract_id=2295953.

33 Yafit Lev-Aretz, "Copyright Lawmaking and Public Choice: From Legislative Battles to Private Ordering," *Harvard Journal of Law & Technology* 27, no. 1 (2012): 203.

34 Cory Doctorow, "Amid Unprecedented Controversy, W3C Greenlights DRM for the Web," Electronic Frontier Foundation, July 6, 2017, www.eff.org/deeplinks/2017/07/amid-unprecedented-controversy-w3c-greenlights-drm-web.

35 Annemarie Bridy, "Notice and Takedown in the Domain Name System: ICANN's Ambivalent Drift into Online Content Regulation," *Washington and Lee Law Review* 74 (2017): 1345–1388.

6 CENSORSHIP

1 Guangchao Charles Feng and Steve Zhongshi Guo, "Tracing the Route of China's Internet Censorship: An Empirical Study," *Telematics and Informatics* 30, no. 4 (November 1, 2013): 335–345, https://doi.org/10.1016/j.tele.2012.09.002.

2 Quoted in an interview with Philip Elmer-Dewitt, "First Nation in Cyberspace," *TIME International*, June 12, 1993, http://kirste.userpage.fu-berlin.de/outerspace/internet-article.html.

3 Bei Qin, David Strömberg, and Yanhui Wu, "Why Does China Allow Freer Social Media? Protests versus Surveillance and Propaganda," *The Journal of Economic Perspectives* 31, no. 1 (2017): 117–140; Fan Yang, "Rethinking China's Internet Censorship: The Practice of Recoding and the Politics of Visibility," *New Media & Society* 18, no. 7 (2016): 1364–1381.

4 Jing Zeng, Chung-hong Chan, and King-wa Fu, "How Social Media Construct 'Truth' Around Crisis Events: Weibo's Rumor Management Strategies After the 2015 Tianjin Blasts," *Policy & Internet* 9, no. 3 (2017): 297–320; see also Gary King, Jennifer Pan, and Margaret E. Roberts, "How Censorship in China Allows Government Criticism but Silences Collective Expression," *American Political Science Review* 107, no. 2 (May 2013): 326–343, https://doi.org/10.1017/S0003055413000014.

5 Justin Clark, Rob Farris, Ryan Morrison-Westphal, Helmi Noman, Casey Tilton, and Jonathan Zittrain, *The Shifting Landscape of Global Internet Censorship* (Berkman Klein Center for Internet & Society, Harvard University, June 2017), 19, https://cyber.harvard.edu/publications/2017/06/GlobalInternetCensorship.

6 Ibid.

7 Freedom House, "Egypt," in *Freedom on the Net 2012* (Freedom House, 2012), https://freedomhouse.org/sites/default/files/Egypt%202012.pdf.

8 Zeynep Tufekci, *Twitter and Tear Gas: The Power and Fragility of Networked Protest* (Yale University Press, 2017), 226.

9 UN Special Rapporteur on the Promotion and Protection of the Right to Freedom of Opinion and Expression, the Organization for Security and Co-operation in Europe Representative on Freedom of the Media, the Organization of American States Special Rapporteur on Freedom of Expression, and the African Commission on Human and Peoples' Rights Special Rapporteur on Freedom of Expression and Access to Information, *Joint Declaration on Freedom of Expression and Responses to Conflict Situations* (Organization for Security and Co-operation in Europe, May 4, 2015), www.osce.org/fom/154846.

10 Justin Clark, Rob Farris, Ryan Morrison-Westphal, Helmi Noman, Casey Tilton, and Jonathan Zittrain, *The Shifting Landscape of Global Internet Censorship* (Berkman Klein Center for Internet & Society, Harvard University, June 2017), https://cyber.harvard.edu/publications/2017/06/GlobalInternetCensorship.

11 Ibid.

12 "Government Requests Report," Facebook, 2017, https://govtrequests.facebook.com/.

13 "Government Requests to Remove Content," Transparency Report, Google, 2017, https://transparencyreport.google.com/government-removals/overview.

14 "2017 Corporate Accountability Index," Ranking Digital Rights and Sustainalytics, 2017, https://rankingdigitalrights.org/index2017.

15 *Jacobellis* v. *Ohio*, 378 US 184 (1964), 197.

16 Daphne Keller, ed., *Law, Borders, and Speech: Proceedings and Materials* (Stanford Law School, 2017), https://cyberlaw.stanford.edu/files/publication/files/12-18%20FINAL%20Conference%20Proceedings.pdf.

17 Daphne Keller, "Ominous: Canadian Court Orders Google to Remove Search Results Globally," The Center for Internet and Society, June 28, 2017, http://cyberlaw.stanford.edu/blog/2017/06/ominous-canadian-court-orders-google-remove-search-results-globally.

18 "Freedom of Expression under Worldwide Attack, UN Rights Expert Warns in New Report," UN Human Rights Office of the High Commissioner, 2016, www.ohchr.org/EN/NewsEvents/Pages/DisplayNews.aspx?NewsID=20717.

19 Gary Elijah Dann and Neil Haddow, "Just Doing Business or Doing Just Business: Google, Microsoft, Yahoo! And the Business of Censoring China's Internet," *Journal of Business Ethics* 79, no. 3 (May 2008): 219–234, https://doi.org/10.1007/s10551-007-9373-9 (discussing Google's operations in China, and concluding that "Wilfully abiding by unjust laws, albeit necessary to do business in China, should not trump moral actions that protect rights.").

20 Dan Svantesson, "Between a Rock and a Hard Place: An International Law Perspective of the Difficult Position of Globally Active Intermediaries," *Computer Law & Security Review* 30 (2014): 348–356.

21 Daphne Keller, "The Right Tools: Europe's Intermediary Liability Laws and the EU 2016 General Data Protection Regulation," *Berkeley Technology Law Journal* 33, no. 1 (2018): 287–364, https://doi.org/10.15779/z38639k53j.

22 Brendan Van Alsenoy and Marieke Koekkoek, "Internet and Jurisdiction after Google Spain: The Extraterritorial Reach of the 'Right to Be Delisted,'" *International Data Privacy Law; Oxford* 5, no. 2 (May 2015): 105–120, https://doi.org/10.1093/idpl/ipv003.

23 Raphael Cohen-Almagor, "The Role of Internet Intermediaries in Tackling Terrorism Online," *Fordham Law Review* 86 (2017): 425–454.

24 "2017 Corporate Accountability Index," Ranking Digital Rights and Sustainalytics, 2017, 28, https://rankingdigitalrights.org/index2017.

25 "2018 Corporate Accountability Index," Ranking Digital Rights and Sustainalytics, April 2018, 57, https://rankingdigitalrights.org/index2018/.

26 Terry Flew, "Post-Globalisation," *Javnost – The Public* 25, no. 1–2 (April 3, 2018): 108, https://doi.org/10.1080/13183222.2018.1418958.

27 Brian Fitzgerald, "*Dow Jones & (and) Co. Inc. v. Gutnick* – Negotiating American Legal Hegemony in the Transnational World of Cyberspace Case Note," *Melbourne University Law Review* 27 (2003): 590–611.

7 LAWLESS

1 John Perry Barlow, "A Declaration of the Independence of Cyberspace," Electronic Frontier Foundation, August 2, 1996, www.eff.org/cyberspace-independence.

2 David R. Johnson and David Post, "Law and Borders: The Rise of Law in Cyberspace," *Stanford Law Review* 48, no. 5 (1996): 1367.

3 Adrienne Massanari, "#Gamergate and the Fappening: How Reddit's Algorithm, Governance, and Culture Support Toxic Technocultures," *New Media & Society* 19, no. 3 (2017): 329–346, https://doi.org/10.1177/1461444815608807.

4 UN Educational, Scientific and Cultural Organization, *Fostering Freedom Online: The Role of Internet Intermediaries* (UN Educational, Scientific and Cultural Organization, 2014), http://unesdoc.unesco.org/images/0023/002311/231162e.pdf; Council of Europe, *Recommendation CM/Rec(2018)2 of the Committee of Ministers to Member States on the Roles and Responsibilities of Internet Intermediaries* (Council of Europe, March 7, 2018), www .coe.int/en/web/freedom-expression/committee-of-ministers-adopted-texts/-/asset_publisher/ aDXmrolovvsU/content/recommendation-cm-rec-2018-2-of-the-committee-of-ministers-to-member-states-on-the-roles-and-responsibilities-of-internet-intermediaries?inheritRedirect= false; Organisation for Economic Co-operation and Development, *The Economic and Social Role of Internet Intermediaries* (Organisation for Economic Co-operation and Development, 2010), www.oecd.org/internet/ieconomy/44949023.pdf.

5 Laura DeNardis, *Protocol Politics: The Globalization of Internet Governance* (MIT Press, 2009); Milton Mueller, *Ruling the Root* (MIT Press, 2002), 162.

6 Lawrence Lessig, *Code: Version 2.0* (Basic Books, 2006).

7 Safiya Umoja Noble, *Algorithms of Oppression: How Search Engines Reinforce Racism* (New York University Press, 2018).

8 Jacqueline Lipton, *Rethinking Cyberlaw: A New Vision for Internet Law* (Edward Elgar, 2015).

9 Jack Goldsmith and Tim Wu, *Who Controls the Internet?: Illusions of a Borderless World* (Oxford University Press, 2006).

10 Laura DeNardis, *The Global War for Internet Governance* (Yale University Press, 2014).

11 Jennifer Holt and Patrick Vonderau, "'Where the Internet Lives': Data Centers as Cloud Infrastructure," in *Signal Traffic: Critical Studies of Media Infrastructures* (University of Illinois Press, 2015), 71–93.

12 Jack Goldsmith and Tim Wu, *Who Controls the Internet? Illusions of a Borderless World* (Oxford University Press, 2006).

13 Tarleton Gillespie, *Custodians of the Internet: Platforms, Content Moderation, and the Hidden Decisions That Shape Social Media*, first edition (Yale University Press, 2018), 28.

14 https://wilmap.law.stanford.edu/.

15 L. M. Sacasas, "The Tech Backlash We Really Need," *The New Atlantis*, no. 55 (2018): 35–42; Isabella Hansen and Darren J. Lim, "Doxing Democracy: Influencing Elections via Cyber Voter Interference," *Contemporary Politics* (July 3, 2018), https://doi.org/10.1080/13569775.2018.1493629.

16 U. S. Government Publishing Office, "Open Hearing: Social Media Influence in the 2016 U.S. Election," U. S. Senate Select Committee on Intelligence, November 1, 2017, www.intelligence.senate.gov/hearings/open-hearing-social-media-influence-2016-us-elections#.

17 Nicky Woolf, "Man Makes $4bn in Two Days Explaining Facebook to Old People," *The New Statesman*, April 12, 2018, www.newstatesman.com/politics/media/2018/04/man-makes-4bn-two-days-explaining-facebook-old-people.

18 Mark R. Warner, "Potential Policy Proposals for Regulation of Social Media and Technology Firms," 2018.

19 Napoli and Caplan, "Why Media Companies Insist They're Not Media Companies, Why They're Wrong, and Why It Matters;" G. Picard and Victor Pickard, *Essential Principles for Contemporary Media and Communications Policymaking* (Reuters Institute for the Study of Journalism: University of Oxford, Recuperado, 2017), https://reutersinstitute.politics.ox.ac.uk/our-research/essential-principles-contemporary-media-and-communications-policymaking.

20 U. S. Government Publishing Office, "Open Hearing: Social Media Influence in the 2016 U.S. Election."

21 Urs Gasser and Wolfgang Schulz, *Governance of Online Intermediaries: Observations from a Series of National Case Studies* (Network of Interdisciplinary Internet & Society Research Centers, February 18, 2015), https://cyber.harvard.edu/publications/2015/online_intermediaries.

22 Angela Daly, "Beyond 'Hipster Antitrust': A Critical Perspective on the European Commission's Google Decision," *European Competition and Regulation Law Review* 1, no. 3 (2017): 188.

23 Rita Barrera and Jessica Bustamante, "The Rotten Apple: Tax Avoidance in Ireland," *The International Trade Journal* 32, no. 1 (January 1, 2018): 150–161, https://doi.org/10.1080/08853908.2017.1356250.

24 *Schrems v. Data Protection Commissioner*, No. Case C-362/14 (Court of Justice of the European Union 2015); *Google Spain SL v. Gonzalez*, No. C-131/12 (Court of Justice of the European Union May 13, 2014).

25 European Parliament and Council of the European Union, "General Data Protection Regulation," 2016/679 § (2016), http://eur-lex.europa.eu/legal-content/EN/TXT/?uri=CELEX%3A32016R0679; "Directive on Copyright in the Digital Single Market," Pub. L. No. 2016/0280(COD) (n.d.).

26 The optimistic view is that we may not need to interfere with how private platforms organize themselves; if they manage to formulate their own legitimate systems of governance, we may be better off leaving platforms to "live and love and law for themselves": F. Gregory Lastowka and Dan Hunter, "The Laws of the Virtual Worlds," *California Law Review*, 92 (2004): 73.

27 Greg Lastowka, *Virtual Justice: The New Laws of Online Worlds*, first edition (Yale University Press, 2010), 195.

28 Philip Elmer-Dewitt, "First Nation in Cyberspace," *TIME International*, June 12, 1993, http://kirste.userpage.fu-berlin.de/outerspace/internet-article.html.

29 Paula Dootson and Nicolas Suzor, "Game of Clones and the Australia Tax: Divergent Views about Copyright Business Models and the Willingness of Australian Consumers to Infringe," *The University of New South Wales Law Journal* 38 (2015): 206–329.

30 Dan Jerker B. Svantesson, *Solving the Internet Jurisdiction Puzzle*, first edition (Oxford University Press, 2017).

8 CONSTITUTIONALIZING INTERNET GOVERNANCE

1 Danny Danziger and John Gillingham, *1215: The Year of Magna Carta* (Touschstone, 2005), 268.

2 Brian Z. Tamanaha, *On the Rule of Law: History, Politics, Theory* (Cambridge University Press, 2004), 122.

3 Julia Black, "Constructing and Contesting Legitimacy and Accountability in Polycentric Regulatory Regimes," *Regulation & Governance* 2, no. 2 (2008): 137–164.

4 T. R. S. Allan, *Constitutional Justice: A Liberal Theory of the Rule of Law* (Oxford University Press, 2001).

5 Albert Venn Dicey, *Introduction to the Study of the Law of the Constitution*, eighth edition (Macmillan, 1982).

6 Tamanaha, *On the Rule of Law: History, Politics, Theory*, 137; E. P. Thompson, *Whigs and Hunters: The Origin of the Black Act* (Penguin, 1990), 266.

7 Tamanaha, *On the Rule of Law: History, Politics, Theory*, 114.

8 M. J. Trebilcock and R. J. Daniels, *Rule of Law Reform and Development: Charting the Fragile Path of Progress* (Edward Elgar, 2008).

9 Lon L. Fuller, *The Morality of Law*, second edition (Yale University Press, 1969).

10 Herbert Lionel Adolphus Hart, *The Concept of Law*, second edition (Oxford, 1994).

11 The requirements of due process are generally accepted as "a necessary, albeit not sufficient condition for the realization of almost any defensible conception of the rule of law;" Trebilcock and Daniels, *Rule of Law Reform and Development*, 30.

12 Mark Zuckerberg, "Update on Terms," Facebook, February 17, 2009, www.facebook.com/notes/facebook/update-on-terms/54746167130.

13 Edoardo Celeste, "Terms of Service and Bills of Rights: New Mechanisms of Constitutionalisation in the Social Media Environment?," *International Review of Law, Computers & Technology*, May 21, 2018, https://doi.org/10.1080/13600869.2018.1475898.

14 Nicolas Suzor, "Digital Constitutionalism: Using the Rule of Law to Evaluate the Legitimacy of Governance by Platforms," *Social Media + Society* 4, no. 3 (July 1, 2018): 2056305118787812, https://doi.org/10.1177/2056305118787812.

15 Centre for International Governance Innovation, "One Internet," 2016, www.ourinternet.org/report.

16 There's a good argument that the fine print of standard form contracts cannot be said to be assented to in any real sense: Karl N. Llewellyn, *The Common Law Tradition: Deciding Appeals* (Little, Brown and Company, 1960); Margaret Jane Radin,

"Boilerplate Today: The Rise of Modularity and the Waning of Consent," *Michigan Law Review* 104 (2006): 1223.

17 Tamanaha, *On the Rule of Law: History, Politics, Theory*, 138–139.

18 John Austin, *The Province of Jurisprudence Determined*, second edition (John Murray, 1861), 117.

19 Colin Scott, "Regulation in the Age of Governance: The Rise of the Post Regulatory State," in *The Politics of Regulation: Institutions and Regulatory Reforms for the Age of Governance*, ed. J. Jordana and D. Levi-Faur (Edward Elgar, 2004), 145–174, http://researchrepository.ucd.ie/handle/10197/6779.

20 Scott Burris, Michael Kempa, and Clifford Shearing, "Changes in Governance: A Cross-Disciplinary Review of Current Scholarship," *Akron Law Review* 41 (2008): 3.

21 Julia Black, "Critical Reflections on Regulation," *Australian Journal of Legal Philosophy* 27 (2002): 1; Scott Burris, Peter Drahos, and Clifford Shearing, "Nodal Governance," *Australian Journal of Legal Philosophy* 30 (2005): 400–419.

22 See, for example, Julia Black, "Constructing and Contesting Legitimacy and Accountability in Polycentric Regulatory Regimes," *Regulation & Governance* 2, no. 2 (2008): 137–164. Scott Burris, Peter Drahos, and Clifford Shearing, "Nodal Governance," *Australian Journal of Legal Philosophy* 30 (2005): 400–419. Peter Grabosky, "Beyond Responsive Regulation: The Expanding Role of Non-State Actors in the Regulatory Process," *Regulation & Governance* 7, no. 1 (March 2013): 114–123, https://doi.org/10.1111/j.1748-5991.2012.01147.x; for an introduction to some of these theories and an overview of the literature, see Scott Burris, Michael Kempa, and Clifford Shearing, "Changes in Governance: A Cross-Disciplinary Review of Current Scholarship," *Akron Law Review* 41 (2008): 3.

23 Rebecca MacKinnon, *Consent of the Networked: The Worldwide Struggle For Internet Freedom* (Basic Books, 2012); Ian Brown and Christopher T. Marsden, eds., *Regulating Code Good Governance and Better Regulation in the Information Age* (MIT Press, 2013); DeNardis, *The Global War for Internet Governance*; Robin Mansell, *Imagining the Internet Communication, Innovation, and Governance* (Oxford University Press, 2012).

24 Ithiel de Sola Pool, *Technologies of Freedom* (Belknap Press, 1983).

25 Jemima Kiss, "An Online Magna Carta: Berners-Lee Calls for Bill of Rights for Web," *The Guardian*, March 12, 2014, www.theguardian.com/technology/2014/mar/12/online-magna-carta-berners-lee-web.

26 Terry Flew, "Platforms on Trial," *Intermedia* 46 (August 2, 2018): 24–29.

27 Dennis Redeker, Lex Gill, and Urs Gasser, "Towards Digital Constitutionalism? Mapping Attempts to Craft an Internet Bill of Rights," *International Communication Gazette* 80, no. 4 (February 16, 2018), https://doi.org/10.1177/1748048518757121.

28 Eleanor Roosevelt, Statement to the United Nations' General Assembly on the Universal Declaration of Human Rights (1948) December 9, 1948, https://erpapers.columbian.gwu.edu/statement-united-nations-general-assembly-universal-declaration-human-rights-1948.

9 PROTECTING FUNDAMENTAL RIGHTS

1 Kate Conger, "Cloudflare CEO on Terminating Service to Neo-Nazi Site: 'The Daily Stormer Are Assholes,'" *Gizmodo Australia*, August 17, 2017, www.gizmodo.com.au/2017/08/cloudflare-ceo-on-terminating-service-to-neo-nazi-site-the-daily-stormer-are-assholes/.

2 What Teubner calls "limitative functions": Gunther Teubner, *Constitutional Fragments: Societal Constitutionalism and Globalization*, Oxford Constitutional Theory (Oxford University Press, 2012), 87.

3 Edoardo Celeste, "Digital Constitutionalism: Mapping the Constitutional Response to Digital Technology's Challenges," July 25, 2018, https://papers.ssrn.com/abstract=3219905.

4 Martin Krygier, "The Rule of Law: Legality, Teleology, Sociology," in *Re-Locating the Rule of Law*, ed., Gianluigi Palombella and Neil Walker (Hart Publishers, 2008), https://papers.ssrn.com/sol3/papers.cfm?abstract_id=1218982.

5 Matthew Prince, "Cloudflare and Free Speech," Cloudflare Blog (blog), August 9, 2013, https://blog.cloudflare.com/cloudflare-and-free-speech/.

6 Kate Conger, "Cloudflare CEO on Terminating Service to Neo-Nazi Site: 'The Daily Stormer Are Assholes,'" *Gizmodo Australia*, August 17, 2017, www.gizmodo.com.au/2017/08/cloudflare-ceo-on-terminating-service-to-neo-nazi-site-the-daily-stormer-are-assholes/.

7 Rebecca MacKinnon, *Consent of the Networked: The Worldwide Struggle For Internet Freedom* (Basic Books, 2012), 172.

8 David Kaye, *Report of the Special Rapporteur to the Human Rights Council on the Role of Digital Access Providers* (Human Rights Council, March 30, 2017), 3, https://documents-dds-ny.un.org/doc/UNDOC/GEN/G17/077/46/PDF/G1707746.pdf?OpenElement.

9 Mashood A. Baderin and Manisuli Ssenyonjo, eds., *International Human Rights Law: Six Decades after the UDHR and Beyond* (Routledge, 2016).

10 John Ruggie, *Protect, Respect and Remedy: A Framework for Business and Human Rights* (UN Human Rights Council, April 7, 2008), http://undocs.org/A/HRC/8/5.

11 Radu Mares, ed., *The UN Guiding Principles on Business and Human Rights: Foundations and Implementation* (Brill Hihojf, 2011).

12 David Bilchitz and Surya Deva, "The Human Rights Obligations of Business: A Critical Framework for the Future," in *Human Rights Obligations of Business*, ed., Surya Deva and David Bilchitz (Cambridge University Press, 2013), 1–26, https://doi.org/10.1017/CBO9781139568333.003; Justine Nolan, "The Corporate Responsibility to Respect Rights: Soft Law or Not Law?," in *Human Rights Obligations of Business: Beyond the Corporate Responsibility to Respect?*, ed., S. Deca and D. Bilchitz (Cambridge University Press, 2013), https://papers.ssrn.com/abstract=2338356.

13 Businesses have a responsibility to "avoid infringing on the human rights of others and should address adverse human rights impacts with which they are involved": UN, *Guiding Principles on Business and Human Rights* (UN, 2011), 13, www.ohchr.org/documents/publications/GuidingprinciplesBusinesshr_en.pdf.

14 Emily B. Laidlaw, "Myth or Promise? The Corporate Social Responsibilities of Online Service Providers for Human Rights," in *The Responsibilities of Online Service Providers*, Law, Governance and Technology Series (Springer, Cham, 2017), 135–155, https://doi.org/10.1007/978-3-319-47852-4_8.

15 Organisation for Economic Co-operation and Development, *The Economic and Social Role of Internet Intermediaries* (Organisation for Economic Co-operation and Development, 2010), www.oecd.org/internet/ieconomy/44949023.pdf.

16 Rikke Frank Jørgensen and Anja Møller Pedersen, "Online Service Providers as Human Rights Arbiters," in The Responsibilities of Online Service Providers, 179–199, https://doi.org/10.1007/978-3-319-47852-4_10.

17 UN Educational, Scientific and Cultural Organization, *Fostering Freedom Online: The Role of Internet Intermediaries* (UN Educational, Scientific and Cultural Organization, 2014), http://unesdoc.unesco.org/images/0023/002311/231162e.pdf.

18 David Kaye, *Report of the Special Rapporteur to the Human Rights Council on Online Content Regulation* (Human Rights Council, April 6, 2018), http://ap.ohchr.org/documents/dpage_e.aspx?si=A/HRC/38/35.

19 Dubravka Šimonović, *Report of the Special Rapporteur on Violence against Women, Its Causes and Consequences on Online Violence against Women and Girls from a Human Rights Perspective* (United Nations General Assembly, June 14, 2018), A/HRC/38/47 http://ap.ohchr.org/documents/dpage_e.aspx?si=A/72/134, paragraph 73.

20 Gunther Teubner, *Constitutional Fragments: Societal Constitutionalism and Globalization*, Oxford Constitutional Theory (Oxford University Press, 2012), 103.

21 Herbert Lionel Adolphus Hart, *The Concept of Law*, second edition (Oxford, 1994).

22 Gunther Teubner, "Substantive and Reflexive Elements in Modern Law," *Law & Society Review* 17, no. 2 (January 1, 1983): 239–285, https://doi.org/10.2307/3053348.

23 Dorothée Baumann-Pauly, Justine Nolan, Auret van Heerden, and Michael Samway, "Industry-Specific Multi-Stakeholder Initiatives That Govern Corporate Human Rights Standards: Legitimacy Assessments of the Fair Labor Association and the Global Network Initiative," *Journal of Business Ethics* 143, no. 4 (July 1, 2017): 771–787, https://doi.org/10.1007/s10551-016-3076-z.

24 Ibid.

25 Zeynep Tufekci, "Why Zuckerberg's 14-Year Apology Tour Hasn't Fixed Facebook," *Wired*, April 6, 2018, www.wired.com/story/why-zuckerberg-15-year-apology-tour-hasnt-fixed-facebook/.

26 Mike Ananny and Tarleton Gillespie, "Public Platforms: Beyond the Cycle of Shocks and Exceptions," The Internet, Policy and Politics Conference, Oxford University, accessed July 9, 2016, http://blogs.oii.ox.ac.uk/ipp-conference/sites/ipp/files/documents/anannyGillespie-publicPlatforms-oii-submittedSept8.pdf.

27 Thomas S. Kuhn, *The Structure of Scientific Revolutions*, fourth edition (University of Chicago Press, 2012).

28 Gunther Teubner, *Constitutional Fragments: Societal Constitutionalism and Globalization*, Oxford Constitutional Theory (Oxford University Press, 2012), 82.

29 Ibid.

30 Steven Bittle and Laureen Snider, "Examining the Ruggie Report: Can Voluntary Guidelines Tame Global Capitalism?," *Critical Criminology* 21, no. 2 (May 1, 2013): 177–192, https://doi.org/10.1007/s10612-013-9177-4; Lee McConnell, "Assessing the Feasibility of a Business and Human Rights Treaty," *International and Comparative Law Quarterly* 66, no. 01 (2017): 143–180, https://doi.org/10.1017/S0020589316000476.

31 Article 19, *Public Interest, Private Infrastructure* (Article 19, 2018), www.article19.org/wp-content/uploads/2018/06/HRIA-report-UNGP_5.6.pdf.

32 Luke O'Brien, "Jailed Chinese Journalist Joins Suit Against Yahoo," *Wired*, June 4, 2007, www.wired.com/2007/06/jailed-chinese-/.

33 Elinor Mills, "Yang Speaks on Yahoo's China Policy," CNET, March 9, 2006, www.cnet.com/news/yang-speaks-on-yahoos-china-policy/.

34 Colin M. Maclay, "Protecting Privacy and Expression Online: Can the Global Network Initiative Embrace the Character of the Net," in *Access Controlled: The Shaping of Power, Rights, and Rule in Cyberspace* (MIT Press, 2010), 87–108.

35 Bobbie Johnson, "Amnesty Criticises Global Network Initiative for Online Freedom of Speech," *The Guardian*, October 30, 2008, www.theguardian.com/technology/2008/oct/30/amnesty-global-network-initiative.

36 "EFF Resigns from Global Network Initiative," Electronic Frontier Foundation, October 10, 2013, www.eff.org/press/releases/eff-resigns-global-network-initiative.

37 Colin Miles Maclay, *An Improbable Coalition: How Businesses, Non-Governmental Organizations, Investors and Academics Formed the Global Network Initiative to Promote Privacy and Free Expression Online.* PhD dissertation, Northeastern University, 2014, 297.

38 *BSR Report 2013–2014: Transparency and Transformation* (BSR, 2014), 27, https://report.bsr.org/files/bsr-report-2013-14.pdf.

39 Rebecca MacKinnon, *Consent of the Networked: The Worldwide Struggle For Internet Freedom* (Basic Books, 2012).

40 Rikke Frank Jørgensen, "What Platforms Mean When They Talk About Human Rights," *Policy & Internet* 9, no. 3 (September 1, 2017): 280–296, https://doi.org/10.1002/poi3.152.

41 Susan Ariel Aaronson and Ian Higham, "Re-Righting Business: John Ruggie and the Struggle to Develop International Human Rights Standards for Transnational Firms," *Human Rights Quarterly* 35 (2013): 333–364.

42 *Charter of Human Rights and Principles for the Internet*, fifth edition (Internet Rights and Principles Coalition, 2014), http://internetrightsandprinciples.org/site/wp-content/uploads/2018/10/IRPC_english_5thedition.pdf/; *Principles on Freedom of Expression and Privacy* (Global Network Initiative, 2012), www.globalnetworkinitiative.org/principles/index.php; "Manila Principles on Intermediary Liability: Best Practices Guidelines for Limiting Intermediary Liability for Content to Promote Freedom of Expression and Innovation," March 24, 2015, www.manilaprinciples.org/.

43 "When Does "Content Moderation" Become Censorship? Policing the Web after Charlottesville," New America, YouTube, 2017, www.youtube.com/watch?time_continue=225&v=X4zy_eBo9kA.

10 WHAT SHOULD WE EXPECT OF INTERMEDIARIES?

1 "Report of the Independent International Fact-Finding Mission on Myanmar," Human Rights Council, August 27, 2018, www.ohchr.org/EN/HRBodies/HRC/MyanmarFFM/Pages/ReportoftheMyanmarFFM.aspx.

2 Penny Green, Thomas MacManus, and Alicia de la Cour Venning, *Countdown to Annihilation: Genocide in Myanmar* (International State Crime Initiative, 2015), www.kaladanpress.org/images/document/genocide%20in%20myanmar.pdf.

3 Ayesha Zainudeen and Helani Galpaya, *Mobile Phones, Internet, and Gender in Myanmar* (GSMA, 2015), www.gsma.com/mobilefordevelopment/wp-content/uploads/2016/02/Mobile-phones-internet-and-gender-in-Myanmar.pdf.

4 Ibid.

5 Christina Fink, "Myanmar: Religious Minorities and Constitutional Questions," *Asian Affairs* 49, no. 2 (2018): 259–277, https://doi.org/10.1080/03068374.2018.1469860; Ronan Lee, "The Dark Side of Liberalization: How Myanmar's Political and Media Freedoms

Are Being Used to Limit Muslim Rights," *Islam and Christian–Muslim Relations* 27, no. 2 (2016): 195–211, https://doi.org/10.1080/09596410.2016.1159045.

6 Min Zin, "Anti-Muslim Violence in Burma: Why Now?," *Social Research; New York* 82, no. 2 (Summer 2015): 375–397.

7 Tom Miles, "U.N. Investigators Cite Facebook Role in Myanmar Crisis," *Reuters*, March 12, 2018, www.reuters.com/article/us-myanmar-rohingya-facebook/u-n-investigators-cite-facebook-role-in-myanmar-crisis-idUSKCN1GO2PN.

8 "Statement by Mr. Marzuki DARUSMAN, Chairperson of the Independent International Fact-Finding Mission on Myanmar, at the 37th Session of the Human Rights Council," OHCHR, 2018, www.ohchr.org/EN/HRBodies/HRC/Pages/NewsDetail.aspx?NewsID= 22798&LangID=E; "Report of the Independent International Fact-Finding Mission on Myanmar."

9 "Warning on the Use of Media and State Accounts to Inflame Rakhine Situation," Burma Human Rights Network, September 1, 2017, www.bhrn.org.uk/en/press-release/18-warning-on-the-use-of-media-and-state-accounts-to-inflame-rakhine-situation.html.

10 Paul Mozur, "A Genocide Incited on Facebook, with Posts from Myanmar's Military," *The New York Times*, October 16, 2018, www.nytimes.com/2018/10/15/technology/myanmar-facebook-genocide.html.

11 Ilana Ullman, Laura Reed, and Rebecca MacKinnon, *Submission to UN Special Rapporteur for Freedom of Expression and Opinion David Kaye: Content Regulation in the Digital Age* (Ranking Digital Rights, December 15, 2017), https://rankingdigitalrights.org/wp-content/uploads/2018/01/RDR-2018-David-Kaye-Submission.pdf.

12 Lee Short, "Facebook Tries to Silence Myanmar's Hateful Monks," Genocide Watch – Prevention, Analysis, Advocacy and Action, July 6, 2018, www.genocidewatch.com/single-post/2018/07/06/Facebook-tries-to-silence-Myanmar%E2%80%99s-hateful-monks.

13 Nikki R. Slocum-Bradley, "Discursive Production of Conflict in Rwanda," in *Global Conflict Resolution through Positioning Analysis* (Springer, 2008), 207–226; Gregory H. Stanton, "Could the Rwandan Genocide Have Been Prevented?," *Journal of Genocide Research* 6, no. 2 (June 1, 2004): 211–228, https://doi.org/10.1080/1462352042000225958.

14 Gunther Teubner, *Constitutional Fragments: Societal Constitutionalism and Globalization*, Oxford Constitutional Theory (Oxford University Press, 2012), 132.

15 Tarleton Gillespie explains that "moderation is, in many ways, the commodity that platforms offer. Though part of the web, social media platforms promise rise above it, by offering a better experience of all this information and sociality: curated, organized, archived, and moderated": Tarleton Gillespie, Custodians of the Internet: Platforms, Content Moderation, and the Hidden Decisions That Shape Social Media, first edition (Yale University Press, 2018), 18.

16 John Ruggie, *Business and Human Rights: Towards Operationalizing the 'Protect, Respect and Remedy' Framework* (UN Human Rights Council, April 22, 2009), para. [71].

17 The requirements that the UNGPs imply for digital intermediaries are specifically set out in more detail in a report by the European Commission. This framework has six basic components: companies must make a firm commitment to respect human rights and embed that commitment into their culture; continuously assess their impact; prevent or mitigate harms in which they are involved; track how well harms are addressed; communicate how harms are addressed; and remediate harm to which they have caused or

contributed. See "ICT Sector Guide on Implementing the UN Guiding Principles on Business and Human Rights," European Commission, 2013, https://ec.europa.eu/anti-trafficking/publications/european-commission-sector-guides-implementing-un-guiding-principles-business-and-hum-o_en.

18 "Human Rights and Transnational Corporations and Other Business Enterprises," Human Rights Council, 2011, https://documents-dds-ny.un.org/doc/RESOLUTION/GEN/G11/144/71/PDF/G1114471.pdf?OpenElement.

19 Rikke Frank Jørgensen, "What Platforms Mean When They Talk About Human Rights," *Policy & Internet* 9, no. 3 (September 1, 2017): 280–296, https://doi.org/10.1002/poi3.152.

20 Nicolas Suzor, Tess Van Geelen, and Sarah Myers West, "Evaluating the Legitimacy of Platform Governance: A Review of Research and a Shared Research Agenda," *International Communication Gazette* 80, no. 4 (February 15, 2018): 385–400, https://doi.org/10.1177/1748048518757142.

21 Lev Grossman, "Inside Facebook's Plan to Wire the World," TIME.com, December 15, 2014, http://time.com/facebook-world-plan/.

22 Sara Su, "Update on Myanmar," Facebook Newsroom (blog), August 15, 2018, https://newsroom.fb.com/news/2018/08/update-on-myanmar/.

23 "Open Letter to Google on Reported Plans to Launch a Censored Search Engine in China," Human Rights Watch, August 28, 2018, www.hrw.org/news/2018/08/28/open-letter-google-reported-plans-launch-censored-search-engine-china; Kate Conger and Daisuke Wakabayashi, "Google Employees Protest Secret Work on Censored Search Engine for China," *The New York Times*, September 10, 2018, www.nytimes.com/2018/08/16/technology/google-employees-protest-search-censored-china.html.

24 Michael A. Samway, "Business & Human Rights," Yahoo! Yodel Blog (blog), May 7, 2008, https://s.yimg.com/ge/brhp/Business_and_Human_Rights.pdf.

25 Michael A. Samway, "Business, Human Rights, and the Internet: A Framework for Implementation," in *Human Dignity and the Future of Global Institutions*, eds, Mark P. Lagon and Anthony Clark Arend (Georgetown University Press, 2014), 295–316, www.jstor.org/stable/j.ctt9qdsd2.21.

26 "2018 Corporate Accountability Index," Ranking Digital Rights and Sustainalytics, April 2018, https://rankingdigitalrights.org/index2018/.

27 Ibid, 22.

28 "2018 Corporate Accountability Index," Ranking Digital Rights and Sustainalytics, April 2018, 24, https://rankingdigitalrights.org/index2018/.

29 Julia Angwin, "Facebook's Secret Censorship Rules Protect White Men from Hate Speech but Not Black Children," *ProPublica*, June 28, 2017, www.propublica.org/article/facebook-hate-speech-censorship-internal-documents-algorithms; Redacted post: www.facebook.com/THEDiDiDelgado/photos/a.271621723285520/278984872549205/?type=1&theater.

30 Anna Grear, *Redirecting Human Rights: Facing the Challenge of Corporate Legal Humanity* (Springer, 2010), 128–134; Bryan S. Turner, *Vulnerability and Human Rights* (Pennsylvania State University Press, 2006), www.jstor.org/stable/10.5325/j.ctt7v124. It is important to note that human rights still operate within a predominantly liberal worldview, and the abstract, disembodied universal language of human rights has been problematic for vulnerable, underprivileged, and oppressed groups: see Lourdes Peroni and Alexandra

Timmer, "Vulnerable Groups: The Promise of an Emerging Concept in European Human Rights Convention Law," *International Journal of Constitutional Law* 11, no. 4 (2013): 1056–1085, https://doi.org/10.1093/icon/mot042.

31 *International Covenant on Civil and Political Rights* (United Nations, 1966), Art 20, https://treaties.un.org/doc/publication/unts/volume%20999/volume-999-i-14668-english.pdf.

32 *International Convention on the Elimination of All Forms of Racial Discrimination* (United Nations, 1969), www.ohchr.org/EN/ProfessionalInterest/Pages/CERD.aspx.

33 Alex Amend, "Silicon Valley's Year in Hate," Southern Poverty Law Center, February 10, 2018, www.splcenter.org/fighting-hate/intelligence-report/2018/silicon-valleys-year-hate.

34 Corynne McSherry, Jillian C. York, and Cindy Cohn, "Private Censorship Is Not the Best Way to Fight Hate or Defend Democracy: Here Are Some Better Ideas," Electronic Frontier Foundation (blog), January 30, 2018, www.eff.org/deeplinks/2018/01/private-censorship-not-best-way-fight-hate-or-defend-democracy-here-are-some.

35 Nicolas Suzor, "Digital Constitutionalism: Using the Rule of Law to Evaluate the Legitimacy of Governance by Platforms," *Social Media + Society* 4, no. 3 (July 1, 2018): 2056305118787812, https://doi.org/10.1177/2056305118787812.

36 Kevin Bankston, Ross Schulman, and Liz Woolery, "Case Study #3: Transparency Reporting," New America, accessed January 16, 2018, www.newamerica.org/in-depth/getting-internet-companies-do-right-thing/case-study-3-transparency-reporting/; Caroline Nolan, Jillian York, Erica Newland, and Cynthia Wong, *Account Deactivation and Content Removal: Guiding Principles and Practices for Companies and Users* (Berkman Klein Center for Internet & Society, 2011), https://cyber.harvard.edu/publications/2011/account_deactivation.

37 "Who Has Your Back? 2011," Electronic Frontier Foundation, 2011, www.eff.org/who-has-your-back-2011.

38 Kevin Bankston, Ross Schulman, and Liz Woolery, "Case Study #3: Transparency Reporting," New America, accessed January 16, 2018, www.newamerica.org/in-depth/getting-internet-companies-do-right-thing/case-study-3-transparency-reporting/

39 Christopher Parsons, "The (In)Effectiveness of Voluntarily Produced Transparency Reports," *Business & Society* 58, no. 1 (2019), https://doi.org/10.1177/0007650317717957.

40 Liz Woolery, Ryan Hal Budish, and Kevin Bankston, *The Transparency Reporting Toolkit: Best Practices for Reporting on U.S. Government Requests for User Information* (New America Foundation and The Berkman Center for Internet & Society, 2016), https://dash.harvard.edu/handle/1/28552578.

41 Nicolas P. Suzor, Sarah Myers West, Andrew Quodling, and Jillian York (2019), What do we mean when we talk about transparency? Towards meaningful transparency in commercial content moderation. *International Journal of Communication*.

42 Oana Brindusa Albu and Mikkel Flyverbom, "Organizational Transparency: Conceptualizations, Conditions, and Consequences," *Business & Society*, July 13, 2016, 0007650316659851, https://doi.org/10.1177/0007650316659851.

43 Hans Krause Hansen and Mikkel Flyverbom, "The Politics of Transparency and the Calibration of Knowledge in the Digital Age," *Organization* 22, no. 6 (November 1, 2015): 872–889, https://doi.org/10.1177/1350508414522315; James Losey, "Surveillance of Communications: A Legitimization Crisis and the Need for Transparency," *International Journal of Communication* 9, no. 0 (October 15, 2015): 10; Christopher Parsons, "The

(In)Effectiveness of Voluntarily Produced Transparency Reports," *Business & Society* 58, no. 1 (2019), https://doi.org/10.1177/0007650317717957.

44 Jonathan Fox, "The Uncertain Relationship between Transparency and Accountability," in *Deconstructing Development Discourse*, eds., Andrea Cornwall and Deborah Eade (Oxfam GB, 2010), 245–256.

45 Archon Fung, Mary Graham, and David Weil, *Full Disclosure: The Perils and Promise of Transparency* (Cambridge University Press, 2007).

46 Rebecca MacKinnon, Nathalie Maréchal, and Priya Kumar, "Corporate Accountability for a Free and Open Internet," Global Commission on Internet Governance Paper Series, December 21, 2016, www.cigionline.org/publications/corporate-accountability-free-and-open-internet.

47 Nathalie Maréchal, "Ranking Digital Rights: Human Rights, the Internet and the Fifth Estate," *International Journal of Communication* 9, no. 10 (2015): 3440–3449.

48 "2018 Corporate Accountability Index," Ranking Digital Rights and Sustainalytics, April 2018, https://rankingdigitalrights.org/index2018/.

49 "Santa Clara Principles on Transparency and Accountability in Content Moderation," May 7, 2018, https://santaclaraprinciples.org/.

50 Jason Bosland and Jonathan Gill, "The Principle of Open Justice and the Judicial Duty to Give Public Reasons," *Melbourne University Law Review* 38, no. 2 (2015): 482–524; Jeremy Waldron, "The Concept and the Rule of Law," *Georgia Law Review* 43 (2009): 1–62.

51 *R* v. *Sussex Justices*, Ex parte McCarthy, 1 KB 256 (High Court of Justice 1924).

52 Sarah Myers West, "Censored, Suspended, Shadowbanned: User Interpretations of Content Moderation on Social Media Platforms," *New Media & Society*, May 8, 2018, https://doi.org/10.1177/1461444818773059.

53 Mike Ananny and Kate Crawford, "Seeing without Knowing: Limitations of the Transparency Ideal and Its Application to Algorithmic Accountability," *New Media & Society* 20, no. 3 (March 1, 2018): 973–989, https://doi.org/10.1177/1461444816676645.

54 Jean Burgess notes that it is a mistake to think about digital media platforms as stable entities – the giant networks we know today have grown extremely quickly and changed substantially in the relatively short time they have been around. See Jean Burgess, "From 'Broadcast Yourself' to 'Follow Your Interests': Making over Social Media," *International Journal of Cultural Studies* 18, no. 3 (2015): 281–285.

55 Safiya Umoja Noble, *Algorithms of Oppression: How Search Engines Reinforce Racism* (New York University Press, 2018). Frank Pasquale, *The Black Box Society* (Harvard University Press, 2015). Christian Sandvig, Kevin Hamilton, Karrie Karahalios, and Caedric Langbort, "Auditing Algorithms: Research Methods for Detecting Discrimination on Internet Platforms," in Data and Discrimination: Converting Critical Concerns into Productive Inquiry, Seattle, WA, 2014.

56 Nicolas Suzor, Tess Van Geelen, and Sarah Myers West, "Evaluating the Legitimacy of Platform Governance: A Review of Research and a Shared Research Agenda," *International Communication Gazette* 80, no. 4 (February 15, 2018): 385–400, https://doi.org/10.1177/1748048518757142.

57 Axel Bruns, "Facebook Shuts the Gate after the Horse Has Bolted, and Hurts Real Research in the Process," Internet Policy Review, April 25, 2018, https://policyreview.info/articles/news/facebook-shuts-gate-after-horse-has-bolted-and-hurts-real-research-process/786.

58 Nicholas Diakopoulos, "Algorithmic Accountability. Journalistic Investigation of Computational Power Structures," *Digital Journalism* 3, no. 3 (2015): 398–415.

59 Christopher Parsons, "The (In)Effectiveness of Voluntarily Produced Transparency Reports," *Business & Society* 58, no. 1 (2019), https://doi.org/10.1177/0007650317717957; Nathalie Maréchal, "Ranking Digital Rights: Human Rights, the Internet and the Fifth Estate," *International Journal of Communication* 9, no. 10 (2015): 3440–3449.

60 Ryan M. Milner, "FCJ-156 Hacking the Social: Internet Memes, Identity Antagonism, and the Logic of Lulz," *The Fibreculture Journal*, no. 22 (2013).

61 Adrienne Massanari, "#Gamergate and the Fappening: How Reddit's Algorithm, Governance, and Culture Support Toxic Technocultures," *New Media & Society* 19, no. 3 (2017): 332, https://doi.org/10.1177/1461444815608807.

62 Ibid.

63 Not all of Reddit supports hateful or harmful speech, but Reddit's design enables niche content to become highly visible if it is popular within a sub-Reddit. Once material has become highly visible, it is harder for other members of the community to supress it; Massanari notes that "because upvotes represent visibility on Reddit, and earlier votes count more heavily than later ones, downvoting after something has become extremely popular is likely to have little effect." Ibid, 338.

64 Tarleton Gillespie, *Custodians of the Internet: Platforms, Content Moderation, and the Hidden Decisions That Shape Social Media*, first edition (Yale University Press, 2018), 136.

65 Adrienne Massanari, "#Gamergate and the Fappening: How Reddit's Algorithm, Governance, and Culture Support Toxic Technocultures," *New Media & Society* 19, no. 3 (2017): 329–346, https://doi.org/10.1177/1461444815608807.

66 Emily van der Nagel and James Meese, "Reddit Tackles 'Revenge Porn' and Celebrity Nudes," The Conversation, accessed April 1, 2016, http://theconversation.com/reddit-tackles-revenge-porn-and-celebrity-nudes-38112.

67 These paragraphs were previously published in Nicolas P. Suzor, Bryony Seignior, and Jennifer Singleton, "Non-Consensual Porn and the Responsibilities of Online Intermediaries," *Melbourne University Law Review* 40, no. 3 (2017): 1057–1097.

68 Emily Van der Nagel, "Faceless Bodies: Negotiating Technological and Cultural Codes on Reddit Gonewild," *Journal of Media Arts Culture* 10, no. 2 (2013), http://scan.net.au/scn/journal/vol10number2/Emily-van-der-Nagel.html.

69 Emily van der Nagel and Jordan Frith, "Anonymity, Pseudonymity, and the Agency of Online Identity: Examining the Social Practices of r/Gonewild," *First Monday* 20, no. 3 (February 22, 2015), https://doi.org/10.5210/fm.v20i3.5615.

70 It must be noted that, while the governance mechanism that prioritizes consent is useful, Gonewild itself reproduces homogenous body standards, prioritizing the bodies of women who are "white, young and slender." See: Jenny Kennedy, James Meese, and Emily van der Nagel, "Regulation and Social Practice Online," *Continuum* 30, no. 2 (2016): 146–157.

71 Stefanie Duguay, Jean Burgess, and Nicolas Suzor, "Queer Women's Experiences of Patchwork Platform Governance on Tinder, Instagram, and Vine, Queer Women's Experiences of Patchwork Platform Governance on Tinder, Instagram, and Vine," *Convergence*, June 19, 2018, 1354856518781530, https://doi.org/10.1177/1354856518781530.

72 Ariadna Matamoros-Fernández, "Platformed Racism: The Mediation and Circulation of an Australian Race-Based Controversy on Twitter, Facebook and YouTube," *Information, Communication & Society* 20, no. 6 (2017): 940, https://doi.org/10.1080/1369118X.2017.1293130.

73 "Manila Principles on Intermediary Liability: Best Practices Guidelines for Limiting Intermediary Liability for Content to Promote Freedom of Expression and Innovation," March 24, 2015, www.manilaprinciples.org/.

74 Kate Crawford and Tarleton Gillespie, "What Is a Flag for? Social Media Reporting Tools and the Vocabulary of Complaint," *New Media & Society* 18, no. 3 (2014): 410–428, https://doi.org/10.1177/1461444814543163.

75 J. Nathan Matias, Amy Johnson, Whitney Erin Boesel, Brian Keegan, Jaclyn Friedman, and Charlie DeTar, *Reporting, Reviewing, and Responding to Harassment on Twitter* (Women, Action, & the Media!, 2015), https://ssrn.com/abstract=2602018.

76 "Manila Principles on Intermediary Liability: Best Practices Guidelines for Limiting Intermediary Liability for Content to Promote Freedom of Expression and Innovation," March 24, 2015, www.manilaprinciples.org/.

77 "Santa Clara Principles on Transparency and Accountability in Content Moderation," May 7, 2018, https://santaclaraprinciples.org/.

78 "Manila Principles on Intermediary Liability: Best Practices Guidelines for Limiting Intermediary Liability for Content to Promote Freedom of Expression and Innovation," March 24, 2015, www.manilaprinciples.org/.

79 David Kaye, *Report of the Special Rapporteur to the Human Rights Council on Online Content Regulation* (Human Rights Council, April 6, 2018), http://ap.ohchr.org/docu ments/dpage_e.aspx?si=A/HRC/38/35.

80 Article 19, *Self-Regulation and 'Hate Speech' on Social Media Platforms* (Article 19, 2018), www.article19.org/resources/self-regulation-hate-speech-social-media-platforms/.

81 Tarleton Gillespie, *Custodians of the Internet: Platforms, Content Moderation, and the Hidden Decisions That Shape Social Media*, first edition (Yale University Press, 2018).

82 Max Read points out that putting in the work to develop a new constitutionalism may actually be the best option for platforms – better than the conceivable alternatives of (a) breaking up the platforms to reduce their power through antitrust law; (b) nationalizing them; or (c) heavy regulatory intervention where the legitimate oversight is imposed from outside: http://nymag.com/selectall/2018/07/does-facebook-need-a-constitution.html.

11 THE ROLE OF STATES AND BINDING LAW

1 "The Techlash against Amazon, Facebook and Google – and What They Can Do – A Memo to Big Tech," *The Economist*, January 20, 2018, www.economist.com/briefing/2018/01/20/the-techlash-against-amazon-facebook-and-google-and-what-they-can-do.

2 Reporters without Borders, "World Press Freedom Index," RSF, 2018, https://rsf.org/en/ranking/2018; Freedom House, "Freedom of the Press 2017," April 18, 2017, https://freedom house.org/report/freedom-press/freedom-press-2017.

3 Justin Clark, Rob Farris, Ryan Morrison-Westphal, Helmi Noman, Casey Tilton, and Jonathan Zittrain, *The Shifting Landscape of Global Internet Censorship* (Berkman Klein Center for Internet & Society, Harvard University, June 2017), https://cyber.harvard.edu/publications/2017/06/GlobalInternetCensorship.

4 Manuel Castells, *Networks of Outrage and Hope: Social Movements in the Internet Age* (Polity Press, 2012), 63.

5 Amy E. Cattle, "Digital Tahrir Square: An Analysis of Human Rights and the Internet Examined through the Lens of the Egyptian Arab Spring," *Duke Journal of Comparative and International Law* 26 (2016): 424–430.

6 Zeynep Tufekci, *Twitter and Tear Gas: The Power and Fragility of Networked Protest* (Yale University Press, 2017).

7 Ibid.

8 UN Special Rapporteur on Freedom of Opinion and Expression, the Organization for Security and Co-operation in Europe Representative on Freedom of the Media, the Organization of American States Special Rapporteur on Freedom of Expression, and the African Commission on Human and Peoples' Rights Special Rapporteur on Freedom of Expression and Access to Information, *Joint Declaration on Freedom of Expression and the Internet* (United Nations, June 1, 2011), www.osce.org/fom/78309.

9 "#KeepItOn," Access Now, accessed October 11, 2018, www.accessnow.org/keepiton/.

10 "The Expression Agenda Report 2016–17," Article 19, 2017, www.article19.org/xpa-17/.

11 Justin Clark, Rob Farris, Ryan Morrison-Westphal, Helmi Noman, Casey Tilton, and Jonathan Zittrain, *The Shifting Landscape of Global Internet Censorship* (Berkman Klein Center for Internet & Society, Harvard University, June 2017), https://cyber.harvard.edu/publications/2017/06/GlobalInternetCensorship.

12 Glenn Greenwald, *No Place to Hide: Edward Snowden, the NSA, and the U.S. Surveillance State* (Henry Holt, 2014). This extensive global network of surveillance has been running for many years before the programs revealed by Edward Snowden: see Nicky Hager, *Secret Power* (Craig Potton Pub, 1996).

13 Derek Bambauer, "Orwell's Armchair," *University of Chicago Law Review* 79, no. 3 (2012): 863.

14 Yochai Benkler, "A Free Irresponsible Press: Wikileaks and the Battle over the Soul of the Networked Fourth Estate," *Harvard Civil Rights Civil Liberties Law Review* 46 (2011): 311–398.

15 The move to avoid constitutional limitations by pressuring internet intermediaries is known as an "invisible handshake": Michael D. Birnhack and Niva Elkin-Koren, "The Invisible Handshake: The Reemergence of the State in the Digital Environment," *Virginia Journal of Law & Technology* 8 (2003): 6–13, http://dx.doi.org/10.2139/ssrn.381020; Niva Elkin-Koren and Eldar Haber, "Governance by Proxy: Cyber Challenges to Civil Liberties," *Brooklyn Law Review* 82 (February 28, 2016).

16 Mike Masnick, "Yes, SOPA Breaks the Internet: By Breaking the Belief in Trust and Sharing That Is the Internet," *Techdirt* (blog), November 16, 2011, www.techdirt.com/articles/20111116/02561516788/yes-sopa-breaks-internet-breaking-belief-trust-sharing-that-is-internet.shtml; Brad Burnham, "I Believe in the Internet – The Content Industry Doesn't," *Unfinished Work* (blog), November 13, 2011, http://bradburnham.tumblr.com/post/12739727902/i-believe-in-the-internet-the-content-industry.

17 Alec Stone Sweet and Jud Mathews, "Proportionality Balancing and Global Constitutionalism," *Columbia Journal of Transnational Law* 47 (2009): 72–164.

18 There are also serious criticisms and disagreements about proportionality reasoning, particularly when it comes to balancing competing rights against each other. See Grant

Huscroft, Bradley W. Miller, and Gregoire Webber, *Proportionality and the Rule of Law: Rights, Justification, Reasoning* (Cambridge University Press, 2014).

19 Loi favorisant la diffusion et la protection de la création sur internet; Nicolas Suzor and Brian Fitzgerald, "The Legitimacy of Graduated Response Schemes in Copyright Law," *University of New South Wales Law Journal* 34, no. 1 (2011): 1–40.

20 Nicolas P. Suzor, Kylie M. Pappalardo, and Natalie McIntosh, "The Passage of Australia's Data Retention Regime: National Security, Human Rights, and Media Scrutiny," *Internet Policy Review* 6, no. 1 (March 2017), https://policyreview.info/ articles/analysis/passage-australias-data-retention-regime-national-security-human-rights-and-media.

21 Wolfgang Schulz and Joris van Hoboken, *Human Rights and Encryption* (UNESCO Publishing, 2016); Adamantia Rachovitsa, "Engineering and Lawyering Privacy by Design: Understanding Online Privacy Both as a Technical and an International Human Rights Issue," *International Journal of Law and Information Technology* 24, no. 4 (December 1, 2016): 374–399, https://doi.org/10.1093/ijlit/eaw012.

22 "Open Letter to Google on Reported Plans to Launch a Censored Search Engine in China," Human Rights Watch, August 28, 2018, www.hrw.org/news/2018/08/28/open-letter-google-reported-plans-launch-censored-search-engine-china; Kate Conger and Daisuke Wakabayashi, "Google Employees Protest Secret Work on Censored Search Engine for China," *The New York Times*, September 10, 2018, www.nytimes.com/2018/08/16/technology/google-employees-protest-search-censored-china.html.

23 Kylie Pappalardo, *A Tort Law Framework for Copyright Authorisation*. PhD thesis, Australian Catholic University, 2016 (considering intermediary liability in copyright law).

24 Jessica Litman, *Digital Copyright* (Prometheus Books, 2006), 144 (explaining that "Copyright legislation written by multiparty negotiation is long, detailed, counterintuitive, kind to the status quo, and hostile to potential new competitors. It is also overwhelmingly likely to appropriate value for the benefit of major stakeholders at the expense of the public at large.").

25 "Manila Principles on Intermediary Liability: Best Practices Guidelines for Limiting Intermediary Liability for Content to Promote Freedom of Expression and Innovation," March 24, 2015, www.manilaprinciples.org/.

26 Eric Goldman, "Online User Account Termination and 47 U.S.C. Sec. 230(c)(2) Governing the Magic Circle: Regulation of Virtual Worlds," *UC Irvine Law Review* 2 (2012): 672.

27 Rebecca Tushnet, "Power without Responsibility: Intermediaries and the First Amendment," *George Washington Law Review* 76, no. 4 (August 6, 2008): 1002.

28 There have been a great many lawsuits over the past two decades challenging the broad application of CDA 230. For a ranked list of the most important decisions, see: Eric Goldman, "The Ten Most Important Section 230 Rulings," *Tulane Journal of Technology and Intellectual Property* 20 (2017): 1–10.

29 Mark A. Lemley, "Rationalizing Internet Safe Harbors," *Journal on Telecommunications & High Technology Law* 6 (2008): 113.

30 James Grimmelmann makes the point that "It seems unlikely that § 230's across-the-board immunity is ideal. Even if in many cases judges are poorly situated to second-guess moderation decisions, they should not be writing blank checks to moderators like Hunter

Moore": James Grimmelmann, "The Virtues of Moderation," *Yale Journal of Law and Technology* 17 (2015): 104–105.

31 Tarleton Gillespie, "Improving Moderation," July 17, 2018, www.custodiansoftheinternet .org/index.php/download_file/view/4/1.

32 Mark A. Lemley, "Rationalizing Internet Safe Harbors," *Journal on Telecommunications & High Technology Law* 6 (2008): 110.

33 Rebecca Tushnet, "Power without Responsibility: Intermediaries and the First Amendment," *George Washington Law Review* 76, no. 4 (August 6, 2008): 1015.

34 Tarleton Gillespie, "Improving Moderation," July 17, 2018, xiii-ix, www.custodiansofthein ternet.org/index.php/download_file/view/4/1.

35 Mark A. Lemley, "Rationalizing Internet Safe Harbors," *Journal on Telecommunications & High Technology Law* 6 (2008): 115.

36 Nicolas Suzor and Brian Fitzgerald, "The Legitimacy of Graduated Response Schemes in Copyright Law," *University of New South Wales Law Journal* 34, no. 1 (2011): 1–40.

37 When we talk to consumers about why they infringe copyright, the most common response is that they have trouble getting access to content legitimately, at a fair price, through a convenient channel: Paula Dootson and Nicolas Suzor, "Game of Clones and the Australia Tax: Divergent Views about Copyright Business Models and the Willingness of Australian Consumers to Infringe," *The University of New South Wales Law Journal* 38 (2015): 206–329.

38 Jack M. Balkin, "Law and Liberty in Virtual Worlds," *New York Law School Law Review* 49 (2004): 69.

39 Sarah Jeong, *The Internet of Garbage*, 1.5 (The Verge, 2018), 60, www.theverge.com/2018/ 8/28/17777330/internet-of-garbage-book-sarah-jeong-online-harassment.

40 Emily Dreyfuss, "Jack Dorsey Has Problems with Twitter, Too," *Wired*, October 16, 2018, www.wired.com/story/wired25-jack-dorsey/.

41 David Kaye, *Report of the Special Rapporteur to the Human Rights Council on Freedom of Expression, States and the Private Sector in the Digital Age* (United Nations, Human Rights Council, May 11, 2016), 5, [11], www.ohchr.org/EN/Issues/FreedomOpinion/Pages/ Privatesectorinthedigitalage.aspx.

42 Tarleton Gillespie, *Custodians of the Internet: Platforms, Content Moderation, and the Hidden Decisions That Shape Social Media*, first edition (Yale University Press, 2018), 47.

43 E. Goldman, "Search Engine Bias and the Demise of Search Engine Utopianism," in *Web Search: Multidisciplinary Perspectives*, ed. Amanda Spink and Michael Zimmer, Information Science and Knowledge Management (Springer, 2008), 121–133, https://doi .org/10.1007/978-3-540-75829-7_8.

44 Safiya Umoja Noble, *Algorithms of Oppression: How Search Engines Reinforce Racism* (New York University Press, 2018).

45 Through the application of the transitive principle, some have also suggested that this means that businesses have binding obligations under human rights law, but this view is not universally accepted. David Bilchitz, "A Chasm between 'is' and 'ought'? A Critique of the Normative Foundations of the SRSG's Framework and the Guiding Principles," in *Human Rights Obligations of Business: Beyond the Corporate Responsibility to Respect?*, ed. Surya Deva and David Bilchitz (Cambridge University Press, 2013), 111–112.

46 Chris Albin-Lackey, "Without Rules: A Failed Approach to Corporate Accountability," in *World Report 2013* (Human Rights Watch, 2013), 32, www.hrw.org/world-report/2013.

47 Surya Deva, "Treating Human Rights Lightly: A Critique of the Consensus Rhetoric and the Language Employed by the Guiding Principles," in Human Rights Obligations of Business, 78–104.

48 Justine Nolan, "The Corporate Responsibility to Respect Rights: Soft Law or Not Law?," in *Human Rights Obligations of Business: Beyond the Corporate Responsibility to Respect?*, ed., S. Deca and D. Bilchitz (Cambridge University Press, 2013), https://papers.ssrn.com/abstract=2338356.

49 *Injustice Incorporated: Corporate Abuses and the Human Right to Remedy*, (Amnesty International, 2014), 202, www.amnesty.org/en/documents/document/?indexNumber=POL30%2f001%2f2014&language=en.

50 Molly Dragiewicz, Jean Burgess, Ariadna Matamoros-Fernández, et al., "Technology Facilitated Coercive Control: Domestic Violence and the Competing Roles of Digital Media Platforms," *Feminist Media Studies* 18, no. 4 (2018): 609–625, https://doi.org/10.1080/14680777.2018.1447341; Nicolas P. Suzor, Molly Dragiewicz, Bridget Harris, Rosalie Gillett, Jean Burgess, and Tess Van Geelen, "Human Rights by Design: The Responsibilities of Social Media Platforms to Address Gender-Based Violence Online," *Policy & Internet*, 2018, https://doi.org/10.1002/poi3.185.

51 Safiya Umoja Noble, *Algorithms of Oppression: How Search Engines Reinforce Racism* (New York University Press, 2018).

52 Gary E. Marchant, Braden R. Allenby, and Joseph R. Herkert, eds., *The Growing Gap between Emerging Technologies and Legal-Ethical Oversight: The Pacing Problem* (Springer, 2011).

53 Braden R. Allenby, "The Dynamics of Emerging Technology Systems," in *Innovative Governance Models for Emerging Technologies*, eds. Kenneth W Abbott, Gary E. Marchant, and Braden R. Allenby (Edward Elgar Publishing, 2013).

54 Roger Brownsword, *Rights, Regulation, and the Technological Revolution* (Oxford Scholarship Online, 2008), www.oxfordscholarship.com/view/10.1093/acprof:oso/9780199276806.001.0001/acprof-9780199276806.

55 Frank Pasquale, *The Black Box Society* (Harvard University Press, 2015).

56 M. C. Stephenson, "Information Acquisition and Institutional Design," *Harvard Law Review* 124, no. 6 (2011): 1422; H. Bakhshi, A. Freedman, and P. J. Heblich, *State of Uncertainty: Innovation Policy through Experimentation* (NESTA, 2011); Gregory N. Mandel, "Regulating Emerging Technologies," *Law, Innovation and Technology* 1, no. 1 (2009): 75–92, https://doi.org/10.1080/17579961.2009.11428365.

57 Mauro Santaniello, Nicola Palladino, Maria Carmela Catone, and Paolo Diana, "The Language of Digital Constitutionalism and the Role of National Parliaments," *International Communication Gazette* 80, no. 4 (2018): 1748048518757138, https://doi.org/10.1177/1748048518757138.

58 Gunther Teubner, *Constitutional Fragments: Societal Constitutionalism and Globalization*, Oxford Constitutional Theory (Oxford University Press, 2012), 84.

59 Julia Black, "Constructing and Contesting Legitimacy and Accountability in Polycentric Regulatory Regimes," *Regulation & Governance* 2, no. 2 (2008): 137–164.

60 Julia Black, "Decentring Regulation: Understanding the Role of Regulation and Self-Regulation in a 'Post-Regulatory' World," *Current Legal Problems* 54, no. 1 (2001): 111, https://doi.org/10.1093/clp/54.1.103.

61 Gunther Teubner, *Constitutional Fragments: Societal Constitutionalism and Globalization*, Oxford Constitutional Theory (Oxford University Press, 2012), 84.

62 See, for example, Nicolas Suzor, Tess Van Geelen, and Sarah Myers West, "Evaluating the Legitimacy of Platform Governance: A Review of Research and a Shared Research Agenda," *International Communication Gazette* 80, no. 4 (February 15, 2018): 385–400, https://doi.org/10.1177/1748048518757142. (discussing the need for a broad range of institutions to help understand complex systems of internet governance).

Index